Algic Researches:
North American Indian
Folktales and Legends

Algic Researches: North American Indian Folktales and Legends

Henry Rowe Schoolcraft

Introduction by
Curtis M. Hinsley
Regents' Professor of History
Northern Arizona University

DOVER PUBLICATIONS, INC.
Mineola, New York

This Dover edition is largely faithful to Schoolcraft's very personalized, often inconsistent, style of writing, spelling, capitalization, punctuation, and the like. A minimum of editorial changes have been made to help clarify the text. Italicized and capitalized words are reproduced as they appeared in the original edition, even when the reason for their emphasis is unclear.

Bibliographical Note

This Dover edition, first published in 1999, is a lightly edited but otherwise unabridged republication of *Algic Researches: Comprising Inquiries Respecting the Mental Characteristics of the North American Indians / First Series: Indian Tales and Legends,* originally published in two volumes by Harper & Brothers, New York, 1839.

This edition has been newly typeset in one volume, with consecutive pagination of the two parts labeled Volume I and Volume II. To help distinguish visually between story and commentary, the editors have introduce a typographical distinction between the two; there was none in the original. In the story "Manabozho," the lengthy footnote on fasting has been repositioned to join the author's Introductory Note to the story.

Dr. Curtis M. Hinsley's introduction has been specially prepared for this edition.

International Standard Book Number: 0-486-40187-1

Schoolcraft, Henry Rowe, 1793–1864.
    Algic researches / Henry Rowe Schoolcraft ; introduction by Curtis M. Hinsley.
        p.   cm.
    Includes bibliographical references.
    ISBN 0-486-40187-1 (pbk.)
    1. Indians of North America—Folklore.   2. Algonquian Indians—Folklore.
I. Title
E98.F6S3   1999
398.2' 089'973—dc21   98–50307
                                                          CIP

Manufactured in the United States of America
Dover Publications, Inc., 31 East 2nd Street, Mineola, N.Y. 11501

CONTENTS

VOLUME I

VOLUME II

Introduction to the Dover Edition

EVEN THOUGH he spent decades in the metropolitan centers of the eastern seaboard—New York, Washington—Henry Rowe Schoolcraft (1793–1864) always lived on the frontiers of his society. A multiple misfit, he became a self-marginalized man, always "positioned on the edge" of his society,[1] repeatedly bankrupt, never financially successful, constantly struggling for economic security and emotional balance. And yet today we can see that Schoolcraft was centrally involved in the processes of American national identity-formation that took place between the Revolutionary period and the Civil War—that is, almost precisely in his lifetime.

The fundamentals of American national identity took shape during the early years of the Republic and, like the elements of all modern nationalities, they took formation as literary texts—the oratory of the Founding Fathers, the narratives of war, the reports of discoveries, the poetry and song of the nation's distinctive regions, and—most importantly—supreme textual moments such as Lincoln's address at Gettysburg. In their seemingly infinite variety these were, to borrow Garry Wills' phrase, "the words that (made and) remade America."[2] Of course, not all of these

---

[1] The phrase is from Frances Karttunen, *Between Worlds: Interpreters, Guides, and Survivors* (New Brunswick: Rutgers University Press, 1994): xii.

[2] Gary Wills, *Lincoln at Gettysburg: The Words that Remade America* (New York: Simon & Schuster, 1992); on the importance of literacy and the widespread distribution of printed materials in the formation of modern nation-states and nationalities, see Benedict Anderson's now-classic study, *Imagined Communities: Reflections on the Origin and Spread of Nationalism* (Verso: London and New York, 1983), *passim*. On the close and critical relationship between national mythologies and the growth in metropolitan printing and audiences in early America, see Richard Slotkin, *Regeneration Through Violence: The Mythology of the American Frontier, 1600–1860* (Middletown, Conn.: Wesleyan University Press, 1973), and its sequels.

American texts were comprised of words. John James Audubon's library of birds, George Catlin's field sketches of aboriginal America, the Hudson River Valley paintings of Thomas Cole, the mappings of Lewis and Clark, Jedediah Morse, and Stephen Long—all of these were attempts to convey, in widely reproduced print formats, the human and natural landscapes that might provide aesthetic (and economic) resources for the expansive, burgeoning young American nation.[3] Together they gave the American people their first, enduring impressions of themselves.

There is considerable irony in the fact that, almost by definition and certainly by experience, most of these textmakers of early America lived on the fringes of settled society; they were obsessed and liminal souls in powerfully ambivalent, frequently rebellious relationship to their origins. Henry Schoolcraft embodied these dynamics almost to the point of caricature. Born in the frontier community of Hamilton, New York, in 1793, the young Schoolcraft decided on a career in either his father's business— glass manufacturing—or geology. Despite his determination to establish himself independently of his powerful father, Schoolcraft's early business ventures repeatedly failed, and the father observed the son's humiliating bankruptcies. In 1819 Schoolcraft fled in desperation from his creditors and his father to the upper Michigan frontier, ostensibly to survey the potential of the district's lead mines for the glass industry. Through his friendship with Lewis Cass, governor of Michigan Territory, Schoolcraft received the federal post of Indian Agent; he saw it as a temporary position, since he hoped for an appointment as Superintendent of Missouri Lead Mines. In Sault Ste. Marie, Schoolcraft boarded with the family of John Johnston, an Irish immigrant who had married the daughter of a prominent Chippewa chief. John and Susan Johnston, and their children, soon became invaluable as informants and interlocutors for Schoolcraft. According to biographer Robert Bieder, Schoolcraft recalled that the Johnston family was the only one "in North America who could, in Indian

---

[3] For an instructive account and analysis of aesthetic confrontations with American landscapes, see Lee Clark Mitchell, *Witnesses to a Vanishing America: The Nineteenth-Century Response* (Princeton: Princeton University Press, 1981).

lore, have acted as my 'guide, philosopher, and friend.'"[4] Cass encouraged his protégé—"as I am told you are somewhat of an aboriginophile"—to gather, through the Johnstons, as much information as possible on Chippewa language, customs, and folklore.[5] The winter of 1822–23 ended with Schoolcraft deeply enmeshed in Chippewa ethnology and language—and married to the eldest Johnston daughter, Jane. This was the period in which Schoolcraft gathered, through the mediating influences of the Johnston family, the stories and legends that he eventually published, in 1839, as *Algic Researches*.

In the same period—the early 1820s—Schoolcraft began an experience of conversion to Presbyterianism which was completed a full decade later and which deeply influenced the course of his work and life. Coincident with his marriage, it was the first of several recreations of his identity that Schoolcraft undertook in a life of many twists and turns.[6] With the publication in 1825 of his *Travels in the Central Portions of the Mississippi Valley*, Schoolcraft made his first serious bid for recognition as a literary figure and as an authority on the peoples and places of the Michigan Territory. Here he struck a sympathetic, even apologetic tone toward the Indians of the region, arguing for the need to overcome White prejudice with greater factual knowledge of the "constitution of the Indian mind." In the coming years, he repeatedly returned to this theme of the Indian mind, as seen in language, customs, and storytelling.

By the mid-1830s, as he was preparing *Algic Researches* for publication, Schoolcraft completed his religious conversion and began to show more definite signs of missionary intentions in his writing. In 1832 he founded the Algic Society—the first use of his neologism that combined "Algonquin" and "Atlantic"—"for encouraging missionary efforts in evangelizing the north western tribes, and promoting education, agriculture, industry, peace and temperance,

---

[4] Quoted in Robert E. Bieder, *Science Encounters the Indian, 1820–1880: The Early Years of American Ethnology* (Norman: University of Oklahoma Press, 1986): 149.
[5] Ibid., 149n13.
[6] The interpretation here is from John F. Freeman, "Religion and Personality in the Anthropology of Henry Schoolcraft," *Journal of the History of the Behavioral Sciences 1* (1965): 301–313. This article, based on Freeman's unpublished 1960 Harvard dissertation, "Henry Rowe Schoolcraft, 1793–1864," is deeply insightful as a psychological profile of Schoolcraft.

among them."[7] By this time Schoolcraft openly subscribed to the increasingly popular belief that America's aboriginal population was in a degenerate, or "fallen," moral state, but he also insisted that the data on language and legends that he was gathering and publishing indicated the Indians' potential for salvation. This theme became more insistent as Schoolcraft aged.[8] With the publication of *Algic Researches* in 1839 Schoolcraft hoped for financial success; he was bitterly disappointed—as he was with all of his literary efforts. By the early 1840s he had lost his government position, his wife Jane had died, his children had been sent off to boarding school, and he had moved to New York City. Tellingly, at this point he briefly changed his name (to "Colcraft")— another critical moment of identity confusion. But once settled in New York, Schoolcraft found a small circle of intellectuals and literary figures with whom to form a community. With the aging Albert Gallatin, he established the American Ethnological Society and enjoyed a position of respect among the New York-based group of American enthusiasts for Indian languages and ethnology.[9] The mid-forties marked the zenith of Schoolcraft's career. He remarried; became a close and influential friend of Joseph Henry, the first secretary of the Smithsonian Institution (and thereby affected the Smithsonian's early policies toward ethnology);[10] and successfully lobbied a reluctant Congress to support his final, massive fact-gathering effort in Indian history

---

[7] Constitution of the Algic Society [pamphlet] (Detroit: Cleland & Sawyer, 1833).

[8] See, especially, his "History and Languages of the North American Tribes," *North American Review* 45 (1837): 34–59. This publication was critical in Schoolcraft's emergent recognition as a *litterateur* and Indian expert. On the prominence of degeneration theory in this period, see George W. Stocking, Jr., "Some Problems in Understanding Nineteenth Century Cultural Evolutionism," in Regna D. Darnell, ed., *Readings in the History of Anthropology* (New York: Harper and Row, 1974): 407–425.

[9] On this period of Schoolcraft's life, and on the others in the circle of the American Ethnological Society, see Bieder, *op. cit.;* for a broader perspective of the AES in American ethnology, see Don D. Fowler and David R. Wilcox, "From Thomas Jefferson to the Pecos Conference: Changing Anthropological Agendas in the American Southwest," unpublished paper presented at the American Philosophical Society Conference on "Surveying the Record: North American Scientific Exploration to 1900," March 1997: pp. 6–11.

[10] Curtis M. Hinsley, *The Smithsonian and the American Indian: Making a Moral Anthropology in Victorian America* (Washington: Smithsonian Institution Press, 1995): 34–63.

and ethnology: *Information Respecting the History, Condition and Prospects of the Indian Tribes of the United States.*[11]

Schoolcraft never achieved the financial rewards for which he hoped, and for most of his career he was dependent on government largesse and the support of influential friends. The 1850s were particularly bittersweet for Schoolcraft in these respects. In 1855 Henry Wadsworth Longfellow, gratefully acknowledging his heavy debts to Schoolcraft's *Algic Researches,* published his epic poem, *Hiawatha,* to immediate popular acclaim.[12] Attempting to capitalize on the connection, Schoolcraft issued a new edition of his Algic/Chippewa stories, which he dedicated to Longfellow. Whereas in the original 1839 edition of *Algic Researches* the heroic figure of Manabozho had appeared in the middle of the first volume in a story entitled "Manabozho; or, the Great Incarnation of the North," now Schoolcraft moved him to the front of his one-volume work and renamed the tale "Hiawatha; or Manabozho." He added some from his *Oneota* series of the 1840s, omitted some from the original 1839 edition of *Algic Researches,* and repackaged them all as *The Myth of Hiawatha, and Other Oral Legends.*[13] Like his previous editions, the book sold poorly. At the same time, Schoolcraft came under fire for the disorganized, poorly edited *History, Condition and Prospects of the Indian Tribes.* Respected literary critic Francis Bowen, reviewing the first three volumes of the series in the influential *North*

---

[11] *Information Respecting . . .* was a six-volume compilation gathered and published, at government expense, between 1851 and 1857.

[12] The relation between Schoolcraft's story of "Manabozho" and Longfellow's "Hiawatha," as well as the much broader issues of borrowing by Longfellow in creating his poem, are explored authoritatively and in detail in Chase and Stellanova Osborn, *Schoolcraft-Longfellow-Hiawatha* (Lancaster, Penna., 1943); and Osborn and Osborn, *"Hiawatha" with Its Original Indian Legends* (Lancaster, Penna., 1944). As Mentor L. Williams appropriately points out, though, "there was never any real doubt about [Longfellow's indebtedness to Schoolcraft], because Longfellow acknowledged his debt handsomely." (Williams, ed., *Schoolcraft's Indian Legends* [East Lansing: Michigan State University Press, 1956]: xix.) For Schoolcraft's enthusiastic reception of Longfellow's epic, see Appendix 6 of Williams' 1956 edition.

[13] The full title was *The Myth of Hiawatha, and Other Oral Legends, Mythologic and Allegoric, of the North American Indians.* The eight-part *Oneota* series (1844–45) was later published by Schoolcraft as, variously, *The Red Race of America, The Indian in His Wigwam, The American Indians,* and *Western Scenes and Reminiscences: Together with Thrilling Legends and Traditions of the Red Men of the Forest* (1853).

American Review in 1853, labelled Schoolcraft's *magnum opus* a "crude and worthless compilation" that might very well "discredit the whole system of publishing works at the government expense." He particularly objected to the illustrations: "sheet after sheet, covered with sprawling outlines of man, bird, and beast, smeared with bright yellow or dirty red."[14]

After years of suffering from a progressive, debilitating paralysis of his right side, Schoolcraft died in the final year of the Civil War. Within a short time several new editions of his Indian tales appeared, diluted and simplified for juvenile audiences, under such titles as *The Indian Fairy Book* and *The Enchanted Mocassins*.[15] In these forms, as well as through the numerous reprintings of Longfellow's *Hiawatha,* the literary labors of Schoolcraft reached the first post-Civil War generations of America's urban, industrial population, providing a generalized and sentimentalized representation of the aboriginal conditions of North America.

The Myth of Hiawatha (originally *Algic Researches*) was, like the Johnston family and, indeed, Schoolcraft's own first marriage, the product of frontier confrontations and mixings.[16] It was a blending of cultures in contact and conflict, and the literary results were of a mixed variety—neither Chippewa/Ojibwa nor Anglo-American, but a unique amalgam of the two—the offspring of long winter nights in the Michigan semi-wilderness, the signs and traces of one culture struggling valiantly to survive and another, half-bred and vigorous, being born.

Curtis M. Hinsley
Regents' Professor of History
Northern Arizona University
November 1998

---

[14] Quoted in Freeman, *op cit.,* 307.

[15] Cornelius Mathews, *The Indian Fairy Book* (New York, 1869; reprinted in 1870, 1871, and 1872); Mathews, *The Enchanted Mocassins* (New York: G. P. Putnam's Sons, 1877); Florence Choate and Elizabeth Curtis, *The Indian Fairy Book* (New York, 1916).

[16] For analysis of Schoolcraft's stylistic contributions to his tales, see William M. Clements, *Native American Verbal Art: Texts and Contexts* (Tucson: The University of Arizona Press, 1996): 111–128.

General Considerations

I T IS proposed by the author to publish the result of his observation on the mythology, distinctive opinions, and intellectual character of the aborigines. Materials exist for separate observations on their oral tales, fictitious and historical; their hieroglyphics, music, and poetry; and the grammatical structure of the languages, their principles of combination, and the actual state of their vocabulary. The former topic has been selected as the commencement of the series. At what time the remaining portions will appear, will depend upon the interest manifested by the public in the subject, and the leisure and health necessary to the examination of a mass of original papers, the accumulation of nearly twenty years.

The character and peculiarities of the tribes have been studied under favourable circumstances and new aspects; offering, it is believed, an insight into their mental constitution, as yet but imperfectly understood. Hitherto our information has related rather to their external customs and manners, their physical traits and historical peculiarities, than to what may be termed the philosophy of the Indian mind. Such an examination required time and diligence. Much of the earlier part of it was necessarily devoted to clearing the ground of inquiry, by acquiring the principles of the languages, and obtaining data for generalization. This was to be done, too, at remote points of the Continent, away from all the facilities and encouragements of literary society, and with the aid of persons profoundly ignorant of the grammatical principles of the languages they spoke, and incapable of discriminating the fabulous from the true in the histories they related. The severe axioms of commerce had, from the first, caused the Indians to be regarded merely as the medium of a peculiar branch of trade, which was pursued at great hazards, excited deep animosity in the breasts of the respective commercial factors, and gave an absorbing interest to all that took place in the Indian country for two centuries. The interpretership of the languages became, of necessity, the business of a class of men who were generally uneducated, and who, imbued strongly with the feelings and prejudices of their employers, sought no higher excellence in their profession than to express the common ideas connected with the transactions of trade. The result was, then as now, that they comprehended the scope and genius of none of the languages they spoke. Whoever will submit to the labour of a critical examination into the subject, will soon become satisfied that the mediums of communication he is compelled to use are jargons, and not languages. It is impossible not to attribute to this imperfect state of oral translation, a considerable share of the errors and misunderstandings which have characterized our intercourse, political and commercial, with the tribes. Made sensible of this defect in the mode of communication, at an early period after my entrance into the Indian territories, my collections in Indian lexicography have been withheld from my journals of travel for further opportunity to examine the principles of the languages themselves. Notwithstanding this impression, and the care adopted to ensure accuracy, much of my earlier information, derived through the ordinary channels of interpretation, proved either wholly fallacious, or required to be tested and amended by a diligent course of subsequent scrutiny.

Language constituted the initial point of inquiry, but it did not limit it. It was found necessary to examine the mythology of the tribes as a means of acquiring an insight into their mode of thinking and reasoning, the sources of their fears and hopes, and the probable origin of their opinions and institutions. This branch of inquiry connected itself, in a manner which could not have been anticipated, with their mode of conveying instruction, moral, mechanical, and religious, to the young, through the intervention of traditionary fictitious tales and legends; and naturally, as the next effort of a barbarous people, to hieroglyphic signs to convey ideas and sounds. Rude as these characters were, however, they furnish very striking illustrations of their intellectual efforts, and exhibit evidences of that desire, implanted in the minds of all men, to convey to their contemporaries and transmit to posterity the prominent facts of their history and attainments. Nothing in the whole inquiry has afforded so ample a clew to their opinions and thoughts, in all the great departments of life and nature, as their oral imaginative tales; and it has, therefore, been deemed proper to introduce copious specimens of these collections from a large number of the tribes, embracing three of the generic stocks of language.

In adopting an original nominative for the series, the object has been to convey definite general impressions. The term ALGIC* is introduced, in a generic sense, for all that family of tribes who, about A. D. 1600, were found spread out, with local exceptions, along the Atlantic, between Pamlico Sound and the Gulf of St. Lawrence, extending northwest to the Missinipi of Hudson's Bay, and west to the Mississippi. The exceptions embrace the Yamassees and Catawbas on the coast, and the Tuscaroras, Iroquois, Wyandots, and Winnebagoes, and a part of the Sioux, in the interior, all of whom appear to have been intruders within the circle, and three of which, namely, the Tuscaroras, Iroquois, and Wyandots, speak dialects of a generic language, which we shall denominate the OSTIC.† The Winnebagoes are clearly of the Abanic‡ stock, and the Yamassees and Catawbas—extinct tribes, of whom but little has been preserved—of the restless and warlike Muscogee race. The latter, who, together with the Cherokees and Choctaws, fill up the southern portion of the Union, quite to the banks of the Mississippi, exist in juxtaposition to, and not as intruders within, the Algic circle. The Chickasaws are a scion of the Choctaws, as the Seminoles are of the Muscogees. The Choctaw and Muscogee are, radically, the same language. The Cherokees do not appear to have put forth any distant branches, and have come down to our times as a distinct people. It thus appears that four mother stocks occupied the entire

---

*Derived from the words Alleghany and Atlantic, in reference to the race of Indians anciently located in this geographical area, but who, as expressed in the text, had extended themselves, at the end of the 15th century, far towards the north and west.
†From the Algic *Oshtegwon,* a head, &c.
‡Denoting occidental. From *Kabeyun,* the west—and embracing the tribes who, at the commencement of 1800, were located west of the Mississippi. The Sioux, Otoes, Omahaws, Osages, and Quapaws, constitute the leading members of this group.

area of North America, east of the Mississippi, and lying between the Gulf of Mexico and Hudson's Bay, with the exception of a single tribe and a portion of another. The Winnebagoes, who are of the Abanic race, had, however, merely crossed from the west to the east banks of the Mississippi, but never proceeded beyond the shores of Green Bay. The Dacotahs had crossed this stream higher north, and proceeded to the west shores of Superior, whence they were beat back by the van of the Algics under the name of Odjibwas.

The object of inquiry is thus defined with general precision, although it is not intended to limit the inquiry itself to geographical boundaries. It will be perceived that the territory formerly occupied by the Algic nations comprehended by far the largest portion of the United States east of the Mississippi, together with a large area of the British possessions. They occupied the Atlantic coast as far south as the river Savannah in Georgia, if Shawnee tradition is entitled to respect, and as high north as the coast of Labrador, where the tribes of this stock are succeeded by the Esquimaux. It was into the limits of these people [Algics] that the Northmen, according to appearances, pushed their daring voyages previous to the discovery of Columbus;* and it was also among these far-spreading and independent hordes that the earliest European colonies were planted. Cabot, and Hudson, and Verrizani made their principal landings among the tribes of this type. The Pilgrims first set foot ashore in their midst, and they landed near the spot where, several centuries before, Thorwald Ericson had fallen a sacrifice to the spirit of Norwegian and Icelandic discovery. If the country had ever been occupied by Esquimaux, as indicated by Scandinavian history, there was not an Esquimaux there at that period. The entire coast of New-England was possessed by the Algics. They extended north of it to Cape Breton. Cartier found them in the Bay of Chaleur, the Pilgrims at Plimouth, Hudson at the island of Manhattan, Barlow and Amidas on the coasts of Virginia. They lined the seaboard; they appear to have migrated along its borders from

---

*For some remarks on this question, see Am. Biblical Repository, second series, No. 2, April, 1839.

southwest to northeast, and were probably attached to the open coast by the double facility which it afforded of a spontaneous subsistence, having the resources of the sea on one side and of the forest on the other. It is probable that these advantages led them to underrate the interior, which, being left unguarded, their enemies pushed in from the west, and seated themselves in Western New-York and Pennsylvania on the sources of the principal streams. It is evident that the Algics did not penetrate the interior to a great extent, their camps and towns forming, as it were, but a hem or cordon along the Atlantic. At the only points where this edging was penetrated, the discoverers found tribes of the Ostic stock, a fierce and indomitable race, of a sanguinary character, and speaking a harsh and guttural language. Such were the Iroquois, who were encountered on the Upper Hudson and the Mohawk, and the Wyandots found by Cartier at the islands of Orleans and Hochelaga. Regard these two leading races of the north in whatever light we may, it is impossible to overlook the strong points of character in which they differed. Both were dexterous and cunning woodsmen, excelling in all the forest arts necessary to their condition, and having much in their manners and appearance in common. But they spoke a radically different language, and they differed scarcely less in their distinctive character and policy. The one was mild and conciliating, the other fierce and domineering. They were alike in hospitality, in their misconception of virtue, and their high estimate of bravery. Independence was strikingly characteristic of both; but the one was satisfied with personal or tribal freedom, while the other sought to secure it by general combination. And if the two races be closely compared, there appears to be grounds for the opinion, that one is descended from a race of shepherds or pastoral nomades, and the other from a line of adventurers and warlike plunderers. It may, perhaps, be deemed among the auspicious circumstances which awaited the Europeans in this hemisphere, that they planted their earliest colonies among the former race.

In giving this enlarged signification to the terms Algic and Ostic, reference has been had to the requisitions of a general philological classification. But it is proper to remark of the Algic tribes, to whom our attention is to be particularly directed, that they were marked by peculiarities and shades of language and customs deemed to be quite striking among themselves. They were separated by large areas of territory, differing considerably in their climate and productions. They had forgotten the general points in their history, and each tribe and sub-tribe was prone to regard itself as independent of all others, if not the leading or parent tribe. Their languages exhibited diversities of sound, where there was none whatever in its syntax. Changes of accent and interchanges of consonants had almost entirely altered the aspect of words, and obscured their etymology. Some of the derivates were local, and not understood beyond a few hundred miles, and all the roots of the language were buried, as we find them at this day, beneath a load of superadded verbiage. The identity of the stock is, however, to be readily traced amid these discrepancies. They are assimilated by peculiar traits of a common physical resemblance; by general coincidence of manners, customs, and opinions; by the rude rites of a worship of spirits, everywhere the same; by a few points of general tradition; and by the peculiar and strongly-marked features of a transpositive language, identified by its grammar, alike in its primitive words, and absolutely fixed in the number and mode of modification of its radical sounds.

One or two additional remarks may be made in relation to the general traits of the Algic race. It was the chiefs of these nomadic bands who welcomed the Europeans to the shore. They occupied the Atlantic States. They everywhere received the strangers with open arms, established pacific relations with them, and evinced, both by their words and their policy, the abiding sense they had of the advantages of the intercourse. They existed so completely in the hunter state as to have no relish for any other kind of labour, looking with an inward and deep contempt on the arts of husbandry and mechanics. They had skill enough to construct their canoes; knew sufficient of the elementary art of weaving to make bags and nets of bark, and the simple tapestry or mats to cover their lodges; and, above all, they were expert in fabricating the proper missiles of war and hunting. They had no smiths, supplying their place by a very considerable skill in the cleavage of silicious stones. They knew enough of pottery to form a mixture which would stand the effects of repeated and sudden heating

and cooling, and had probably retained the first simple and effec-
tual arts of the human race in this branch. They had but little
knowledge of numbers, and none of letters; but found a substitute
for the latter in a system of hieroglyphics of a general character,
but quite exact in their mode of application, and absolutely fixed
in the elements. They were formal, and inclined to stateliness in
their councils and public intercourse, and very acute and expert
in the arrangement and discussion of minor matters, but failed in
comprehensive views, deep-reaching foresight, and powers of
generalization. Hence they were liable to be called cunning rather
than wise. They were, emphatically, men of impulse, capable of
extraordinary exertions on the instant, but could not endure the
tension, mental and physical, of long-continued exertions.
Action appeared to be always rather the consequence of nervous,
than of intellectual excitement. Above all, they were characterized by habits of sloth, which led them utterly to despise the
value of time; and this has appeared so constant a trait, under
every vicissitude of their history, that it may be regarded as the
probable effect of a luxurious effeminacy, produced upon the
race under a climate more adverse to personal activity. It should
be borne in mind, that the character first drawn of the Algic race
is essentially that which has been attributed to the whole of the
North American tribes, although it is not minutely applicable to
some of the interior nations. The first impressions made upon
the strangers from the Old World, sank deep; and there was,
naturally, but little disposition to re-examine the justice of the
conclusions thus formed. These people were, from the outset,
regarded as of eastern origin; and, if nothing before adverted to
had been suited to give colouring to the idea, it would have resulted,
almost as a matter of course, from their having, in all their tribes
and every band of them, a class of Magii, who affected to exert
the arts of magic, offered sacrifices to idolatrous things, and were
consulted as oracles both in peace and war. These pseudo priests
were called *Powows* by the English, *Jongleurs* by the French, and
by various other terms by themselves and by others; but their office
and general character were identical. They upheld a spurious
worship, and supported it by all sorts of trick and deception.
There was no regular succession in this priesthood, so far as is

known; but the office, like that of the war-captain, was generally assumed and exercised by men of more than ordinary acuteness and cunning. In other words, it was conferred by the election of opinion, but not of votes.

The Algics entered the present limits of the United States from the southwest. They appear to have crossed the Mississippi at the point where the heavy formations of boulder and gravel, southwest of the Alleghanies, are heaved up close along its banks. They were followed, at distinct eras, by the Ostic, the Muskogee, and the Tsallanic* hordes, by the first of whom they were driven, scattered, and harassed, and several of the tribes not only conquered, but exterminated. The Iroquois, who, in their sixfold dialects, constitute the type of the Ostics, appear to have migrated up the Valley of the Ohio, which they occupied and named; and, taking a most commanding and central position in Western New-York, interposed themselves between the New-England and the Algonquin sub-types, and thus cut off their communication with each other. This separation was complete. They pushed their conquests successfully down the Hudson, the Delaware, the Susquehanna, and the St. Lawrence, and westward up the great lakes. The Wyandots, an Ostic tribe, who, at the discovery of the St. Lawrence by the French, were posted as low down as the island of Orleans, formed an alliance with the French and with the Algonquins north of that stream. This exposed them to dissension with their warlike and jealous relatives the Iroquois, and led to their expulsion into the region of the upper lakes, even to the farther shores of Lake Superior. They were, however, supported by all the influence of the French, and by the whole of the confederate Algic tribes, and finally fixed themselves upon the Straits of Detroit, where they were privileged with a high political power, as keepers of the great council fire, and enjoyed much respect among the Western tribes through the whole of the eighteenth century. It was this tribe whom it required most address to bring over, in the combined struggle which the lake tribes made for independence under the noted Algic leader Pontiac, between 1759 and 1764.

------

*From *Tsallakee*—the name by which, according to David Brown, the Cherokees call themselves.

History first takes notice of the Algics in Virginia, and some parts of the Carolinas and Georgia. The Powhattanic tribes were a clearly-marked scion of this stock. They occupied all the streams of Virginia and Maryland flowing into the Ocean or into Chesapeake Bay. They were ever prone to divide and assume new names, which were generally taken from some prominent or characteristic feature in the geography or natural productions of the country. The farther they wandered, the more striking were their diversities, and the more obscure became every link by which identity is traced. Under the name of Lenawpees and of Mohegans, they extended along the seashore through the present limits of Delaware, Pennsylvania, New-Jersey, and New-York, and various petty independent tribes of the same race swept round the whole coast of New-England, and the British provinces beyond it, to Cape Breton and the Gulf of St. Lawrence. The traditions of all these tribes pointed southwest as the place of their origin, and it was there that they located the residence of their God. The Odjibwas and Algonquins proper, and their numerous progeny of tribes in the west and northwest, date their origin in the east, and to this day call the north and northwest winds the *home wind,* * indicating, probably, that it blows back on the track of their migration. Whether this be considered in a local or general sense, it is equally interesting of a people whose original terms are simple in meaning, and constitute, as it were, so many links in the investigation of their history. The whole of these tribes, interior and Atlantic, spoke branches of one radical language. Scattered as they were in geographical position, and marked by peculiarities of language and history, they are yet readily recognised as descendants from a common stock. Wherever the process of philological analysis is applied, the Algic roots are found. The tribes coincide also in their general character-istics, mental and physical. They employed the same hieroglyphic signs to express names and events; possessed the same simple, and, in some respects, childlike attainments in music and poetry, and brought with them to this Continent, and extensively propa-gated, a mythology, the strong belief in which furnishes the best

---

* *Keewaydin.*

clew to their hopes and fears, and lies at the foundation of the Indian character. Simple although their music is, there is something strikingly characteristic in it. Their Pib-e-gwun is but another name for the Arcadian pipe; but they did not appropriate the same music to love and religion. The latter was of a totally different, and of a louder and harsher kind. Their hieroglyphics, bearing quite a resemblance to the Egyptian, express a series of whole images, without adjuncts, and stand as general memoranda to help the recollection, and to be interpreted according to the mythology, customs, and arts of the people. There is nothing whatever in this system analogous to the Runic character. Nor does there appear to be, in either language or religion, anything approximating either to the Scandinavian or to the Hindoo races. With a language of a strongly Semitic cast, they appear to have retained leading principles of syntax where the lexicography itself has changed; and while they fell into a multiplicity of bands from the most common causes, they do not appear to have advanced an iota in their original stock of knowledge, warlike arts, or political tact, but rather fell back. The ancient bow and arrow, javelin, and earth kettle remained precisely the same things in their hands. And whatever mechanical skill they had in architecture, weaving, or any other arts, dwindled to a mere knowledge of erecting a wigwam, and weaving nets and garters. At least, if they possessed superior attainments in the Southern portions of this Continent, where they certainly dwelt, these were lost amid the more stern vicissitudes and frigid climate of the North. And this was perfectly natural. Of what use were these arts to a comparatively sparse population, who occupied vast regions, and lived, very well, by hunting the flesh and wearing the skins of animals? To such men a mere subsistence was happiness, and the killing of a few men in war glory. It may be doubted whether the very fact of the immensity of an unoccupied country, spread out before a civilized or half civilized people, with all its allurements of wild game and personal independence, would not be sufficient, in the lapse of a few centuries, to throw them back into a complete state of barbarism.

But we will not anticipate the results of research, where the object is merely to direct attention to the interest of the inquiry itself. To discover and fix the comprehensive points of their national resemblance, and the concurring circumstances of their history and traditions; to point out the affinities of their languages, and to unveil the principles of their mythology, are conceived to be essential prerequisites to the formation of right notions of their probable origin and mental peculiarities. And it is obvious that the true period for this inquiry must be limited to the actual existence of the tribes themselves. Every year is diminishing their numbers and adding to the obscurity of their traditions. Many of the tribes and languages are already extinct, and we can allude to at least one of the still existing smaller tribes who have lost the use of their vernacular tongue and adopted the English.* Distinct from every benevolent consideration, weighty as these are, it is exceedingly desirable that the record of facts, from which they are to be judged, should be completed as early as possible. It is conceived that, in rescuing their oral tales and fictitious legends, an important link in the chain has been supplied. But it is believed that still higher testimony remains. History, philosophy, and poetry regard with deep interest these recorded and accumulating materials on the character and origin of races of men, who are associated with the geographical nomenclature of the country, and to whom at least, it may be assumed, posterity will render poetic justice. But revelation has a deeper stake in the question, and it is one calculated to infuse new energy in the case of benevolence, and awaken fresh ardour in the heart of piety.

It is not the purpose of these remarks to excite the expectation that a long residence in the Indian country, and official intercourse with the tribes, have given the author such access to the Indian mind, or enabled him to push his inquiries so far into their former history and mental characteristics, as to clear up fully the obscurities referred to; but the hope is indulged that data have been obtained of a new and authentic character, which will prove important in any future researches on these topics.

---

*The Brothertons.

Preliminary Observations
on the Tales

T HE FOLLOWING tales are published as specimens of an oral
imaginative lore existing among the North American aborigines. In the long period of time in which these tribes
have been subjects of observation, we are not aware that powers
of this kind have been attributed to them. And it may be asked,
Why the discovery of this peculiar trait in their intellectual character has not been made until the first quarter of the nineteenth
century? The force of the query is acknowledged; and, in asserting
the claim for them, the writer of these pages proposes first to
offer to the public some proofs of the correctness of his own conclusions on this point.

The era of the discovery was the era of maritime adventure.
The master spirits of those times were men of shrewd, keen sense
and adventurous tempers, who wished to get ahead in the world,
and relied for their success, rather upon the compass and sword,
than upon their pens. It was the age of action and not of research.
Least of all, had they the means or the inclination to inquire into
the mental capacities of fierce and warlike races of hunters and
warriors, who claimed to be lords of the soil, and actually exterminated the first settlements made in St. Domingo and in
Virginia. They set out from Europe with a lamentable want of
true information respecting them, and were disappointed in not
finding them wild animals on two legs. Long after the discovery,
it was debated whether any faith ought to be kept with them; and
the chief point of inquiry was, not whether they had any right to
the soil, but how they could be turned to the best account in the
way of trade and merchandise. The Spaniards, who occupy the
foreground in the career of discovery, began by selling the Indian

and compelling him to feudal servitude, and would probably have driven as profitable a traffic as was subsequently carried on with the Africans, had it not soon appeared that the Indian was a lazy man, and not a productive labourer. He sank under the overwhelming idea of hopeless servitude, lingered a few years an unprofitable miner, and died. The project was therefore relinquished, not because of the awakened sensibilities of the conquerors, but because it was (in the mercantile acceptation of the term) a bad business. The history of the manners, customs, and languages of the ancient nations, and particularly of the oriental branches of the human family, from whom they were thought to have descended, was deeply in the dark. Comparative philology was unknown, and the spirit of critical and historical acumen, which has evinced itself in Germany in modern days, and is rapidly extending itself over the world, still slumbered under the intellectual darkness which spellbound the human mind after the overthrow of Greece and Rome, and the dispersion of the Jews. To expect, therefore, that the hardy commanders of exploring voyages should have, at the opening of the sixteenth century, entered into any minute inquiries of the kind referred to, would be to expect that the human mind should reverse its ordinary mode of operation. These men do not appear to have troubled themselves with the inquiry whether the Indians *had* a history: certainly they took no pains to put on record facts in the department of inquiry to which our attention is now directed. This view results from an attentive examination of the earlier voyages and histories of adventure in this hemisphere, in which is exhibited the coldest air of mercantile calculation. The journals themselves are mere logbooks, rigid and dry in their details, destitute of any powers of reflection upon the events they narrate, and unrelieved by exact research, tact of observation, or high-souled sentiment.

History is required to pass a less censorious judgment on the moral character of those of the colonists who settled north of the latitudes of the West Indies. The great Anglo-Saxon stock, which spread along the shores of the North Atlantic, carried with it notions of liberty and justice, which shielded the aboriginal tribes from the curse of slavery. They treated them as having a just right to the occupancy of the soil, and formed treaties with them. They acknowledged, by these acts, their existence as independent political communities, and maintained, in their fullest extent, the doctrine of political faith and responsibility. Some of the colonies went farther, and early directed their attention to their improvement and conversion to Christianity. The two powers were, however, placed in circumstances adverse to the prosperous and contemporaneous growth of both, while they occupied a territory over which there was a disputed sovereignty. It must needs have happened, that the party which increased the fastest in numbers, wanted most land, and had most knowledge (to say nothing of the influence of temperance and virtue), should triumph, and those who failed in these requisites, decline. It is believed that this is the true cause why the transplanted European race overspread the land, and the Indians were driven before them. And that the result is by no means owing to a proper want of sympathy for the latter, or of exertions both to better their condition and avert their fate. The Indians could not, however, be made to understand this. They did not look to causes, but reasoned wholly from effects. They saw the white race occupying the prominent harbours, pushing up the navigable streams, spreading over the uplands, and multiplying in numbers "like sands on the sea-shore." And they attributed to hostile purpose, breach of faith, and cupidity, what was, to a very great extent, owing to their own idle habits, vices, and short-sightedness. The two races soon came to measure swords; and this contest extended, with short periods of intervening peace, from about A. D. 1600 to the close of 1814. The Indians staked stratagem and the geographical obstacles of a vast unknown wilderness, against knowledge, resources, and discipline. Their policy was to fly when pursued, and pursue when relieved from pursuit; to avoid field fights, and carry on a most harassing war of detail. By avoiding concentration in camps, and occupying a comparatively large area of country, they have compelled their assailants, at all times, to employ a force entirely disproportioned to that required to cope with the same number of civilized troops. The result of this long-continued, and often renewed contest for supremacy, it is only necessary to advert to. It has been anything but favourable to the production of right feelings and a reciprocal knowledge of real character on both sides. The Indians could never be made to appreciate the offers of education and Christianity by one portion of the community, while others were arrayed against them in arms. Their idea of government was, after all, the Eastern notion of a unity or despotism, in which everything emanates from the governing power, and is responsible to it. Nor has their flitting and feverish position on the frontiers been auspicious to the acquisition of a true knowledge of their character, particularly in those things which have relation to the Indian mind, their opinions on abstract subjects, their mythology, and other kindred topics. Owing to illiterate interpreters and dishonest men, the parties have never more than half understood each other. Distrust and misapprehension have existed by the century together. And it is, therefore, no cause for astonishment, that the whole period of our contemporaneous history should be filled up with so many negotiations and cessions, wars and treaties.

These remarks are offered to indicate that the several periods of our colonial and confederate history, and wars, were unfavourable to the acquisition of that species of information respecting their mental capacities and social institutions, of which it is our purpose to speak. The whole tendency of our intercourse with them has been to demonstrate rather the physical than moral capabilities of the Indian, his expertness in war, his skill, stratagem, powers of endurance, and contempt of suffering. Indian fortitude has been applauded at the stake, and Indian kindness and generosity acknowledged in the wigwam, and in the mazes of the wilderness. Admiration had been excited by his noble sentiments of independence and exaltation above personal fear. Above all, perhaps, had he been accredited for intellect in his acuteness in negotiation and the simple force of his oratory. But the existence of an intellectual invention had never been traced, so far as it is known, to the amusements of his domestic fireside; nor could it well have been conjectured to occupy so wide a field for its display in legendary tales and fables.

My attention was first arrested by the fact of the existence of such tales among the Odjibwa nation inhabiting the region about Lake Superior in 1822. Two years previous, I had gone out in that quarter as one of the members of a corps of observation, on an exploratory expedition to the head waters of the Mississippi. The large area of territory which it was found this tribe occupied, together with their number and warlike character, induced the department of war to extend a military post to the Falls or *Sault* of St. Mary's, near the outlet of Lake Superior, in the year above named. I accompanied this force, and assumed, at the same time, an official relation to this tribe, as Agent of Indian Affairs, which led me to inquire into their distinctive history, language, and characteristic traits. It was found that they possessed a story-telling faculty, and I wrote down from their narration a number of these fictitious tales;* some of which were amusing merely, others were manifestly intended to convey mythologic or allegoric information. The boundaries between truth and fiction are but feebly defined among the aborigines of this Continent, and it was found in this instance, that the individuals of the tribe who related the tales were also the depositories of their historical traditions, such as they were; and these narrators wove the few and scattered incidents and landmarks of their history into the web and woof of their wildest tales. I immediately announced this interesting discovery in their moral character to a few friends and correspondents, who were alike interested in the matter; and a new zest was thus given to the inquiry, and the field of observation greatly extended. The result was the finding of similar tales among all the northwestern tribes whose traditions were investigated. They were also found among some of the tribes west of the Mississippi, and the present state of the inquiry demonstrates that this species of oral lore is common to the Algic, the Ostic, and some tribes of the Abanic stock. It is conjectured to exist among the rather extended branches of the Muskogee, and also the Cherokee, although no actual proof is possessed. And it becomes a question of interest to ascertain how far a similar trait can be traced among the North American tribes, and where the exceptions and limitations are to be found. To find a trait which

---

*Some specimens of these tales were published in my "Travels in the Central Portions of the Mississippi Valley" in 1825, and a "Narrative of the Expedition to Itasca Lake" in 1834, and a few of them have been exhibited to literary friends, who have noticed the subject. *Vide* Dr. Gilman's "Life on the Lakes," and Mrs. Jameson's "Winter Studies and Summer Rambles," received at the moment these sheets are going through the press.

must hereafter be deemed characteristic of the mental habits of these tribes, so diffused, furnishes a strong motive for extending inquiries farther and wider. It may be asked whether the South American aborigines possessed or still possess, this point of intellectual affinity with the tribes of the North. Did Manco Capac and Montezuma employ this means to strengthen political power, inspire courage, or console themselves under misfortune? Do the ice-bound and impoverished natives of the Arctic circle draw inspiration in their cruel vicissitudes from a similar intellectual source? What sound deductions can be drawn from a comparison of Eastern with Western fable, as thus developed? And, finally, is this propensity connected, in other of the American stock tribes, with a hieroglyphic system of notation, as we find it in the Algic, which will bear any useful comparison with the phonetic system of Egypt, the Runic of Iceland and Norway, or with any other mode of perpetuating the knowledge of events or things known to the human race?

A few remarks may be added respecting the character of the tales now submitted to inspection. And the first is, that they appear to be of a homogeneous and vernacular origin. There are distinctive tribal traits, but the general features coincide. The ideas and incidents do not appear to be borrowed or unnatural. The situations and circumstances are such as are common to the people. The language and phraseology are of the most simple kind. Few adjectives are used, and few comparisons resorted to. The style of narration, the cast of invention, the theory of thinking, are eminently peculiar to a people who wander about in woods and plains, who encounter wild beasts, believe in demons, and are subject to the vicissitudes of the seasons. The tales refer themselves to a people who are polytheists; not believers in one God or Great Spirit, but of thousands of spirits; a people who live in fear, who wander in want, and who die in misery. The machinery of spirits and necromancy, one of the most ancient and prevalent errors of the human race, supplies the framework of these fictitious creations. Language to carry out the conceptions might seem to be wanting, but here the narrator finds a ready resource in the use of metaphor, the doctrine of metamorphosis, and the personification of inanimate objects; for the latter of which, the grammar of the language has a peculiar adaptation. Deficiencies of the vocabulary are thus supplied, life and action are imparted to the whole material creation, and every purpose of description is answered. The belief of the narrators and listeners in every wild and improbable thing told, helps wonderfully, in the original, in joining the sequence of parts together. Nothing is too capacious for Indian belief. Almost every declaration is a prophecy, and every tale a creed. He believes that the whole visible and invisible creation is animated with various orders of malignant or benign spirits, who preside over the daily affairs and over the final destinies of men. He believes that these spirits must be conciliated by sacrifices, and a series of fasts and feasts either follow or precede these rites, that by the one they may be rendered acceptable, and by the other, his gratitude may be shown. This constitutes the groundwork of the Algic religion: but superstition has ingrafted upon the original stock, till the growth is a upas of giant size, bearing the bitter fruits of demonology, witchcraft, and necromancy. To make the matter worse, these tribes believe that animals of the lowest, as well as highest class in the chain of creation, are alike endowed with reasoning powers and faculties. And as a natural conclusion, they endow birds, and bears, and all other animals with souls, which, they believe, will be encountered in other shapes in another state of existence. So far the advantages of actual belief come in aid of their fictitious creations, and this is the true cause why so much importance is attached to the flight and appearance of particular birds, who, being privileged to ascend in the air, are supposed by them to be conversant with the wishes, or to act in obedience to the mandates of the spirits: and the circumstance of this belief deserves to be borne in mind in the perusal of their tales, as it will be found that the words put into the mouths of the actors express the actual opinions of the natives on life, death, and immortality, topics which have heretofore been impenetrably veiled.

The value of these traditionary stories appeared to depend, very much, upon their being left, as nearly as possible, in their original forms of thought and expression. In the original there is no attempt at ornament. Great attention is paid, in the narration, to repeating the conversations and speeches, and imitating the very tone and gesture of the actors. This is sometimes indulged at the risk of tautology. Moral point has been given to no tale which does not, in the original, justify it; and it is one of the unlooked-for features connected with the subject, that so considerable a proportion of them possess this trait. It is due to myself, and to those who have aided me in the collection and translation of the materials, to say, that the advantages enjoyed in this respect have been of the most favourable character. The whole examination, extending, with intervals, through a period of seventeen years, has been conducted not only with the aid that a public station, as an executive officer for the tribes, has supplied, but with the super-added intelligence and skill in the languages existing within the range of my domestic and affiliated circle.

Of the antiquity of the tales, the surest external evidence may probably be drawn from the lexicography. In a language in which the actor and the object are riveted, so to speak, by transitive inflections, it must needs happen that the history of its names for objects, whether preserved orally or by letters, is, in fact, the history of the introduction of the objects named, and this fixes eras in the enlargement of the vocabulary. Although it is true, that without letters these eras cannot be accurately fixed, yet valuable inferences may be drawn from an examination of this branch of the inquiry. Words are like coins, and may, like them, be examined to illustrate history. It has been found that those of the highest antiquity are simple and brief. Most of the primitive nouns are monosyllabic, and denote but a single object or idea. A less number are dissyllabic; few exceed this; and it may be questioned, from the present state of the examination, whether there is a single primitive trisyllable. The primitives become polysyllabic by adding an inflection indicating the presence or absence of vitality (which is the succedaneum for gender), and a farther inflection to denote number. They also admit of adjective terminations. Pronouns are denoted by particles prefixed or suffixed. The genius of the language is accumulative, and tends rather to add syllables or letters, making farther distinctions in objects already before the mind, than to introduce new words. A simple word is thus oftentimes converted into a descriptive phrase, at once formidable to the eye and the ear. And it is only by dissecting such compounds that the radix can be attained.

Judged by this test, most of the tales are of the era of flint arrow-heads, earthen pots, and skin clothes. Their fish-nets are represented as being made of the bark of trees. No mention is made of a blanket, gun, knife, or any metallic instrument; we do not hear of their cutting down trees, except in a single instance, yet there is nothing to indicate that their economical labours were not well performed. *Au* is an original, causitive particle, and appears to be the root of a numerous class of words, sometimes with, and sometimes without a consonant added. *Aukee* is earth, and may be, but is rather too remote for a derivative from אֶרֶץ.*
By adding *k* to this root the term is made specific, and denotes an earthen pot or kettle. *Aubik* is the radix for metal, ore, rock. By prefixing the particle *Pe,* we have the name for iron, *Misk* for copper, and so forth; but as euphony requires, in forming compounds, that two vowels should not come together, the sound of *w* is interposed in these particular instances. *Gunzh* is the radix for plant; *Tig* for tree; *Asee* for animal, &c.; and either by suffixing or prefixing syllabical increments, the terminology of the three great departments of nature is formed. The terms of consanguinity are derived from *Ai,* a heart, hence *Si-ai,* elder brother, *Sheem-ai,* younger brother, or younger sister, &c. *Konaus,* a loose wrapper, is the most ancient and generic term for a garment which has been found. The principal female garment, leggon, &c., are derivatives from it. *Muttataus,* a beaver robe, is from the same root. *Wyaun,* a furred skin, and *Waigin,* a dressed skin, appear to form the bases of the nomenclature for the Indian wardrobe. Blanket is a modern term, meaning white furred skin. Woollen cloth took the name of dressed skin, and its various colours and qualities are indicated by adjective prefixes. Calicoes or printed cottons are named for a generic, meaning speckled or spotted. All these are modern terms, as modern as those for a horse, a sheep, or a hog, and, like the latter, are descriptive and polysyllabic. Tobacco and the zea mays, both indigenous productions, are mentioned. The latter is the subject of a simple allegoric tale.

These particulars may suffice to indicate the importance of

---

*[For commentary on the Hebrew, see the note, pp. 40–41.]

etymological analysis in examining the antiquity of the tales. Narrations of a later era are denoted by the introduction of the modern compounds, such as their names for the domestic animals of Europe, a gun, a rifle, a ship, a spyglass, compass, watch, hat, &c. The bow and arrow, club and lance, are the only species actually described as in use, except in a single instance, and this tale is manifestly an interpolated version of an ancient story. The father of the winds makes battle with a huge flagroot, and the king of reptiles is shot with a dart.

Geographical terms and allusions to the climate supply another branch of comparison. Some of the grand features of the country are referred to by their modern Indian names, but this is nearly restricted to what may be termed the historical legends. There are frequent allusions to the Northern hemisphere. Snow, ice, and lakes are referred to. Warm latitudes are once or twice mentioned, and the allusions are coupled with admonitions against the danger of corrupt and effeminate manners and habits.

Astronomy and cosmogony constitute subjects of frequent notice; and this might naturally be expected from a people who are quick in their perceptions of external nature, and pass a large share of time under the open sky. The phenomena of thunder, lightning, the aurora borealis, meteors, the rainbow, the galaxy of the milky way, the morning and evening stars, and the more prominent groups of the fixed and minor stars, are specifically named and noticed. The cardinal points are accurately distinguished. They entertain the semi-ancient theory that the earth is spheroidal, and the sun and moon perform their circuits round it. The visiters to these luminaries, described in the text, personify the former as a male and the latter as a female, under the idea of brother and sister. We are left to infer, from another passage, that they believe the sky revolves. Nothing, however, in the "open firmament," is a subject of more constant and minute observation, and a more complex terminology, than the clouds. Their colour, shape, transparency or obscurity, movements, and relative position to the sun and to each other, constitute objects of minute notice and deep importance. A large proportion of the names of individuals in the Algic tribes is drawn from this fruitful source of Indian observation. The Great Spirit is invariably located in the sky, and the Evil Spirit, and the train of minor malignant Spirits, in the earth. Their notions of the position of seas and continents are altogether vague and confused. Nor has it been observed that they have any knowledge of volcanic action. The idea of a universal deluge appears to be equally entertained by the tribes of North and South America.* The Algics certainly have it incorporated in their traditionary tales, and I have found the belief in these traditions the most firmly seated among the bands the farthest removed from the advances of civilization and Christianity.

It is the mythology, however, of these tribes which affords the deepest insight into their character, and unfolds, perhaps, some of the clearest coincidences with Oriental rites and opinions. Were the terms Baalim and Magii introduced into the descriptions of their worship, instead of Manito and Meeta, this coincidence would be very apparent. Medical magic spread the charms of its delusion over the semi-barbaric tribes who, at a very early epoch, spread from the Persian and the Arabian Gulfs to the Mediterranean; and it would not be a light task to find branches of the human race who are more completely characterized by its doctrines and practices than the wide-spreading members of the Algic stock of this Continent. Their prophets, jugglers, and meetays occupy the same relative importance in the political scale. They advise the movement of armies, and foretell the decrees of fate to individuals. They interpret dreams, affect the performance of miraculous cures, and preside over the most sacred rites. Oracles alike to chiefs and kings, warriors and hunters, nothing can be accomplished without their aid, and it would be presumptuous and impious to attempt anything, in war or peace, which they had decreed to be wrong. But our more immediate object is the class of oral fictions among the Western tribes, and for the growth and development of which their peculiar belief in the doctrine of spirits and magicians has furnished so wide a field. Come from what quarter of the world they may, the propensity to amusing and serio-comic fiction appears to have been brought with them.

*Humboldt found it among the traditions of the Auricanians.

What traits, if any, of the original threadwork of foreign story remain, it would be premature, in the present state of these collections, to decide. The character and incidents of the narrations are adapted to the condition they are now in, as well as the position they now occupy. There is, it is true, a spirit of reminiscence apparent which pleases itself in allusions to the past; they speak of a sort of golden age, when all things were better with them than they now are; when they had better laws and leaders; when crimes were more promptly punished; when their language was spoken with greater purity, and their manners were freer from barbarism. But all this seems to flit through the Indian mind as a dream, and furnishes him rather the source of a pleasing secret retrospection than any spring to present and future exertions. He pines away as one that is fallen, and despairs to rise. He does not seem to open his eyes on the prospect of civilization and mental exaltation held up before him, as one to whom the scene is new or attractive. These scenes have been pictured before him by teachers and philanthropists for more than two centuries; but there has been nothing in them to arouse and inspire him to press onward in the career of prospective civilization and refinement. He has rather turned away with the air of one to whom all things "new" were "old," and chosen emphatically to re-embrace his woods, his wigwam, and his canoe.

Perhaps the trait that was least to have been anticipated in the tales is the moral often conveyed by them. But, on reflection, this is in accordance with the Indian maxim, which literally requires "an eye for an eye, and a tooth for a tooth." And the more closely this feature of poetic justice is scrutinized, the more striking does it appear. Cruelty, murder, and sorcery are eventually punished, although the individual escapes for the time and his career may be long drawn out. Domestic infidelity meets the award of death in the only instance narrated. Religious vows are held inviolate. Respect for parents and for age, fraternal affection, hospitality, bravery, self-denial, endurance under fatigue or suffering, and disinterestedness, are uniformly inculcated. Presumption and pride are rebuked, and warnings given against the allurements of luxury and its concomitant vices. With a people who look back to some ancient and indefinite period in their history as an age of glory, an adherence to primitive manners and customs naturally occupies the place of virtue. The stories are generally so constructed as to hold up to admiration a bold and independent spirit of enterprise and adventure. Most of their heroes are drawn from retired or obscure places, and from abject circumstances. Success is seen to crown the efforts of precocious boys, orphans, or castaways. But whatever success is had, it is always through the instrumentality of the spirits or Manitoes—the true deities worshipped by all the Algic tribes.

The legend of Manabozho reveals, perhaps, the idea of an incarnation. He is the great spirit-man of northern mythology. The conception of the character reveals rather a monstrosity than a deity, displaying in strong colours far more of the dark and incoherent acts of a spirit of carnality than the benevolent deeds of a god. His birth is shrouded in allegoric mystery. He is made to combine all that is brave, warlike, strong, wise, and great in Indian conception, both of mortal and immortal. He conquers the greatest magician, overcomes fiery serpents, and engages in combats and performs exploits the most extravagant. He has no small share in the Adamic-like labour of naming the animals. He destroys the king of the reptile creation, is drawn into the mouth of a gigantic fish with his canoe, survives a flood by climbing a tree, and recreates the earth from a morsel of ground brought up in the paws of a muskrat. In contrast with these high exploits, he goes about playing low tricks, marries a wife, travels the earth, makes use of low subterfuges, is often in want of food, and, after being tricked and laughed at, is at one time made to covet the ability of a woodpecker, and at another outdone by the simple skill of a child. The great points in which he is exultingly set forth in the story-telling circle, are his great personal strength, readiness of resource, and strong powers of necromancy. Whatever other parts he is made to play, it is the Indian Hercules, Samson, or Proteus that is prominently held up to admiration. It is perhaps natural that rude nations in every part of the world should invent some such mythological existence as the Indian Manabozho to concentrate their prime exploits upon; for it is the maxim of such nations that "the race *is* always to the swift, and the battle to the strong."

In closing these remarks, it will not be irrelevant to notice the evidence of the vernacular character and antiquity of the tales, which is furnished by the Pontiac manuscript, preserved in the collections of the Historical Society of Michigan. By this document, which is of the date of 1763, it is shown that this shrewd and talented leader of the Algic tribes, after he had formed the plan of driving the Saxon race from the Continent, appealed to the mythologic belief of the tribes to bring them into his views. It was the Wyandots whom he found it the hardest to convert; and in the general council which he held with the Western chiefs, he narrated before them a tale of a Delaware magician, which is admirably adapted in its incidents to the object he had in view, and affords proof of his foresight and powers of invention. It is deemed of further interest in this connexion, as carrying back the existence of the tales and fables to a period anterior to the final fall of the French power in the Canadas, reaching to within a fraction more than sixty years of their establishment at Detroit.* While, however, the authenticity of this curious politico-mythologic tale is undisputed, the names and allusions would show it to be of the modern class of Indian fictions, were not the fact historically known. The importance of this testimony, in the absence of any notice of this trait in the earlier writers, has induced me to submit a literal translation of the tale, from the original French MS., executed by Professor Fasquelle.

---

*Although Quebec was taken in 1759, the Indians did not acquiesce in the transference of power, in the upper lakes, till the *raising of the siege* of Detroit in 1763. This is the true period of the Pontiac war.

VOLUME I

NOTE

THE MATERIALS of these tales and legends have been derived
from the aborigines, and interpreted from their languages by various individuals, among whom it is deemed important to name
the following: Mrs. Henry R. Schoolcraft, Mr. William Johnston,
of Mackinac; Mrs. James Lawrence Schoolcraft, Henry Connor,
Esq., of Detroit; Mrs. [Rev.] William M'Murray, of Dundas,
George C. Martin, of Amherstburg, U. Canada; Mrs. La Chapelle,
of Prairie du Chien; Mr. John Quinney, Stockbridge Reserve,
Wisconsin; John H. Kinzie, Esq., of Chicago; Miss Eleanor
Bailly, of Konamik, Illinois; Mr. George Johnston, Miss Mary
Holiday, of Sault Ste. Marie, Michigan. These persons are well
versed in the respective tongues from which they have given
translations; and being residents of the places indicated, a reference to them for the authenticity of the materials is thus brought
within the means of all who desire it.

It is also deemed proper to refer, in this connexion, to Gen. Cass,
American Minister at Paris, and to C. C. Trowbridge, Esq., of
Detroit, and James D. Doty, Esq., Green Bay, whose inquiries
have been, at my instance, respectively directed to this new feature
in the oral traditions of the Indians.

New-York, January 31, 1839.

OJEEG ANNUNG*

or

THE SUMMER-MAKER

An Odjibwa Tale†

THERE LIVED a celebrated hunter on the southern shores of Lake Superior, who was considered a Manito by some, for there was nothing but what he could accomplish. He lived off the path, in a wild, lonesome place, with a wife whom he loved, and they were blessed with a son, who had attained his thirteenth year. The hunter's name was Ojeeg, or the Fisher, which is the name of an expert, sprightly little animal common to the region. He was so successful in the chase, that he seldom returned without bringing his wife and son a plentiful supply of venison, or other dainties of the woods. As hunting formed his constant occupation, his son began early to emulate his father in the same employment, and would take his bow and arrows, and exert his skill in trying to kill birds and squirrels. The greatest impediment he met with was the coldness and severity of the climate. He often returned home, his little fingers benumbed with cold, and crying with vexation at his disappointment. Days, and months, and years passed away, but still the same perpetual depth of snow was seen, covering all the country as with a white cloak.

---

*There is a group of stars in the Northern hemisphere which the Odjibwas call *Ojeeg Annung,* or the Fisher Stars. It is believed to be identical with the group of the Plough. They relate the following tale respecting it.
†This term is used, in these tales, as synonymous with Chippewa.

3

One day, after a fruitless trial of his forest skill, the little boy was returning homeward with a heavy heart, when he saw a small red squirrel gnawing the top of a pine bur. He had approached within a proper distance to shoot, when the squirrel sat up on its hind legs and thus addressed him:

"My grandchild, put up your arrows, and listen to what I have to tell you." The boy complied rather reluctantly, when the squirrel continued: "My son, I see you pass frequently, with your fingers benumbed with cold, and crying with vexation for not having killed any birds. Now, if you will follow my advice, we will see if you cannot accomplish your wishes. If you will strictly pursue my advice, we will have perpetual summer, and you will then have the pleasure of killing as many birds as you please; and I will also have something to eat, as I am now myself on the point of starvation.

"Listen to me. As soon as you get home you must commence crying. You must throw away your bow and arrows in discontent. If your mother asks you what is the matter, you must not answer her, but continue crying and sobbing. If she offers you anything to eat, you must push it away with apparent discontent, and continue crying. In the evening, when your father returns from hunting, he will inquire of your mother what is the matter with you. She will answer that you came home crying, and would not so much as mention the cause to her. All this while you must not leave off sobbing. At last your father will say, 'My son, why is this unnecessary grief? Tell me the cause. You know I am a spirit, and that nothing is impossible for me to perform.' You must then answer him, and say that you are sorry to see the snow continually on the ground, and ask him if he could not cause it to melt, so that we might have perpetual summer. Say it in a supplicating way, and tell him this is the cause of your grief. Your father will reply, 'It is very hard to accomplish your request, but for your sake, and for my love for you, I will use my utmost endeavours.' He will tell you to be still, and cease crying. He will try to bring summer with all its loveliness. You must then be quiet, and eat that which is set before you."

The squirrel ceased. The boy promised obedience to his advice, and departed. When he reached home, he did as he had been instructed, and all was exactly fulfilled, as it had been predicted by the squirrel.

Ojeeg told him that it was a great undertaking. He must first make a feast, and invite some of his friends to accompany him on a journey. Next day he had a bear roasted whole. All who had been invited to the feast came punctually to the appointment. There were the Otter, Beaver, Lynx, Badger, and Wolverine. After the feast, they arranged it among themselves to set out on the contemplated journey in three days. When the time arrived, the Fisher took leave of his wife and son, as he foresaw that it was for the last time. He and his companions travelled in company day after day, meeting with nothing but the ordinary incidents. On the twentieth day they arrived at the foot of a high mountain, where they saw the tracks of some person who had recently killed an animal, which they knew by the blood that marked the way. The Fisher told his friends that they ought to follow the track, and see if they could not procure something to eat. They followed it for some time; at last they arrived at a lodge, which had been hidden from their view by a hollow in the mountain. Ojeeg told his friends to be very sedate, and not to laugh on any account. The first object that they saw was a man standing at the door of the lodge, but of so deformed a shape that they could not possibly make out who or what sort of a man it could be. His head was enormously large; he had such a queer set of teeth, and no arms. They wondered how he could kill animals. But the secret was soon revealed. He was a great Manito. He invited them to pass the night, to which they consented.

He boiled his meat in a hollow vessel made of wood, and took it out of this singular kettle in some way unknown to his guests. He carefully gave each their portion to eat, but made so many odd movements that the Otter could not refrain from laughing, for he is the only one who is spoken of as a jester. The Manito looked at him with a terrible look, and then made a spring at him, and got on him to smother him, for that was his mode of killing animals. But the Otter, when he felt him on his neck, slipped his head back and made for the door, which he passed in safety; but went out with the curse of the Manito. The others passed the night, and they conversed on different subjects. The Manito told the Fisher that he would accomplish his object, but that it would probably cost him his life. He gave them his advice, directed them how to act, and described a certain road which they must follow, and they would thereby be led to the place of action.

They set off in the morning, and met their friend, the Otter, shivering with cold; but Ojeeg had taken care to bring along some of the meat that had been given him, which he presented to his friend. They pursued their way, and travelled twenty days more before they got to the place which the Manito had told them of. It was a most lofty mountain. They rested on its highest peak to fill their pipes and refresh themselves. Before smoking, they made the customary ceremony, pointing to the heavens, the four winds, the earth, and the zenith; in the meantime, speaking in a loud voice, addressed the Great Spirit, hoping that their object would be accomplished. They then commenced smoking.

They gazed on the sky in silent admiration and astonishment, for they were on so elevated a point that it appeared to be only a short distance above their heads. After they had finished smoking, they prepared themselves. Ojeeg told the Otter to make the first attempt to try and make a hole in the sky. He consented with a grin. He made a leap, but fell down the hill stunned by the force of his fall; and the snow being moist, and falling on his back, he slid with velocity down the side of the mountain. When he found himself at the bottom, he thought to himself, it is the last time I make such another jump, so I will make the best of my way home. Then it was the turn of the Beaver, who made the attempt, but fell down senseless; then of the Lynx and Badger, who had no better success.

"Now," says the Fisher to the Wolverine, "try your skill; your ancestors were celebrated for their activity, hardihood, and perseverance, and I depend on you for success. Now make the attempt." He did so, but also without success. He leaped the second time, but now they could see that the sky was giving way to their repeated attempts. Mustering strength, he made the third leap, and went in. The Fisher nimbly followed him.

They found themselves in a beautiful plain, extending as far as the eye could reach, covered with flowers of a thousand different hues and fragrance. Here and there were clusters of tall, shady trees, separated by innumerable streams of the purest water, which wound around their courses under the cooling shades, and filled the plain with countless beautiful lakes, whose banks and bosom were covered with waterfowl, basking and sporting in the sun. The trees were alive with birds of different plumage, warbling their sweet notes, and delighted with perpetual spring.

The Fisher and his friend beheld very long lodges, and the celestial inhabitants amusing themselves at a distance. Words cannot express the beauty and charms of the place. The lodges were empty of inhabitants, but they saw them lined with mocuks* of different sizes, filled with birds and fowls of different plumage. Ojeeg thought of his son, and immediately commenced cutting open the mocuks and letting out the birds, who descended in whole flocks through the opening which they had made. The warm air of those regions also rushed down through the opening, and spread its genial influence over the north.

When the celestial inhabitants saw the birds let loose, and the warm gales descending, they raised a shout like thunder, and ran for their lodges. But it was too late. Spring, summer, and autumn had gone; even perpetual summer had almost gone; but they separated it with a blow, and only a part descended; but the ends were so mangled, that, wherever it prevails among the lower inhabitants, it is always sickly.†

When the Wolverine heard the noise, he made for the opening and safely descended. Not so the Fisher. Anxious to fulfill his son's wishes, he continued to break open the mocuks. He was, at last, obliged to run also, but the opening was now closed by the inhabitants. He ran with all his might over the plains of heaven, and, it would appear, took a northerly direction. He saw his pursuers so close that he had to climb the first large tree he came to. They commenced shooting at him with their arrows, but without effect, for all his body was invulnerable except the space of about an inch near the tip of his tail. At last one of the arrows hit the spot, for he had in this chase assumed the shape of the Fisher after whom he was named.

He looked down from the tree, and saw some among his

---

*Baskets, or cages.
†The idea here indicated is among the peculiar notions of these tribes, and is grafted in the forms of their language, which will be pointed out in the progress of these researches.

assailants with the totems* of his ancestors. He claimed relationship, and told them to desist, which they only did at the approach of night. He then came down to try and find an opening in the celestial plain, by which he might descend to the earth. But he could find none. At last, becoming faint from the loss of blood from the wound on his tail, he laid himself down towards the north of the plain, and, stretching out his limbs, said, "I have fulfilled my promise to my son, though it has cost me my life; but I die satisfied in the idea that I have done so much good, not only for him, but for my fellow-beings. Hereafter I will be a sign to the inhabitants below for ages to come, who will venerate my name for having succeeded in procuring the varying seasons. They will now have from eight to ten moons without snow."

He was found dead next morning, but they left him as they found him, with the arrow sticking in his tail, as it can be plainly seen, at this time, in the heavens.

---

*Family arms, or armorial mark.

THE CELESTIAL SISTERS

A Shawnee Tale

WAUPEE, OR the White Hawk, lived in a remote part of the forest, where animals and birds were abundant. Every day he returned from the chase with the reward of his toil, for he was one of the most skillful and celebrated hunters of his tribe. With a tall, manly form, and the fire of youth beaming from his eye, there was no forest too gloomy for him to penetrate, and no track made by the numerous kinds of birds and beasts which he could not follow.

One day he penetrated beyond any point which he had before visited. He travelled through an open forest, which enabled him to see a great distance. At length he beheld a light breaking through the foliage, which made him sure that he was on the borders of a prairie. It was a wide plain covered with grass and flowers. After walking some time without a path, he suddenly came to a ring worn through the sod, as if it had been made by footsteps following a circle. But what excited his surprise was, that there was no path leading to or from it. Not the least trace of footsteps could be found, even in a crushed leaf or broken twig. He thought he would hide himself, and lie in wait to see what this circle meant. Presently he heard the faint sounds of music in the air. He looked up in the direction they came from, and saw a small object descending from above. At first it looked like a mere speck, but rapidly increased, and, as it came down, the music became plainer and sweeter. It assumed the form of a basket, and was filled with twelve sisters of the most lovely forms and enchanting beauty. As soon as the basket touched the ground, they leaped out, and began to dance round the magic ring, striking, as they did so, a shining ball as we strike the drum. Waupee gazed upon their graceful forms and motions from his place of concealment. He admired them all, but was most pleased with the youngest. Unable longer to restrain his admiration, he rushed out and endeavoured to seize her. But the sisters, with the quickness of birds, the moment they descried the form of a man, leaped back into the basket and were drawn up into the sky.

Regretting his ill luck and indiscretion, he gazed till he saw them disappear, and then said, "They are gone, and I shall see them no more." He returned to his solitary lodge, but found no relief to his mind. Next day he went back to the prairie, and took his station near the ring; but in order to deceive the sisters, he assumed the form of an opossum. He had not waited long, when he saw the wicker car descend, and heard the same sweet music. They commenced the same sportive dance, and seemed even more beautiful and graceful than before. He crept slowly towards the ring, but the instant the sisters saw him they were startled, and sprang into their car. It rose but a short distance, when one of the elder sisters spoke. "Perhaps," said she, "it is come to show us how the game is played by mortals." "Oh no!" the youngest replied; "quick, let us ascend." And all joining in a chant, they rose out of sight.

The White Hawk returned to his own form again, and walked sorrowfully back to his lodge. But the night seemed a very long one, and he went back betimes the next day. He reflected upon the sort of plan to follow to secure success. He found an old stump near by, in which there were a number of mice. He thought their small form would not create alarm, and accordingly assumed it. He brought the stump and sat it up near the ring. The sisters came down and resumed their sport. "But see," cried the younger sister, "that stump was not there before." She ran affrighted towards the car. They only smiled, and gathering round the stump, struck it in jest, when out ran the mice, and Waupee among the rest. They killed them all but one, which was pursued by the youngest sister; but just as she had raised her stick to kill it, the form of White Hawk arose, and he clasped his prize in his arms. The other eleven sprang to their basket and were drawn up to the skies.

Waupee exerted all his skill to please his bride and win her affections. He wiped the tears from her eyes. He related his adventures in the chase. He dwelt upon the charms of life on the earth. He was incessant in his attentions, and picked out the way for her to walk as he led her gently towards his lodge. He felt his heart glow with joy as she entered it, and from that moment he was one of the happiest of men. Winter and summer passed rapidly away, and their happiness was increased by the addition of a beautiful boy to their lodge. Waupee's wife was a daughter of one of the stars, and as the scenes of earth began to pall upon her sight, she sighed to revisit her father. But she was obliged to hide these feelings from her husband. She remembered the charm that would carry her up, and took occasion, while the White Hawk was engaged in the chase, to construct a wicker basket, which she kept concealed. In the mean time she collected such rarities from the earth as she thought would please her father, as well as the most dainty kinds of food. When all was in readiness, she went out one day, while Waupee was absent, to the charmed ring, taking her little son with her. As soon as they got into the car, she commenced her song and the basket rose. As the song was wafted by the wind, it caught her husband's ear. It was a voice which he well knew, and he instantly ran to the prairie. But he could not reach the ring before he saw his wife and child ascend. He lifted up his voice in loud appeals, but they were unavailing. The basket still went up. He watched it till it became a small speck, and finally it vanished in the sky. He then bent his head down to the ground, and was miserable.

Waupee bewailed his loss through a long winter and a long summer. But he found no relief. He mourned his wife's loss sorely, but his son's still more. In the mean time his wife had reached her home in the stars, and almost forgot, in the blissful employments there, that she had left a husband on the earth. She was reminded of this by the presence of her son, who, as he grew up, became anxious to visit the scene of his birth. His grandfather said to his daughter one day, "Go, my child, and take your son down to his father, and ask him to come up and live with us. But tell him to bring along a specimen of each kind of bird and animal he kills in the chase." She accordingly took the boy and descended. The White Hawk, who was ever near the enchanted spot, heard her voice as she came down the sky. His heart beat with impatience as he saw her form and that of his son, and they were soon clasped in his arms.

He heard the message of the Star, and began to hunt with the greatest activity, that he might collect the present. He spent whole nights, as well as days, in searching for every curious and beautiful bird or animal. He only preserved a tail, foot, or wing of each, to identify the species; and, when all was ready, they went to the circle and were carried up.

Great joy was manifested on their arrival at the starry plains. The Star Chief invited all his people to a feast, and, when they had assembled, he proclaimed aloud, that each one might take of the earthly gifts such as he liked best. A very strange confusion immediately arose. Some chose a foot, some a wing, some a tail, and some a claw. Those who selected tails or claws were changed into animals, and ran off; the others assumed the form of birds, and flew away. Waupee chose a white hawk's feather. His wife and son followed his example, when each one became a white hawk. He spread his wings, and followed by his wife and son, descended with the other birds to the earth, where his species are still to be found.

Tau-Wau-Chee-Hezkaw

or

THE WHITE FEATHER

A Sioux Tale

THERE WAS an old man living in the centre of a forest, with his grandson, whom he had taken when quite an infant. The child had no parents, brothers, or sisters; they had all been destroyed by six large giants, and he had been informed that he had no other relative living besides his grandfather. The band to whom he belonged had put up their children on a wager in a race against those of the giants, and had thus lost them. There was an old tradition in the band, that it would produce a great man, who would wear a white feather, and who would astonish every one with his skill and feats of bravery.

The grandfather, as soon as the child could play about, gave him a bow and arrows to amuse himself. He went into the edge of the woods one day, and saw a rabbit; but, not knowing what it was, he ran home and described it to his grandfather. He told him what it was, that its flesh was good to eat, and that, if he would shoot one of his arrows into its body, he would kill it. He did so, and brought the little animal home, which he asked his grandfather to boil, that they might feast on it. He humoured the boy in this, and encouraged him to go on in acquiring the knowledge of hunting, until he could kill deer and larger animals; and he became, as he grew up, an expert hunter. As they lived alone, and away from the other Indians, his curiosity was excited to know what was passing in the world. One day he came to the edge of a

13

prairie, where he saw ashes like those at his grandfather's lodge, and lodge-poles left standing. He returned and inquired whether his grandfather had put up the poles and made the fire. He was answered no, nor did he believe that he had seen anything of the kind. It was all imagination.

Another day he went out to see what there was curious; and, on entering the woods, he heard a voice calling out to him, "Come here, you destined wearer of the White Feather. You do not yet wear it, but you are worthy of it. Return home and take a short nap. You will dream of hearing a voice, which will tell you to rise and smoke. You will see in your dream a pipe, smoking-sack, and a large white feather. When you awake you will find these articles. Put the feather on your head, and you will become a great hunter, a great warrior, and a great man, capable of doing anything. As a proof that you will become a great hunter, when you smoke the smoke will turn into pigeons." The voice then informed him who he was, and disclosed the true character of his grandfather, who had imposed upon him. The voice-spirit then gave him a *vine,* and told him he was of an age to revenge the injuries of his relations. "When you meet your enemy," continued the spirit, "you will run a race with him. He will not see the vine, because it is enchanted. While you are running, you will throw it over his head and entangle him, so that you will win the race."

Long ere this speech was ended he had turned to the quarter from which the voice proceeded, and was astonished to behold a man, for as yet he had never seen any man besides his grandfather, whose object it was to keep him in ignorance. But the circumstance that gave him the most surprise was, that this man, who had the looks of great age, was composed of *wood* from his breast downward, and appeared to be fixed in the earth.

He returned home, slept, heard the voice, awoke, and found the promised articles. His grandfather was greatly surprised to find him with a white feather on his forehead, and to see flocks of pigeons flying out of his lodge. He then recollected what had been predicted, and began to weep at the prospect of losing his charge.

Invested with these honours, the young man departed the next morning to seek his enemies and gratify his revenge. The giants lived in a very high lodge in the middle of a wood. He travelled on till he came to this lodge, where he found that his coming had been made known by *the little spirits who carry the news*. The giants came out, and gave a cry of joy as they saw him coming. When he approached nearer, they began to make sport of him, saying, "Here comes the little man with the white feather, who is to achieve such wonders." They, however, spoke very fair to him when he came up, saying he was a brave man, and would do brave things. This they said to encourage, and the more surely to deceive him. He, however, understood the object.

He went fearlessly up to the lodge. They told him to commence the race with the smallest of their number. The point to which they were to run was a peeled tree towards the rising sun, and then back to the starting-place, which was marked by a CHAUNKAHPEE, or war-club, made of iron. This club was the stake, and whoever won it was to use it in beating the other's brains out. If he beat the first giant, he was to try the second, and so on until they had all measured speed with him. He won the first race by a dexterous use of the vine, and immediately despatched his competitor, and cut off his head. Next morning he ran with the second giant, whom he also outran, killed, and decapitated. He proceeded in this way for five successive mornings, always conquering by the use of his vine, and cutting off the heads of the vanquished. The survivers acknowledged his power, but prepared secretly to deceive him. They wished him to leave the heads he had cut off, as they believed they could again reunite them with the bodies, by means of one of their *medicines*. White Feather insisted, however, in carrying all the heads to his grandfather. One more contest was to be tried, which would decide the victory; but, before going to the giant's lodge on the sixth morning, he met his old counsellor in the woods, who was stationary. He told him that he was about to be deceived. That he had never known any other sex but his own; but that, as he went on his way to the lodge, he would meet the most beautiful woman in the world. He must pay no attention to her, but, on meeting her, he must wish himself changed into a male elk. The transformation would take place immediately, when he must go to feeding and not regard her.

He proceeded towards the lodge, met the female, and became

an elk. She reproached him for having turned himself into an elk on seeing her; said she had travelled a great distance for the purpose of seeing him, and becoming his wife. Now this woman was the sixth giant, who had assumed this disguise; but Tau-Wau-Chee-Hezkaw remained in ignorance of it. Her reproaches and her beauty affected him so much, that he wished himself a man again, and he at once resumed his natural shape. They sat down together, and he began to caress her, and make love to her. He finally ventured to lay his head in her lap and went to sleep. She pushed his head aside at first, for the purpose of trying if he was really asleep; and when she was satisfied he was, she took her axe and broke his back. She then assumed her natural shape, which was in the form of the sixth giant, and afterward changed him into a dog, in which degraded form he followed his enemy to the lodge. He took the white feather from his brow, and wore it as a trophy on his own head.

There was an Indian village at some distance, in which there lived two girls, who were rival sisters, the daughters of a chief. They were fasting to acquire power for the purpose of enticing the wearer of the white feather to visit their village. They each secretly hoped to engage his affections. Each one built herself a lodge at a short distance from the village. The giant, knowing this, and having now obtained the valued plume, went immediately to visit them. As he approached, the girls saw and recognised the feather. The eldest sister prepared her lodge with great care and parade, so as to attract the eye. The younger, supposing that he was a man of sense, and would not be enticed by mere parade, touched nothing in her lodge, but left it as it ordinarily was. The eldest went out to meet him, and invited him in. He accepted her invitation, and made her his wife. The younger invited the enchanted dog into her lodge, and made him a good bed, and treated him with as much attention as if he were her husband.

The giant, supposing that whoever possessed the white feather possessed also all its virtues, went out upon the prairie to hunt, but returned unsuccessful. The dog went out the same day a-hunting upon the banks of a river. He drew a stone out of the water, which immediately became a beaver. The next day the giant followed the dog, and, hiding behind a tree, saw the manner in which the dog went into the river and drew out a stone, which at once turned into a beaver. As soon as the dog left the place, the giant went to the river, and observing the same manner, drew out a stone, and had the satisfaction of seeing it transformed into a beaver. Tying it to his belt, he carried it home, and, as is customary, threw it down at the door of the lodge before he entered. After being seated a short time, he told his wife to bring in his belt or hunting girdle. She did so, and returned with it, with nothing tied to it but a *stone*.

The next day, the dog, finding his method of catching beavers had been discovered, went to a wood at some distance, and broke off a charred limb from a burned tree, which instantly became a bear. The giant, who had again watched him, did the same, and carried a bear home; but his wife, when she came to go out for it, found nothing but a black stick tied to his belt.

The giant's wife determined she would go to her father, and tell him what a valuable husband she had, who furnished her lodge with abundance. She set out while her husband went to hunt. As soon as they had departed, the dog made signs to his mistress to sweat him after the manner of the Indians. She accordingly made a lodge just large enough for him to creep in. She then put in heated stones, and poured on water. After this had been continued the usual time, he came out a very handsome young man, but had not the power of speech.

Meantime the elder daughter had reached her father's, and told him of the manner in which her sister supported a dog, treating him as her husband, and of the singular skill this animal had in hunting. The old man, suspecting there was some magic in it, sent a deputation of young men and women to ask her to come to him, and bring the dog along. When this deputation arrived, they were surprised to find, in the place of the dog, so fine a young man. They both accompanied the messengers to the father, who was no less astonished. He assembled all the old and wise men of the nation to see the exploits which, it was reported, the young man could perform. The giant was among the number. He took his pipe and filled it, and passed it to the Indians, to see if anything would happen when they smoked. It was passed around to the dog, who made a sign to hand it to the giant first, which was done, but nothing effected. He then took it himself. He made a sign to them to put the white feather upon his head. This was done, and immediately he regained his speech. He then commenced smoking, and behold! immense flocks of white and blue pigeons rushed from the smoke.

The chief demanded of him his history, which he faithfully recounted. When it was finished, the chief ordered that the giant should be transformed into a dog, and turned into the middle of the village, where the boys should pelt him to death with clubs. This sentence was executed.

The chief then ordered, on the request of the White Feather, that all the young men should employ themselves four days in making arrows. He also asked for a buffalo robe. This robe he cut into thin shreds, and sowed in the prairie. At the end of the four days he invited them to gather together all their arrows, and accompany him to a buffalo hunt. They found that these shreds of skin had grown into a very large herd of buffalo. They killed as many as they pleased, and enjoyed a grand festival, in honour of his triumph over the Giants.

Having accomplished their labour, the White Feather got his wife to ask her father's permission to go with him on a visit to his grandfather. He replied to this solicitation, that a woman must follow her husband into whatever quarter of the world he may choose to go.

The young man then placed the white feather in his frontlet, and, taking his war-club in his hand, led the way into the forest, followed by his faithful wife.

PEBOAN AND SEEGWUN

AN ALLEGORY OF THE SEASONS

From the Odjibwa

A N OLD man was sitting alone in his lodge, by the side of a frozen stream. It was the close of winter, and his fire was almost out. He appeared very old and very desolate. His locks were white with age, and he trembled in every joint. Day after day passed in solitude, and he heard nothing but the sounds of the tempest, sweeping before it the new-fallen snow.

One day, as his fire was just dying, a handsome young man approached and entered his dwelling. His cheeks were red with the blood of youth, his eyes sparkled with animation, and a smile played upon his lips. He walked with a light and quick step. His forehead was bound with a wreath of sweet grass, in place of a warrior's frontlet, and he carried a bunch of flowers in his hand.

"Ah, my son," said the old man, "I am happy to see you. Come in. Come, tell me of your adventures, and what strange lands you have been to see. Let us pass the night together. I will tell you of my prowess and exploits, and what I can perform. You shall do the same, and we will amuse ourselves."

He then drew from his sack a curiously-wrought antique pipe, and having filled it with tobacco, rendered mild by an admixture of certain leaves, handed it to his guest. When this ceremony was concluded they began to speak.

"I blow my breath," said the old man, "and the streams stand still. The water becomes stiff and hard as clear stone."

"I breathe," said the young man, "and flowers spring up all over the plains."

"I shake my locks," retorted the old man, "and snow covers the land. The leaves fall from the trees at my command, and my breath blows them away. The birds get up from the water, and fly to a distant land. The animals hide themselves from my breath, and the very ground becomes as hard as flint."

"I shake my ringlets," rejoined the young man, "and warm showers of soft rain fall upon the earth. The plants lift up their heads out of the earth, like the eyes of children glistening with delight. My voice recalls the birds. The warmth of my breath unlocks the streams. Music fills the groves wherever I walk, and all nature rejoices."

At length the sun began to rise. A gentle warmth came over the place. The tongue of the old man became silent. The robin and bluebird began to sing on the top of the lodge. The stream began to murmur by the door, and the fragrance of growing herbs and flowers came softly on the vernal breeze.

Daylight fully revealed to the young man the character of his entertainer. When he looked upon him, he had the icy visage of Peboan.* Streams began to flow from his eyes. As the sun increased, he grew less and less in stature, and anon had melted completely away. Nothing remained on the place of his lodge fire but the miskodeed,† a small white flower, with a pink border, which is one of the earliest species of Northern plants.

---

*Winter.
†The *Claytonia Virginica.*

THE RED LOVER

A Chippewa Tale

MANY YEARS ago there lived a warrior on the banks of Lake Superior, whose name was Wawanosh. He was the chief of an ancient family of his tribe, who had preserved the line of chieftainship unbroken from a remote time, and he consequently cherished a pride of ancestry. To the reputation of birth he added the advantages of a tall and commanding person, and the dazzling qualities of personal strength, courage, and activity. His bow was noted for its size, and the feats he had performed with it. His counsel was sought as much as his strength was feared, so that he came to be equally regarded as a hunter, a warrior, and a counsellor. He had now passed the meridian of his days, and the term AKKEE-WAIZEE, i. e., one who has been long on the earth, was applied to him.

Such was Wawanosh, to whom the united voice of the nation awarded the first place in their esteem, and the highest authority in council. But distinction, it seems, is apt to engender haughtiness in the hunter state as well as civilized life. Pride was his ruling passion, and he clung with tenacity to the distinctions which he regarded as an inheritance.

Wawanosh had an only daughter, who had now lived to witness the budding of the leaves of the eighteenth spring. Her father was not more celebrated for his deeds of strength than she for her gentle virtues, her slender form, her full beaming hazel eyes, and her dark and flowing hair.

"And through her cheek
The blush would make its way, and all but speak.
The sunborn blood suffused her neck, and threw
O'er her clear brown skin a lucid hue,
Like coral reddening through the darken'd wave,
Which draws the diver to the crimson cave."

Her hand was sought by a young man of humble parentage, who had no other merits to recommend him but such as might arise from a tall and commanding person, a manly step, and an eye beaming with the tropical fires of youth and love. These were sufficient to attract the favourable notice of the daughter, but were by no means satisfactory to the father, who sought an alliance more suitable to the rank and the high pretensions of his family.

"Listen to me, young man," he replied to the trembling hunter, who had sought the interview, "and be attentive to my words. You ask me to bestow upon you my daughter, the chief solace of my age, and my choicest gift from the Master of Life. Others have asked of me this boon, who were as young, as active, and as ardent as yourself. Some of these persons have had better claims to become my son-in-law. Have you reflected upon the deeds which have raised me in authority, and made my name known to the enemies of my nation? Where is there a chief who is not proud to be considered the friend of Wawanosh? Where, in all the land, is there a hunter who has excelled Wawanosh? Where is there a warrior who can boast the taking of an equal number of scalps? Besides, have you not heard that my fathers came from the East, bearing the marks of chieftaincy?

"And what, young man, have *you* to boast? Have *you* ever met your enemies in the field of battle? Have *you* ever brought home a trophy of victory? Have *you* ever proved your fortitude by suffering protracted pain, enduring continued hunger, or sustaining great fatigue? Is your *name* known beyond the humble limits of your native village? Go, then, young man, and earn a name for yourself. It is none but the brave that can ever hope to claim an alliance with the house of Wawanosh. Think not my warrior blood shall mingle with the humble mark of the Awasees*—fit totem for fishermen!"

The intimidated lover departed, but he resolved to do a deed that should render him worthy of the daughter of Wawanosh, or die in the attempt. He called together several of his young companions and equals in years, and imparted to them his design of conducting an expedition against the enemy, and requested their assistance. Several embraced the proposal immediately; others were soon brought to acquiesce; and, before ten suns set, he saw himself at the head of a formidable party of young warriors, all eager, like himself, to distinguish themselves in battle. Each warrior was armed, according to the custom of the period, with a bow and a quiver of arrows, tipped with flint or jasper. He carried a sack or wallet, provided with a small quantity of parched and pounded corn, mixed with pemmican or maple sugar. He was furnished with a PUGGAMAUGUN, or war-club of hard wood, fastened to a girdle of deer skin, and a stone or copper knife. In addition to this, some carried the ancient *shemagun,* or lance, a smooth pole about a fathom in length, with a javelin of flint, firmly tied on with deer's sinews. Thus equipped, and each warrior painted in a manner to suit his fancy, and ornamented with appropriate feathers, they repaired to the spot appointed for the war-dance.

A level, grassy plain extended for nearly a mile from the lodge of Wawanosh along the lake shore. Lodges of bark were promiscuously interspersed over this green, and here and there a cluster of trees, or a solitary tall pine. A belt of yellow sand skirted the lake shore in front, and a tall, thick forest formed the background. In the centre of this plain stood a high shattered pine, with a clear space about, renowned as the scene of the war-dance time out of mind. Here the youths assembled, with their tall and graceful leader, distinguished by the feathers of the bald eagle, which he wore on his head. A bright fire of pine wood blazed upon the green. He led his men several times around this fire, with a measured and solemn chant. Then suddenly halting, the

---

*Catfish.

war-whoop was raised, and the dance immediately began. An old man, sitting at the head of the ring, beat time upon the drum, while several of the elder warriors shook their rattles, and "ever and anon" made the woods re-echo with their yells. Each warrior chanted alternately the verse of a song, all the rest joining in chorus.

FIRST VOICE.
The eagles scream on high,
   They whet their forked beaks:
Raise—raise the battle cry,
   'Tis fame our leader seeks.

SECOND VOICE.
'Tis fame my soul desires,
   By deeds of martial strife:
Give—give me warlike fires,
   Or take—ah take my life.

THIRD VOICE.
The deer a while may go
   Unhunted o'er the heath,
For now I seek a nobler foe,
   And prize a nobler death.

FOURTH VOICE.
Lance and quiver, club and bow,
   Now alone attract my sight;
I will go where warriors go,
   I will fight where warriors fight.

Thus they continued the dance, with short intermissions, for two successive days and nights. Sometimes the village seer, who led the ceremony, would embrace the occasion of a pause to address them with words of encouragement.

In the dreamy hours of night
I beheld the bloody fight.
As reclined upon my bed,

Holy visions crowned my head;
High our guardian spirit bright
Stood above the dreadful fight;
Beaming eye and dazzling brand
Gleamed upon my chosen band,
While a black and awful shade
O'er the faithless foeman spread.
Soon they wavered, sunk, and fled,
Leaving wounded, dying, dead,
While my gallant warriors high
Waved their trophies in the sky.

At every recurrence of this kind, new energy was infused into the dance, and the warriors renewed their gesticulations, and stamped upon the ground as if they were trampling their enemies under their feet.

FIFTH VOICE.
Now my heart with valour burns,
I my lance in fury shake;
He who falters, he who turns,
Give him fagot, fire, and stake.

SIXTH VOICE.
See my visage scarred and red—
See my brows with trophies bright—
Such the brows that warriors dread,
Such the trophies of the fight.

At length the prophet uttered his final prediction of success; and the warriors dropping off, one by one, from the fire, each sought his way to the place appointed for the rendezvous, on the confines of the enemy's country. Their leader was not among the last to depart, but he did not leave the village without seeking an interview with the daughter of Wawanosh. He disclosed to her his firm determination never to return, unless he could establish his name as a warrior. He told her of the pangs he had felt at the bitter reproaches of her father, and declared that his soul spurned the imputation of effeminacy and cowardice implied by his language. He averred that he never could be happy, either with or without her, until he had proved to the whole tribe the strength of his heart, which is the Indian term for courage. He said that his dreams had not been propitious, but he should not cease to invoke the power of the Great Spirit. He repeated his protestations of inviolable attachment, which she returned, and, pledging vows of mutual fidelity, they parted.

All she ever heard from her lover after this interview was brought by one of his successful warriors, who said that he had distinguished himself by the most heroic bravery, but, at the close of the fight, he had received an arrow in his breast. The enemy fled, leaving many of their warriors dead on the field. On examining the wound, it was perceived to be beyond their power to cure. They carried him towards home a day's journey, but he languished and expired in the arms of his friends. From the moment the report was received, no smile was ever seen in the once happy lodge of Wawanosh. His daughter pined away by day and by night. Tears and sighs, sorrow and lamentation, were heard continually. Nothing could restore her lost serenity of mind. Persuasives and reproofs were alternately employed, but employed in vain. She would seek a sequestered spot, where she would sit under a shady tree, and sing her mournful laments for hours together.

It was not long before a small bird of beautiful plumage flew upon the tree under which she usually sat, and with its sweet and artless notes seemed to respond to her voice. It was a bird of strange character, such as had not before been observed. It came every day and sang, remaining until dark. Her fond imagination soon led her to suppose it was the spirit of her lover, and her visits were repeated with greater frequency. She passed her time in fasting, and singing her plaintive songs. Thus she pined away, until that death she so fervently desired came to her relief. After her decease the bird was never more seen, and it became a popular opinion that this mysterious bird had flown away with her spirit.

But bitter tears of regret fell in the lodge of Wawanosh. Too late he regretted his false pride and his harsh treatment of the noble youth.

IAMO

or

THE UNDYING HEAD

An Ottowa Tale

I N A remote part of the north lived a man and his only sister, who had never seen a human being. Seldom, if ever, had the man any cause to go from home; for, as his wants demanded food, he had only to go a little distance from the lodge, and there, in some particular spot, place his arrows, with their barbs in the ground. Telling his sister where they had been placed, every morning she would go in search, and never fail of finding each struck through the heart of a deer. She had then only to drag them into the lodge and prepare their food. Thus she lived till she attained womanhood, when one day her brother, whose name was Iamo, said to her, "Sister, the time is near at hand when you will be ill. Listen to my advice. If you do not, it will probably be the cause of my death. Take the implements with which we kindle our fires. Go some distance from our lodge, and build a separate fire. When you are in want of food, I will tell you where to find it. You must cook for yourself, and I will for myself. When you are ill, do not attempt to come near the lodge, or bring any of the utensils you use. Be sure always to fasten to your belt the implements you need, for you do not know when the time will come. As for myself, I must do the best I can." His sister promised to obey him in all he had said.

Shortly after, her brother had cause to go from home. She was alone in her lodge, combing her hair. She had just untied the belt

27

to which the implements were fastened, when suddenly the event, to which her brother had alluded, occurred. She ran out of the lodge, but in her haste forgot the belt. Afraid to return, she stood for some time thinking. Finally she decided to enter the lodge and get it. For, thought she, my brother is not at home, and I will stay but a moment to catch hold of it. She went back. Running in suddenly, she caught hold of it, and was coming out when her brother came in sight. He knew what was the matter. "Oh," he said, "did I not tell you to take care? But now you have killed me." She was going on her way, but her brother said to her, "What can you do there now? the accident has happened. Go in, and stay where you have always stayed. And what will become of you? You have killed me."

He then laid aside his hunting dress and accoutrements, and soon after both his feet began to inflame and turn black, so that he could not move. Still he directed his sister where to place the arrows, that she might always have food. The inflammation continued to increase, and had now reached his first rib; and he said, "Sister, my end is near. You must do as I tell you. You see my medicine-sack, and my war-club tied to it. It contains all my medicines, and my war-plumes, and my paints of all colours. As soon as the inflammation reaches my breast, you will take my war-club. It has a sharp point, and you will cut off my head. When it is free from my body, take it, place its neck in the sack, which you must open at one end. Then hang it up in its former place. Do not forget my bow and arrows. One of the last you will take to procure food. The remainder tie to my sack, and then hang it up, so that I can look towards the door. Now and then I will speak to you, but not often." His sister again promised to obey.

In a little time his breast was affected. "Now," said he, "take the club and strike off my head." She was afraid, but he told her to muster courage. "*Strike,*" said he, and a smile was on his face. Mustering all her courage, she gave the blow and cut off the head. "Now," said the head, "place me where I told you." And fearfully she obeyed it in all its commands. Retaining its animation, it looked around the lodge as usual, and it would command its sister to go to such places as it thought would procure for her the flesh of different animals she needed. One day the head said,

"The time is not distant when I shall be freed from this situation, but I shall have to undergo many sore evils. So the Superior Manito decrees, and I must bear all patiently." In this situation we must leave the head.

In a certain part of the country was a village inhabited by a numerous and warlike band of Indians. In this village was a family of ten young men—brothers. It was in the spring of the year that the youngest of these blackened his face and fasted. His dreams were propitious. Having ended his fast, he sent secretly for his brothers at night, so that none in the village could overhear or find out the direction they intended to go. Though their drum was heard, yet that was a common occurrence. Having ended the usual formalities, he told them how favourable his dreams were, and that he had called them together to know if they would accompany him in a war excursion. They all answered they would. The third brother from the eldest, noted for his oddities, coming up with his war-club when his brother had ceased speaking, jumped up, "Yes," said he, "*I* will go, and this will be the way I will treat those we are going to fight"; and he struck the post in the centre of the lodge, and gave a yell. The others spoke to him, saying, "Slow, slow, Mudjikewis, when you are in other people's lodges." So he sat down. Then, in turn, they took the drum, and sang their songs, and closed with a feast. The youngest told them not to whisper their intention even to their wives, but secretly to prepare for their journey. They all promised obedience, and Mudjikewis was the first to say so.

The time for their departure drew near. Word was given to assemble on a certain night, when they would depart immediately. Mudjikewis was loud in his demands for his moccasins. Several times his wife asked him the reason. "Besides," said she, "you have a good pair on." "Quick, quick," he said, "since you must know, we are going on a war excursion. So be quick." He thus revealed the secret. That night they met and started. The snow was on the ground, and they travelled all night, lest others should follow them. When it was daylight, the leader took snow and made a ball of it; then tossing it into the air, he said, "It was in this way I saw snow fall in a dream, so that I could not be tracked." And he told them to keep close to each other for fear of losing themselves, as the snow began to fall in very large flakes. Near as they walked, it was with difficulty they could see each other. The snow continued falling all that day and the following night. So it was impossible to track them.

They had now walked for several days, and Mudjikewis was always in the rear. One day, running suddenly forward, he gave the *Saw-saw-quan,** and struck a tree with his war-club, which broke into pieces as if struck with lightning. "Brothers," said he, "this will be the way I will serve those whom we are going to fight." The leader answered, "Slow, slow, Mudjikewis. The one I lead you to is not to be thought of so lightly." Again he fell back and thought to himself, "What, what: Who can this be he is leading us to?" He felt fearful, and was silent. Day after day they travelled on, till they came to an extensive plain, on the borders of which human bones were bleaching in the sun. The leader spoke. "They are the bones of those who have gone before us. None has ever yet returned to tell the sad tale of their fate." Again Mudjikewis became restless, and, running forward, gave the accustomed yell. Advancing to a large rock which stood above the ground, he struck it, and it fell to pieces. "See brothers," said he, "thus will I treat those whom we are going to fight." "Still, still," once more said the leader; "he to whom I am leading you is not to be compared to that rock."

Mudjikewis fell back quite thoughtful, saying to himself, "I wonder who this can be that he is going to attack." And he was afraid. Still they continued to see the remains of former warriors, who had been to the place where *they* were now going, some of whom had retreated as far back as the place where they first saw the bones, beyond which no one had ever escaped. At last they came to a piece of rising ground, from which they plainly distinguished, sleeping on a distant mountain, a mammoth bear.

The distance between them was very great, but the size of the animal caused him plainly to be seen. "There," said the leader, "it is he to whom I am leading you; here our troubles only will commence, for he is a MISHEMOKWA† and a Manito. It is he who has

---

*War-cry.

†A she-bear—also a male having the ferocity of a she-bear.

that we prize so dearly (i.e., *wampum*), to obtain which, the warriors whose bones we saw sacrificed their lives. You must not be
fearful. Be manly. We shall find him asleep." They advanced
boldly till they came near, when they stopped to view him more
closely. He was asleep. Then the leader went forward and touched
the belt around the animal's neck. "This," he said, "is what we
must get. It contains the wampum." They then requested the
eldest to try and slip the belt over the bear's head, who appeared
to be fast asleep, as he was not in the least disturbed by the attempt
to obtain the belt. All their efforts were in vain, till it came to the
one next the youngest. He tried, and the belt moved nearly over
the monster's head, but he could get it no farther. Then the
youngest one and leader made his attempt, and succeeded.
Placing it on the back of the oldest, he said, "Now we must run,"
and off they started. When one became fatigued with its weight,
another would relieve him. Thus they ran till they had passed the
bones of all former warriors, and were some distance beyond,
when, looking back, they saw the monster slowly rising. He stood
some time before he missed his wampum. Soon they heard his
tremendous howl, like distant thunder, slowly filling all the sky;
and then they heard him speak and say, "Who can it be that has
dared to steal my wampum? Earth is not so large but that I can
find them." And he descended from the hill in pursuit. As if con-
vulsed, the earth shook with every jump he made. Very soon he
approached the party. They however kept the belt, exchanging it
from one to another, and encouraging each other. But he gained
on them fast. "Brothers," said the leader, "has never any one of
you, when fasting, dreamed of some friendly spirit who would
aid you as a guardian?" A dead silence followed. "Well," said he,
"fasting, I dreamed of being in danger of instant death, when I
saw a small lodge, with smoke curling from its top. An old man
lived in it, and I dreamed he helped me. And may it be verified
soon," he said, running forward and giving the peculiar yell, and
a howl as if the sounds came from the depths of his stomach, and
which is called *Checaudum*. Getting upon a piece of rising
ground, behold! a lodge, with smoke curling from its top, appeared.
This gave them all new strength, and they ran forward and entered it. The leader spoke to the old man who sat in the lodge,

saying, "*Nemesho,* * help us. We claim your protection, for the great bear will kill us." "Sit down and eat, my grandchildren," said the old man. "Who is a great Manito?" said he, "there is none but me; but let me look," and he opened the door of the lodge, when lo! at a little distance he saw the enraged animal coming on, with slow but powerful leaps. He closed the door. "Yes," said he, "*he* is indeed a great Manito. My grandchildren, you will be the cause of my losing my life. You asked my protection, and I granted it; so now, come what may, I will protect you. When the bear arrives at the door, you must run out of the other end of the lodge." Then putting his hand to the side of the lodge where he sat, he brought out a bag, which he opened. Taking out two small black dogs, he placed them before him. "These are the ones I use when I fight," said he; and he commenced patting, with both hands, the sides of one of them, and he began to swell out, so that he soon filled the lodge by his bulk. And he had great strong teeth. When he attained his full size he growled, and from that moment, as from instinct, he jumped out at the door and met the bear, who in another leap would have reached the lodge. A terrible combat ensued. The skies rang with the howls of the fierce monsters. The remaining dog soon took the field. The brothers, at the onset, took the advice of the old man, and escaped through the opposite side of the lodge. They had not proceeded far before they heard the dying cry of one of the dogs, and soon after of the other. "Well," said the leader, "the old man will share their fate; so run, run, he will soon be after us." They started with fresh vigour, for they had received food from the old man; but very soon the bear came in sight, and again was fast gaining upon them. Again the leader asked the brothers if they could do nothing for their safety. All were silent. The leader, running forward, did as before. "I dreamed," he cried, "that, being in great trouble, an old man helped me who was a Manito. We shall soon see his lodge." Taking courage, they still went on. After going a short distance they saw the lodge of the old Manito. They entered immediately and claimed his protection, telling him a Manito was after them.

---

*"My grandfather."

The old man, setting meat before them, said, "Eat. Who is a Manito? there is no Manito but me. There is none whom I fear." And the earth trembled as the monster advanced. The old man opened the door and saw him coming. He shut it slowly, and said, "Yes, my grandchildren, you have brought trouble upon me." Procuring his medicine sack, he took out his small war-clubs of black stone, and told the young men to run through the other side of the lodge. As he handled the clubs they became very large, and the old man stepped out just as the bear reached the door. Then striking him with one of the clubs, it broke in pieces. The bear stumbled. Renewing the attempt with the other war-club, that also was broken, but the bear fell senseless. Each blow the old man gave him sounded like a clap of thunder, and the howls of the bear ran along till they filled the heavens.

The young men had now run some distance, when they looked back. They could see that the bear was recovering from the blows. First he moved his paws, and soon they saw him rise on his feet. The old man shared the fate of the first, for they now heard his cries as he was torn in pieces. Again the monster was in pursuit, and fast overtaking them. Not yet discouraged, the young men kept on their way; but the bear was now so close that the leader once more applied to his brothers, but they could do nothing. "Well," said he, "my dreams will soon be exhausted. After this I have but one more." He advanced, invoking his guardian spirit to aid him. "Once," said he, "I dreamed that, being sorely pressed, I came to a large lake, on the shore of which was a canoe, partly out of water, having ten paddles all in readiness. Do not fear," he cried, "we shall soon get to it." And so it was, even as he had said. Coming to the lake, they saw the canoe with the ten paddles, and immediately they embarked. Scarcely had they reached the centre of the lake when they saw the bear arrive at its borders. Lifting himself on his hind legs, he looked all around. Then he waded into the water; then losing his footing, he turned back, and commenced making the circuit of the lake. Meanwhile, the party remained stationary in the centre to watch his movements. He travelled around, till at last he came to the place from whence he started. Then he commenced drinking up the water, and they saw the current fast setting in towards his open mouth. The leader encouraged them to paddle hard for the opposite shore. When only a short distance from land, the current had increased so much, that they were drawn back by it, and all their efforts to reach it were vain.

Then the leader again spoke, telling them to meet their fates manfully. "Now is the time, Mudjikewis," said he, "to show your prowess. Take courage, and sit in the bow of the canoe; and when it approaches his mouth, try what effect your club will have on his head." He obeyed, and stood ready to give the blow, while the leader, who steered, directed the canoe for the open mouth of the monster.

Rapidly advancing, they were just about to enter his mouth when Mudjikewis struck him a tremendous blow on the head, and gave the saw-saw-quan. The bear's limbs doubled under him, and he fell, stunned by the blow. But before Mudjikewis could renew it, the monster disgorged all the water he had drunk, with a force which sent the canoe with great velocity to the opposite shore. Instantly leaving the canoe, again they fled, and on they went till they were completely exhausted. The earth again shook, and soon they saw the monster hard after them. Their spirits drooped, and they felt discouraged. The leader exerted himself, by actions and words, to cheer them up; and once more he asked them if they thought of nothing, or could do nothing for their rescue; and, as before, all were silent. "Then," he said, "this is the last time I can apply to my guardian spirit. Now if we do not suc-ceed, our fates are decided." He ran forward, invoking his spirit with great earnestness, and gave the yell. "We shall soon arrive," said he to his brothers, "to the place where my last guardian spirit dwells. In him I place great confidence. Do not, do not be afraid, or your limbs will be fear-bound. We shall soon reach his lodge. Run, run," he cried.

Returning now to Iamo, he had passed all the time in the same condition we left him, the head directing its sister, in order to procure food, where to place the magic arrows, and speaking at long intervals. One day the sister saw the eyes of the head brighten, as if through pleasure. At last it spoke. "Oh, sister," it said, "in what a pitiful situation you have been the cause of placing me. Soon, very soon, a party of young men will arrive and apply to me for aid; but, alas! how can I give what I *would* have done with so much pleasure. Nevertheless, take two arrows, and place them where you have been in the habit of placing the others, and have meat prepared and cooked before they arrive. When you hear them coming and calling on my name, go out and say, 'Alas! it is long ago that an accident befell him. I was the cause of it.' If they still come near, ask them in and set meat before them. And now you must follow my directions strictly. When the bear is near, go out and meet him. You will take my medicine sack, bows and arrows, and my head. You must then untie the sack, and spread out before you my paints of all colours, my war eagle feathers, my tufts of dried hair, and whatever else it contains. As the bear approaches, you will take all these articles, one by one, and say to him, 'This is my deceased brother's paint,' and so on with all the other articles, throwing each of them as far from you as you can. The virtues contained in them will cause him to totter; and, to complete his destruction, you will take my head, and that too you will cast as far off as you can, crying aloud, 'See, this is my deceased brother's head.' He will then fall senseless. By this time the young men will have eaten, and you will call them to your assistance. You must then cut the carcass into pieces, yes, into *small* pieces, and scatter them to the four winds; for, unless you do this, he will again revive." She promised that all should be done as he said. She had only time to prepare the meat, when the voice of the leader was heard calling upon Iamo for aid. The woman went out and said as her brother had directed. But the war party, being closely pursued, came up to the lodge. She invited them in, and placed the meat before them. While they were eating they heard the bear approaching. Untying the medicine sack and taking the head, she had all in readiness for his approach. When he came up she did as she had been told; and, before she had expended the paints and feathers, the bear began to totter, but, still advancing, came close to the woman. Saying as she was commanded, she then took the head, and cast it as far from her as she could. As it rolled along the ground, the blood, excited by the feelings of the head in this terrible scene, gushed from the nose and mouth. The bear, tottering, soon fell with a tremendous noise. Then she cried for help, and the young men came rushing out, having partially regained their strength and spirits.

Mudjikewis, stepping up, gave a yell and struck him a blow upon the head. This he repeated till it seemed like a mass of brains; while the others, as quick as possible, cut him into very small pieces, which they then scattered in every direction. While thus employed, happening to look around where they had thrown the meat, wonderful to behold! they saw starting up and running off in every direction small black bears, such as are seen at the present day. The country was soon overspread with these black animals. And it was from this monster that the present race of bears derived their origin.

Having thus overcome their pursuer, they returned to the lodge. In the mean time, the woman, gathering the implements she had used and the head, placed them again in the sack. But the head did not speak again, probably from the effects of its great exertion to overcome the monster.

Having spent so much time and traversed so vast a country in their flight, the young men gave up the idea of ever returning to their own country, and game being plenty, they determined to remain where they now were. One day they moved off some distance from the lodge for the purpose of hunting, having left the wampum with the woman. They were very successful, and amused themselves, as all young men do when alone, by talking and jesting with each other. One of them spoke and said, "We have all this sport to ourselves; let us go and ask our sister if she will not let us bring the head to this place, as it is still alive. It may be pleased to hear us talk and be in our company. In the mean time, take food to our sister." They went, and requested the head. She told them to take it, and they took it to their hunting-grounds and tried to amuse it, but only at times did they see its eyes beam with pleasure. One day, while busy in their encampment, they were unexpectedly attacked by unknown Indians. The skirmish was long contested and bloody. Many of their foes were slain, but still they were thirty to one. The young men fought desperately till they were all killed. The attacking party then retreated to a heighth of ground, to muster their men, and to count the number of missing and slain. One of their young men had strayed away, and, in endeavouring to overtake them, came to the place where the head was hung up. Seeing that alone retain animation, he eyed it for some time with fear and surprise. However, he took it down and opened the sack, and was much pleased to see the beautiful feathers, one of which he placed on his head.

Starting off, it waved gracefully over him till he reached his party, when he threw down the head and sack, and told them how he had found it, and that the sack was full of paints and feathers. They all looked at the head and made sport of it. Numbers of the young men took the paint and painted themselves, and one of the party took the head by the hair and said, "Look, you ugly thing, and see your paints on the faces of warriors." But the feathers were so beautiful, that numbers of them also placed *them* on their heads. Then again they used all kinds of indignity to the head, for which they were in turn repaid by the death of those who had used the feathers. Then the chief commanded them to throw all away except the head. "We will see," said he, "when we get home, what we can do to it. We will try to make it shut its eyes."

When they reached their homes they took it to the council lodge, and hung it up before the fire, fastening it with raw hide soaked, which would shrink and become tightened by the action of the fire. "We will then see," they said, "if we cannot make it shut its eyes."

Meanwhile, for several days the sister had been waiting for the young men to bring back the head; till at last, getting impatient, she went in search of it. The young men she found lying within short distances of each other, dead, and covered with wounds. Various other bodies lay scattered in different directions around them. She searched for the head and sack, but they were nowhere to be found. She raised her voice and wept, and blackened her face. Then she walked in different directions, till she came to the place from whence the head had been taken. There she found the magic bow and arrows, where the young men, ignorant of their qualities, had left them. She thought to herself that she would find her brother's head, and came to a piece of rising ground, and there saw some of his paints and feathers. These she carefully put up, and hung upon the branch of a tree till her return.

At dusk she arrived at the first lodge of a very extensive village.

Here she used a charm, common among Indians when they wish
to meet with a kind reception. On applying to the old man and
woman of the lodge, she was kindly received. She made known
her errand. The old man promised to aid her, and told her that
the head was hung up before the council fire, and that the chiefs
of the village, with their young men, kept watch over it continually. The former are considered as Manitoes. She said she only
wished to see it, and would be satisfied if she could only get to
the door of the lodge. She knew she had not sufficient power to
take it by force. "Come with me," said the Indian, "I will take you
there." They went, and they took their seats near the door. The
council lodge was filled with warriors, amusing themselves with
games, and constantly keeping up a fire to smoke the head, as
they said, to make dry meat. They saw the head move, and not
knowing what to make of it, one spoke and said, "Ha! ha! it is
beginning to feel the effects of the smoke." The sister looked up
from the door, and her eyes met those of her brother, and tears
rolled down the cheeks of the head. "Well," said the chief, "I
thought we would make you do something at last. Look! look at
it—shedding tears," said he to those around him; and they all
laughed and passed their jokes upon it. The chief, looking
around and observing the woman, after some time said to the
man who came with her, "Who have you got there? I have never
seen that woman before in our village." "Yes," replied the man,
"you have seen her; she is a relation of mine, and seldom goes
out. She stays in my lodge, and asked me to allow her to come
with me to this place." In the centre of the lodge sat one of those
young men who are always forward, and fond of boasting and
displaying themselves before others. "Why," said he, "I have seen
her often, and it is to his lodge I go almost every night to court
her." All the others laughed and continued their games. The
young man did not know he was telling a lie to the woman's
advantage, who by that means escaped.

She returned to the man's lodge, and immediately set out for
her own country. Coming to the spot where the bodies of her
adopted brothers lay, she placed them together, their feet towards
the east. Then taking an axe which she had, she cast it up into the
air, crying out, "Brothers, get up from under it, or it will fall on

you." This she repeated three times, and the third time the brothers all arose and stood on their feet.

Mudjikewis commenced rubbing his eyes and stretching himself. "Why," said he, "I have overslept myself." "No, indeed," said one of the others, "do you not know we were all killed, and that it is our sister who has brought us to life?" The young men took the bodies of their enemies and *burned* them. Soon after, the woman went to procure wives for them, in a distant country, they knew not where; but she returned with ten young females, which she gave to the young men, beginning with the eldest. Mudjikewis stepped to and fro, uneasy lest he should not get the one he liked. But he was not disappointed, for she fell to his lot. And they were well matched, for she was a female magician. They then all moved into a very large lodge, and their sister told them that the women must now take turns in going to her brother's head every night, trying to untie it. They all said they would do so with pleasure. The eldest made the first attempt, and with a rushing noise she fled through the air.

Towards daylight she returned. She had been unsuccessful, as she succeeded in untying only one of the knots. All took their turns regularly, and each one succeeded in untying only one knot each time. But when the youngest went, she commenced the work as soon as she reached the lodge; although it had always been occupied, still the Indians never could see any one. For ten nights now, the smoke had not ascended, but filled the lodge and drove them out. This last night they were all driven out, and the young woman carried off the head.

The young people and the sister heard the young woman coming high through the air, and they heard her saying, "Prepare the body of our brother." And as soon as they heard it, they went to a small lodge where the black body of Iamo lay. His sister commenced cutting the neck part, from which the head had been severed. She cut so deep as to cause it to bleed; and the others who were present, by rubbing the body and applying medicines, expelled the blackness. In the meantime the one who brought it, by cutting the neck of the head, caused that also to bleed.

As soon as she arrived, they placed that close to the body, and by the aid of medicines and various other means, succeeded in restoring Iamo to all his former beauty and manliness. All rejoiced in the happy termination of their troubles, and they had spent some time joyfull together, when Iamo said, "Now I will divide the wampum"; and getting the belt which contained it, he commenced with the eldest, giving it in equal proportions. But the youngest got the most splendid and beautiful, as the bottom of the belt held the richest and rarest.

They were told that, since they had all once died, and were restored to life, they were no longer mortals, but *spirits,* and they were assigned different stations in the invisible world. Only Mudjikewis's place was, however, named. He was to direct the *west wind,* hence generally called Kabeyun, there to remain for ever. They were commanded, as they had it in their power, to do good to the inhabitants of the earth; and forgetting their sufferings in procuring the wampum, to give all things with a liberal hand. And they were also commanded that it should also be held by them *sacred;* those grains or shells of the pale hue to be emblematic of peace, while those of the darker hue would lead to evil and to war.

The spirits then, amid songs and shouts, took their flight to their respective abodes on high; while Iamo, with his sister Iamoqua, descended into the depths below.

Some of the incidents of this tale furnish references to both Occidental as well as Oriental customs, which are appropriate subjects of comment. This is not the place to enter into their discussion. It may be sufficient to mention, that the burning of the dead is an Eastern, not an Algic custom. Burying with the feet towards the east is common to the present and to many Eastern tribes; but there are tumuli or barrows in the Northwest, in which the bones lie north and south, indicating its occupancy by tribes of a prior race. The idea of the immortality of man is clearly indicated; but an idea more clearly shadowed forth here, than perhaps in any other of these fictions, is the necessity of a great boon or Saviour to render men happy. This is placed symbolically in this tale in wampum, the most sacred of all objects known to these tribes, and its acquirement is the work of the Indian Mudjikewis or heir. It is not presumable that they possess, or ever possessed, the true idea of the Saviour of mankind, as revealed by Holy Writ. The allusions are thought rather to show the original tendency of the human mind, unenlightened and uninstructed, to seek for some moral or physical panacea which is to introduce happiness to the race. Such an idea appears compatible with the condition of the erratic nations immediately at, and posterior to, the great biblical era of the introduction of new languages, and the consequent dispersion of men over the world. For it is rather to this era, than to the comparatively newer one of the fall of the Israelitish kingdom, that we are to look as the *first* point of historical and philological comparison. It is hence that the Hebrew, the initial language, becomes so important in the investigation. We may, indeed, regard it as furnishing a key to the principles of grammatical utterance in the East.

It has been observed, that the custom of female separation, upon the violation of which the present tale is founded, is a Hebrew custom, identified with the written institutions of the Pentateuch. A lodge of separation is established at these periods by all the Algic tribes. Nothing is better attested, by those who have given attention to this subject, than that everything touched by the female during this period is polluted and rendered unclean. To cross her pathway even, is to fall under the bane of impurity; and a hunter or a warrior who should thus trespass, would feel his hopes blighted and his prospect of success destroyed.

MON-DAW-MIN

or

THE ORIGIN OF INDIAN CORN

An Odjibwa Tale

———————

I N TIMES past, a poor Indian was living with his wife and children in a beautiful part of the country. He was not only poor, but inexpert in procuring food for his family, and his children were all too young to give him assistance. Although poor, he was a man of a kind and contented disposition. He was always thankful to the Great Spirit for everything he received. The same disposition was inherited by his eldest son, who had now arrived at the proper age to undertake the ceremony of the Ke-ig-uish-im-o-win, or fast, to see what kind of a spirit would be his guide and guardian through life. Wunzh, for this was his name, had been an obedient boy from his infancy, and was of a pensive, thoughtful, and mild disposition, so that he was beloved by the whole family. As soon as the first indications of spring appeared, they built him the customary little lodge, at a retired spot some distance from their own, where he would not be disturbed during this solemn rite. In the meantime he prepared himself, and immediately went into it and commenced his fast. The first few days he amused himself in the mornings by walking in the woods and over the mountains, examining the early plants and flowers, and in this way prepared himself to enjoy his sleep, and, at the same time, stored his mind with pleasant ideas for his dreams. While he rambled through the woods, he felt a strong desire to know how the plants, herbs, and berries grew, without any aid from man, and why it was that some species were good to eat, and others possessed medicinal or poisonous juices. He recalled these thoughts to mind after he became too languid to walk about, and had confined himself strictly to the lodge; he wished he could dream of something that would prove a benefit to his father and family, and to all others. "True!" he thought, "the Great Spirit made all things, and it is to him that we owe our lives. But could he not make it easier for us to get our food, than by hunting animals and taking fish? I must try to find out this in my visions."

On the third day he became weak and faint, and kept his bed. He fancied, while thus lying, that he saw a handsome young man coming down from the sky and advancing towards him. He was richly and gayly dressed, having on a great many garments of green and yellow colours, but differing in their deeper or lighter shades. He had a plume of waving feathers on his head, and all his motions were graceful.

"I am sent to you, my friend," said the celestial visiter, "by that Great Sprit who made all things in the sky and on the earth. He has seen and knows your motives in fasting. He sees that it is from a kind and benevolent wish to do good to your people, and to procure a benefit for them, and that you do not seek for strength in war or the praise of warriors. I am sent to instruct you, and show you how you can do your kindred good." He then told the young man to arise, and prepare to wrestle with him, as it was only by this means that he could hope to succeed in his wishes. Wunzh knew he was weak from fasting, but he felt his courage rising in his heart, and immediately got up, determined to die rather than fail. He commenced the trial, and, after a protracted effort, was almost exhausted, when the beautiful stranger said, "My friend, it is enough for once; I will come again to try you"; and, smiling on him, he ascended in the air in the same direction from which he came. The next day the celestial visiter reappeared at the same hour and renewed the trial. Wunzh felt that his strength was even less than the day before, but the courage of his mind seemed to increase in proportion as his body became weaker. Seeing this, the stranger again spoke to him in the same words he used before, adding, "To-morrow will be your last trial. Be strong, my friend, for this is the only way you can overcome me, and obtain the boon you seek." On the third day he again appeared at the same time and renewed the struggle. The poor youth was very faint in body, but grew stronger in mind at every contest, and was determined to prevail or perish in the attempt. He exerted his utmost powers, and after the contest had been continued the usual time, the stranger ceased his efforts and declared himself conquered. For the first time he entered the lodge, and sitting down beside the youth, he began to deliver his instructions to him, telling him in what manner he should proceed to take advantage of his victory.

"You have won your desires of the Great Spirit," said the stranger. "You have wrestled manfully. To-morrow will be the seventh day of your fasting. Your father will give you food to strengthen you, and as it is the last day of trial, you will prevail. I know this, and now tell you what you must do to benefit your family and your tribe. To-morrow," he repeated, "I shall meet you and wrestle with you for the last time; and, as soon as you have prevailed against me, you will strip off my garments and throw me down, clean the earth of roots and weeds, make it soft, and bury me in the spot. When you have done this, leave my body in the earth, and do not disturb it, but come occasionally to visit the place, to see whether I have come to life, and be careful never to let the grass or weeds grow on my grave. Once a month cover me with fresh earth. If you follow my instructions, you will accomplish your object of doing good to your fellow-creatures by teaching them the knowledge I now teach you." He then shook him by the hand and disappeared.

In the morning the youth's father came with some slight refreshments, saying, "My son, you have fasted long enough. If the Great Spirit will favour you, he will do it now. It is seven days since you have tasted food, and you must not sacrifice your life. The Master of Life does not require that." "My father," replied the youth, "wait till the sun goes down. I have a particular reason for extending my fast to that hour." "Very well," said the old man, "I shall wait till the hour arrives, and you feel inclined to eat."

At the usual hour of the day the sky-visiter returned, and the trial of strength was renewed. Although the youth had not availed himself of his father's offer of food, he felt that new strength had been given to him, and that exertion had renewed his strength and fortified his courage. He grasped his angelic antagonist with supernatural strength, threw him down, took from him his beautiful garments and plume, and finding him dead, immediately buried him on the spot, taking all the precautions he had been told of, and being very confident, at the same time, that his friend would again come to life. He then returned to his father's lodge, and partook sparingly of the meal that had been prepared for him. But he never for a moment forgot the grave of his friend. He carefully visited it throughout the spring, and weeded out the grass, and kept the ground in a soft and pliant state. Very soon he saw the tops of the green plumes coming through the ground; and the more careful he was to obey his instructions in keeping the ground in order, the faster they grew. He was, however, careful to conceal the exploit from his father. Days and weeks had passed in this way. The summer was now drawing towards a close, when one day, after a long absence in hunting, Wunzh invited his father to follow him to the quiet and lonesome spot of his former fast. The lodge had been removed, and the weeds kept from growing on the circle where it stood, but in its place stood a tall and graceful plant, with bright-coloured silken hair, surmounted with nodding plumes and stately leaves, and golden clusters on each side. "It is my friend," shouted the lad; "it is the friend of all mankind. It is *Mondawmin*.* We need no longer rely on hunting alone; for, as long as this gift is cherished and taken care of, the ground itself will give us a living." He then pulled an ear. "See, my father," said he, "this is what I fasted for. The Great Spirit has listened to my voice, and sent us something new,† and henceforth our people will not alone depend upon the chase or upon the waters."

He then communicated to his father the instructions given him

---

*The Algic name for corn. The word is manifestly a trinary compound from *monedo*, spirit; *min*, a grain or berry; and *iaw*, the verb substantive.

†The Zea mays, it will be recollected, is indigenous to America, and was unknown in Europe before 1495.

by the stranger. He told him that the broad husks must be torn away, as he had pulled off the garments in his wrestling; and having done this, directed him how the ear must be held before the fire till the outer skin became brown, while all the milk was retained in the grain. The whole family then united in a feast on the newly-grown ears, expressing gratitude to the Merciful Spirit who gave it. So corn came into the world, and has ever since been preserved.

PEETA KWAY

or

THE TEMPEST

An Algic Tale

THERE ONCE lived a woman called Monedo Kway* on the sand mountains called "the Sleeping Bear" of Lake Michigan, who had a daughter as beautiful as she was modest and discreet. Everybody spoke of the beauty of this daughter. She was so handsome that her mother feared she would be carried off, and to prevent it she put her in a box on the lake, which was tied by a long string to a stake on the shore. Every morning the mother pulled the box ashore, and combed her daughter's long, shining hair, gave her food, and then put her out again on the lake.

One day a handsome young man chanced to come to the spot at the moment she was receiving her morning's attentions from her mother. He was struck with her beauty, and immediately went home and told his feelings to his uncle, who was a great chief and a powerful magician. "My nephew," replied the old man, "go to the mother's lodge, and sit down in a modest manner, without saying a word. You need not ask her the question. But whatever *you think* she will understand, and what *she thinks* in answer you will also understand." The young man did so. He sat down, with his head dropped in a thoughtful manner, without

---

*Female spirit or prophetess.

uttering a word. He then thought, "I wish she would give me her daughter." Very soon he understood the mother's thoughts in reply. "Give you my daughter?" thought she; *"you!* No, indeed, my daughter shall never marry *you."* The young man went away and reported the result to his uncle. "Woman without good sense," said he, "who is she keeping her daughter for? Does she think she will marry the Mudjikewis?* Proud heart! we will try her magic skill, and see whether she can withstand our power." The pride and haughtiness of the mother was talked of by the spirits living on that part of the lake. They met together and determined to exert their power in humbling her. For this purpose they resolved to raise a great storm on the lake. The water began to toss and roar, and the tempest became so severe, that the string broke, and the box floated off through the straits down Lake Huron, and struck against the sandy shores at its outlet. The place where it struck was near the lodge of a superannuated old spirit called Ishkwon Daimeka, or the keeper of the gate of the lakes. He opened the box and let out the beautiful daughter, took her into his lodge, and married her.

When the mother found that her daughter had been blown off by the storm, she raised very loud cries and lamented exceedingly. This she continued to do for a long time, and would not be comforted. At length, after two or three years, the spirits had pity on her, and determined to raise another storm and bring her back. It was even a greater storm than the first; and when it began to wash away the ground and encroach on the lodge of Ishkwon Daimeka, she leaped into the box, and the waves carried her back to the very spot of her mother's lodge on the shore. Monedo Equa was overjoyed; but when she opened the box, she found that her daughter's beauty had almost all departed. However, she loved her still because she was her daughter, and now thought of the young man who had made her the offer of marriage. She sent a formal message to him, but he had altered his mind, for he knew that she had been the wife of another. *"I* marry your daughter?" said he; *"your* daughter! No, indeed! I shall never marry her."

---

*A term indicative of the heir or successor to the first place in power.

The storm that brought her back was so strong and powerful that it tore away a large part of the shore of the lake, and swept off Ishkwon Daimeka's lodge, the fragments of which, lodging in the straits, formed those beautiful islands which are scattered in the St. Clair and Detroit rivers. The old man himself was drowned, and his bones are buried under them. They heard him singing as he was driven off on a portion of his lodge; some fragments of his words are still repeated, which show what his thoughts were in the midst of his overthrow.

ISHKWON DAIMEKA'S LAMENT.

The waves, the waves, the angry waves,
   Have borne my bless'd away,
And cast me forth all reft and lone,
   With wrecks of wood and clay.

My power is gone, my guardian dead,
   My loved, my cherish'd lost,
And every dream of pleasure fled,
   And every bright hope cross'd.

I go—I go, a floating ball,
   A speck of earth at best;
But with my dying breath I call
   On Peeta Kway the bless'd.

Oh! was it kind in spirits high,
   Who rule these waters free,
To call the vengeance of the sky,
   And turn its wrath on me?

Yet shall I triumph; for the storm
   That sounds my funeral knell,
Shall lands, and coasts, and islands form,
   Where joy and peace shall dwell.

And every vestige of my lodge,
   And all my simple store,
Shall turn to pastures green and sweet,
   And many a winding shore.

There other tribes of men shall dwell,
    Who serve a purer power,
And oft of me the story tell,
    To while away the hour.

So shall I live, though now I'm toss'd,
    A poor, dishonour'd thing,
And where one Peeta Kway was lost,
    A thousand more shall spring.

MANABOZHO

or

THE GREAT INCARNATION
OF THE NORTH

An Algic Legend

Introductory Note.—The accounts which the Indians hand down of a remarkable personage of miraculous birth, who waged a warfare with monsters, performed the most extravagant and heroic feats, underwent a catastrophe like Jonah's, and survived a general deluge, constitute a very prominent portion of their cabin lore. Interwoven with these leading traits are innumerable tales of personal achievement, sagacity, endurance, miracle, and trick, which place him in almost every scene of deep interest that could be imagined, from the competitor on the Indian playground, to a giant-killer, or a mysterious being of stern, all-knowing, superhuman power. Whatever man could do, he could do. He affected all the powers of a necromancer. He wielded the arts of a demon, and had the ubiquity of a god. But in proportion as Manabozho exercises powers and performs exploits wild or wonderful, the chain of narration which connects them is broken or vague. He leaps over extensive regions of country like an ignis fatuus. He appears suddenly like an avatar, or saunters over weary wastes a poor and starving hunter. His voice is at one moment deep and sonorous as a thunder-clap, and at another clothed with the softness of feminine supplication. Scarcely any two persons agree in all the minor circumstances of the story, and scarcely any omit the leading traits. The several tribes who speak dialects of the mother language from which the narration is taken, differ, in like manner, from each other in the particulars of his exploits. But he is not presented here as an historical personage, or in any other light than as the native narrators themselves depict him, when they have assembled a group of listeners in the lodge, and begin the story of Manabozho. His birth and parentage are obscure. Story says his grandmother was the daughter of the moon. Having been married but a short time, her rival attracted her to a grapevine swing on the banks of a lake, and by one bold exertion pitched her into its centre, from which she fell through to the earth. Having a daughter, the fruit of her lunar marriage, she was very careful in instructing her, from early infancy, to beware of the west wind, and never, in stooping, to expose herself to its influence. In some unguarded moment this precaution was neglected. In an instant, the gale, invading her robes, scattered them upon its wings, and accomplishing its Tarquinic purpose, at the same moment annihilated her. At the scene of this catastrophe her mother found a fœtus-like mass, which she carefully and tenderly nursed till it assumed the beautiful and striking lineaments of the infant Manabozho.

Very little is told of his early boyhood. We take him up in the following legend at a period of advanced youth, when we find him living with his grandmother. And at this time he possessed, although he had not yet *exercised,* all the anomalous and contradictory powers of body and mind, of manship and divinity, which he afterward evinced. The timidity and rawness of the boy quickly gave way in the courageous developments of the man. He soon evinced the sagacity, cunning, perseverance, and heroic courage which constitute the admiration of the Indians. And he relied largely upon these in the gratification of an ambitious, vainglorious, and mischief-loving disposition. In wisdom and energy he was superior to any one who had ever lived before. Yet he was simple when circumstances required it, and was ever the object of tricks and ridicule in others. He could transform himself into any animal he pleased, being man or manito, as circumstances rendered necessary. He often conversed with animals, fowls, reptiles, and fishes. He deemed himself related to them, and invariably addressed them by the term "my brother"; and one of his greatest resources, when hard pressed, was to change himself into their shapes.

Manitoes constitute the great power and absorbing topic of Indian lore. Their agency is at once the groundwork of their mythology and demonology. They supply the machinery of their poetic inventions, and the belief in their multitudinous existence exerts a powerful influence upon the lives and character of individuals. As their Manitoes are of all imaginary kinds, grades, and powers, benign and malicious, it seems a grand conception among the Indians to create a personage strong enough in his necromantic and spiritual powers to baffle the most malicious, beat the stoutest, and overreach the most cunning. In carrying out this conception in the following tale, they have, however, rather exhibited an incarnation of the power of Evil than of the genius of Benevolence.

Fasts.—The rite of fasting is one of the most deep-seated and universal in the Indian ritual. It is practised among all the American tribes, and is deemed by them essential to their success in life in every situation. No young man is fitted and prepared to begin the career of life until he has accomplished his great fast. Seven days appear to have been the ancient maximum limit of endurance, and the success of the devotee is inferred from the length of continued abstinence to which he is known to have attained. These fasts are anticipated by the youth as one of the most important events of his life. They are awaited with interest, prepared for with solemnity, and endured with a self-devotion bordering on the heroic. Character is thought to be fixed from this period, and the primary fast, thus prepared for and successfully established, seems to hold that relative importance to subsequent years that is attached to a public profession of religious faith in civilized communities. It is at this period that the young men and the young women "see visions and dream dreams," and fortune or misfortune is predicted from the guardian spirit chosen during this, to them, religious ordeal. The hallucinations of the mind are taken for divine inspiration. The effect is deeply felt and strongly impressed on the mind; too deeply, indeed, to be ever obliterated in after life. The father in the circle of his lodge, the hunter in the pursuit of the chase, and the warrior in the field of battle, think of the guardian genius which they fancy to accompany them, and trust to his power and benign influence under every circumstance. This genius is the absorbing theme of their silent meditations, and stands to them in all respects in place of the Christian's hope, with the single difference that, however deeply mused upon, the *name* is never uttered, and every circumstance connected with its selection, and the devotion paid to it, is most studiously and professedly concealed even from their nearest friends.

Fasts in subsequent life appear to have for their object a renewal of the powers and virtues which they attribute to the rite. And they are observed more frequently by those who strive to preserve unaltered the ancient state of society among them, or by men who assume austere habits for the purpose of acquiring influence in the tribe, or as preparatives for war or some extraordinary feat. It is not known that there is any fixed day observed as a general fast. So far as a rule is followed, a general fast seems to have been observed in the spring, and to have *preceded* the general and customary feasts at that season.

It will be inferred from these facts, that the Indians believe fasts to be very meritorious. They are deemed most acceptable to the Manitoes or spirits whose influence and protection they wish to engage or preserve. And it is thus clearly deducible, that a very large proportion of the time devoted by the Indians to secret worship, so to say, is devoted to these guardian or intermediate spirits, and not to the Great Spirit or Creator.

MANABOZHO WAS living with his grandmother near the edge of a wide prairie. On this prairie he first saw animals and birds of every kind. He there also saw exhibitions of divine power in the sweeping tempests, in the thunder and lightning, and the various shades of light and darkness, which form a never-ending scene of observation. Every new sight he beheld in the heavens was a subject of remark; every new animal or bird an object of deep interest; and every sound uttered by the animal creation a new lesson, which he was expected to learn. He often trembled at what he heard and saw. To this scene his grandmother sent him at an early age to watch. The first sound he heard was that of the owl, at which he was greatly terrified, and, quickly descending the tree he had climbed, he ran with alarm to the lodge. "Noko! Noko!"* he cried, "I have heard a monedo." She laughed at his fears, and asked him what kind of a noise it made. He answered, "It makes a noise like this: Ko-ko-ko-ho." She told him that he was young and foolish; that what he had heard was only a bird, deriving its name from the noise it made.

He went back and continued his watch. While there, he thought to himself, "It is singular that I am so simple, and my grandmother so wise, and that I have neither father nor mother. I have never heard a word about them. I must ask and find out." He went home and sat down silent and dejected. At length his grandmother asked him, "Manabozho, what is the matter with you?" He answered, "I wish you would tell me whether I have any

---

*An abbreviated term for "my grandmother," derived from *no-kó-miss.*

parents living, and who my relatives are." Knowing that he was of a wicked and revengeful disposition, she dreaded telling him the story of his parentage, but he insisted on her compliance. "Yes," she said, "you have a father and three brothers living. Your mother is dead. She was taken without the consent of her parents by your father, the West. Your brothers are the North, East, and South, and, being older than yourself, your father has given them great power with the winds, according to their names. You are the youngest of his children. I have nourished you from your infancy, for your mother died in giving you birth, owing to the ill treatment of your father. I have no relations besides you this side of the planet in which I was born, and from which I was precipitated by female jealousy. Your mother was my only child, and you are my only hope."

He appeared to be rejoiced to hear that his father was living, for he had already thought in his heart to try and kill him. He told his grandmother he should set out in the morning to visit him. She said it was a long distance to the place where Ningabiun* lived. But that had no effect to stop him, for he had now attained manhood, possessed a giant's height, and was endowed by nature with a giant's strength and power. He set out and soon reached the place, for every step he took covered a large surface of ground. The meeting took place on a high mountain in the West. His father was very happy to see him. He also appeared pleased. They spent some days in talking with each other. One evening Manabozho asked his father what he was most afraid of on earth. He replied, "Nothing." "But is there not something you dread here? tell me." At last his father said, yielding, "Yes, there is a black stone found in such a place. It is the only thing earthly I am afraid of; for if it should hit me or any part of my body, it would injure me very much." He said this as a secret, and in return asked his son the same question. Knowing each other's power, although the son's was limited, the father feared him on account of his great strength. Manabozho answered, "Nothing!" intending to avoid the question, or to refer to some harmless object as the

---

*This is a term for the west wind. It is a derivative from *Ka-bian-oong,* the proper appellation for the occident.

one of which he was afraid. He was asked again and again, and answered "Nothing!" But the West said, "There must be something you are afraid of." "Well! I will tell you," says Manabozho, "what it is." But, before he would pronounce the word, he affected a great dread. "*Ie-ee—Ie-ee*—it is—it is," said he, "yeo! yeo!* I cannot name it, I am seized with a dread." The West told him to banish his fears. He commenced again, in a strain of mock sensitiveness repeating the same words; at last he cried out, "It is the root of the *apukwa.*"** He appeared to be exhausted by the effort of pronouncing the word, in all this skilfully acting a studied part.

Some time after he observed, "I will get some of the black rock." The West said, "Far be it from you; do not do so, my son." He still persisted. "Well," said the father, "I will also get the apukwa root." Manabozho immediately cried out, *"Kago! kago!"*† affecting, as before, to be in great dread of it, but really wishing, by this course, to urge on the West to procure it, that he might draw him into combat. He went out and got a large piece of the black rock, and brought it home. The West also took care to bring the dreaded root.

In the course of conversation, he asked his father whether he had been the cause of his mother's death. The answer was "Yes!" He then took up the rock and struck him. Blow led to blow, and here commenced an obstinate and furious combat, which continued several days. Fragments of the rock, broken off under Manabozho's blows, can be seen in various places to this day.‡ The root did not prove as mortal a weapon as his well-acted fears had led his father to expect, although he suffered severely from the blows. This battle commenced on the mountains. The West was forced to give ground. Manabozho drove him across rivers, and over mountains and lakes, and at last he came to the brink of this world.

---

*An interjection indicating pain.
**The scirpus or bulrush.
†"Do not—do not."
‡The Northern Indians, when traveling in company with each other, or with white persons who possess their confidence, so as to put them at ease, are in the habit of making frequent allusions to Manabozho and his exploits. "There," said a young Chippewa, pointing to some huge boulders of greenstone, "are pieces of the rock broken off in Manabozho's combat with his father." "This is the duck," said an Indian interpreter on the sources of the Mississippi, "that Manabozho kicked." "Under that island," said a friend conversant with their language, "Manabozho lost a beaver."

"Hold!" cried he, "my son, you know my power, and that it is impossible to kill me. Desist, and I will also portion you out with as much power as your brothers. The four quarters of the globe are already occupied; but you can go and do a great deal of good to the people of this earth, which is infested with large serpents, beasts, and monsters,* who make great havoc among the inhabitants. Go and do good. You have the power now to do so, and your fame with the beings of this earth will last for ever. When you have finished your work, I will have a place provided for you. You will then go and sit with your brother Kabibboonocca in the north."

Manabozho was pacified. He returned to his lodge, where he was confined by the wounds he had received. But from his grandmother's skill in medicines he was soon recovered. She told him that his grandfather, who had come to the earth in search of her, had been killed by MEGISSOGWON,† who lived on the opposite side of the great lake. "When he was alive," she continued, "I was never without oil to put on my head, but now my hair is fast falling off for want of it." "Well!" said he, "Noko, get cedar bark and make me a line, whilst I make a canoe." When all was ready, he went out to the middle of the lake to fish. He put his line down, saying, "Me-she-nah-ma-gwai (the name of the kingfish), take hold of my bait." He kept repeating this for some time. At last the king of the fishes said, "Manabozho troubles me. Here, Trout, take hold of his line." The trout did so. He then commenced drawing up his line, which was very heavy, so that his canoe stood nearly perpendicular; but he kept crying out, "Wha-ee-he! wha-ee-he!" till he could see the trout. As soon as he saw him, he spoke to him. "Why did you take hold of my hook? Esa! esa!‡ you ugly fish." The trout, being thus rebuked, let go.

Manabozho put his line again in the water, saying, "King of

---

*The term *weendigo,* translated here monster, is commonly applied, at this time, by the Indians, to cannibals. Its ancient use appears, however, to have embraced giants and anomalous voracious beasts of the land, to the former existence of which, on this Continent, their traditions refer.

The word *genàbik,* rendered serpent, appears likewise to have been used in a generic sense for amphibious animals of large and venomous character. When applied to existing species of serpents, it requires an adjective prefix or qualifying term.

†The wampum or pearl feather.

‡An interjection equivalent to "Shame! Shame!"

fishes, take hold of my line." But the king of the fishes told a monstrous sunfish to take hold of it; for Manabozho was tiring him with his incessant calls. He again drew up his line with difficulty, saying as before, "Wha-ee-he! wha-ee-he!" while his canoe was turning in swift circles. When he saw the sunfish, he cried, "Esa! esa! you odious fish! why did you dirty my hook by taking it in your mouth? Let go, I say, let go." The sunfish did so, and told the king of fishes what Manabozho said. Just at that moment the bait came near the king, and hearing Manabozho continually crying out, "Me-she-nah-ma-gwai, take hold of my hook," at last he did so, and allowed himself to be drawn up to the surface, which he had no sooner reached than, at one mouthful, he took Manabozho and his canoe down. When he came to himself, he found that he was in the fish's belly, and also his canoe. He now turned his thoughts to the way of making his escape. Looking in his canoe, he saw his war-club, with which he immediately struck the heart of the fish. He then felt a sudden motion, as if he were moving with great velocity. The fish observed to the others, "I am sick at stomach for having swallowed this dirty fellow Manabozho." Just at this moment he received another more severe blow on the heart. Manabozho thought, "If I am thrown up in the middle of the lake, I shall be drowned; so I must prevent it." He drew his canoe and placed it across the fish's throat, and just as he had finished the fish commenced vomiting, but to no effect. In this he was aided by a squirrel, who had accompanied him unperceived until that moment. This animal had taken an active part in helping him to place his canoe across the fish's throat. For this act he named him, saying, "For the future, boys shall always call you Ajidaumo."*

He then renewed his attack upon the fish's heart, and succeeded, by repeated blows, in killing him, which he first knew by the loss of motion, and by the sound of the beating body against the shore. He waited a day longer to see what would happen. He heard birds scratching on the body, and all at once the rays of light broke in. He could see the heads of gulls, who were looking

---

*Animal tail, or bottom upward.

in by the opening they had made. "Oh!" cried Manabozho, "my younger brothers, make the opening larger, so that I can get out." They told each other that their brother Manabozho was inside of the fish. They immediately set about enlarging the orifice, and in a short time liberated him. After he got out he said to the gulls, "For the future you shall be called Kayoshk* for your kindness to me."

The spot where the fish happened to be driven ashore was near his lodge. He went up and told his grandmother to go and prepare as much oil as she wanted. All besides, he informed her, he should keep for himself.

Some time after this, he commenced making preparations for a war excursion against the Pearl Feather, the Manito who lived on the opposite side of the great lake, who had killed his grandfather. The abode of this spirit was defended, first, by fiery serpents, who hissed fire so that no one could pass them; and, in the second place, by a large mass of gummy matter lying on the water, so soft and adhesive that whoever attempted to pass, or whatever came in contact with it, was sure to stick there.

He continued making bows and arrows without number, but he had no heads for his arrows. At last Noko told him that an old man who lived at some distance could make them. He sent her to get some. She soon returned with her conaus, or wrapper, full.† Still he told her he had not enough, and sent her again. She returned with as much more. He thought to himself, "I must find out the way of making these heads." Cunning and curiosity prompted him to make the discovery. But he deemed it necessary to deceive his grandmother in so doing. "Noko," said he, "while I take my drum and rattle, and sing my war songs, go and try to get me some larger heads for my arrows, for those you brought me are all of the same size. Go and see whether the old man cannot make some a little larger." He followed her as she went, keeping

---

*A free translation of this expression might be rendered as noble scratchers or grabbers.
†The *conaus* is the most ancient garment known to these tribes, being a simple extended single piece, without folds. The word is the apparent root of *godaus*, a female garment. *Waub-e-wion*, a blanket, is a comparatively modern phrase for a wrapper, signifying, literally, a white skin with the wool on.

at a distance, and saw the old artificer at work, and so discovered his process. He also beheld the old man's daughter, and perceived that she was very beautiful. He felt his breast beat with a new emotion, but said nothing. He took care to get home before his grandmother, and commenced singing as if he had never left his lodge. When the old woman came near, she heard his drum and rattle, without any suspicion that he had followed her. She delivered him the arrow-heads.

One evening the old woman said, "My son, you ought to *fast*** before you go to war, as your brothers frequently do, to find out whether you will be successful or not." He said he had no objection, and immediately commenced a fast for several days. He would retire every day from the lodge so far as to be out of reach of his grandmother's voice. It seems she had indicated this spot, and was very anxious he should fast there, and not at another place. She had a secret motive, which she carefully hid from him. Deception always begets suspicion. After a while he thought to himself, "I must find out why my grandmother is so anxious for me to fast at this spot." Next evening he went but a short distance. She cried out, "A little farther off"; but he came nearer to the lodge, and cried out in a low, counterfeited voice, to make it appear that he was distant. She then replied, "That is far enough." He had got so near that he could see all that passed in the lodge. He had not been long in his place of concealment when a paramour in the shape of a bear entered the lodge. He had very long hair. They commenced talking about him, and appeared to be improperly familiar. At that time people lived to a very great age, and he perceived, from the marked attentions of this visiter, that he did not think a grandmother too old to be pleased with such attentions. He listened to their conversation some time. At last he determined to play the visiter a trick. He took some fire, and when the bear had turned his back, touched his long hair. When the animal felt the flame, he jumped out, but

---

*FASTS: [Originally introduced as a lengthy footnote where the old woman implores her grandson to fast before going off to war. The author's footnote now appears as part of his commentary at the beginning of the chapter.]

the open air only made it burn the fiercer, and he was seen running off in a full blaze.

Manabozho ran to his customary place of fasting, and, assuming a tone of simplicity, began to cry out, "Noko! Noko! is it time for me to come home?" "Yes," she cried. When he came in she told him what had taken place, at which he appeared to be very much surprised.

After having finished his term of fasting and sung his war-song—from which the Indians of the present day derive the custom—he embarked in his canoe, fully prepared for war. In addition to the usual implements, he had a plentiful supply of oil. He travelled rapidly night and day, for he had only to will or speak, and the canoe went. At length he arrived in sight of the fiery serpents. He stopped to view them. He saw they were some distance apart, and that the flame only which issued from them reached across the pass. He commenced talking as a friend to them; but they answered, "We know you, Manabozho, you cannot pass." He then thought of some expedient to deceive them, and hit upon this. He pushed his canoe as near as possible. All at once he cried out, with a loud and terrified voice, "What is that behind you?" The serpents instantly turned their heads, when, at a single word, he passed them. "Well!" said he, placidly, after he had got by, "how do you like my exploit?" He then took up his bow and arrows, and with deliberate aim shot them, which was easily done, for the serpents were stationary, and could not move beyond a certain spot. They were of enormous length and of a bright colour.

Having overcome the sentinel serpents, he went on in his canoe till he came to a soft gummy portion of the lake, called PIGIU-WAGUMEE, or Pitch-water. He took the oil and rubbed it on his canoe, and then pushed into it. The oil softened the surface and enabled him to slip through it with ease, although it required frequent rubbing, and a constant reapplication of the oil. Just as his oil failed, he extricated himself from this impediment, and was the first person who ever succeeded in overcoming it.

He now came in view of land, on which he debarked in safety, and could see the lodge of the Shining Manito, situated on a hill. He commenced preparing for the fight, putting his arrows and clubs in order, and just at the dawn of day began his attack, yelling and shouting, and crying with triple voices, "Surround him! surround him! run up! run up!" making it appear that he had many followers. He advanced, crying out, "It was you that killed my grandfather," and with this shot his arrows. The combat continued all day. Manabozho's arrows had no effect, for his antagonist was clothed with pure wampum. He was now reduced to three arrows, and it was only by extraordinary agility that he could escape the blows which the Manito kept making at him. At that moment a large woodpecker (the ma-ma) flew past, and lit on a tree. "Manabozho," he cried, "your adversary has a vulnerable point; shoot at the lock of hair on the crown of his head." He shot his first arrow so as only to draw blood from that part. The Manito made one or two unsteady steps, but recovered himself. He began to parley, but, in the act, received a second arrow, which brought him to his knees. But he again recovered. In so doing, however, he exposed his head, and gave his adversary a chance to fire his third arrow, which penetrated deep and brought him, a lifeless corpse, to the ground. Manabozho uttered his saw-saw-quan, and taking his scalp as a trophy, he called the woodpecker to come and receive a reward for his information. He took the blood of the Manito and rubbed it on the woodpecker's* head, the feathers of which are red to this day.

After this victory he returned home, singing songs of triumph and beating his drum. When his grandmother heard him, she came to the shore and welcomed him with songs and dancing. Glory fired his mind. He displayed the trophies he had brought in the most conspicuous manner, and felt an unconquerable desire for other adventures. He felt himself urged by the consciousness of his power to new trials of bravery, skill, and necromantic prowess. He had destroyed the Manito of Wealth, and killed his guardian serpents, and eluded all his charms. He did not long remain inactive. His next adventure was upon the water, and proved him the prince of fishermen. He captured a fish of such monstrous size that the fat and oil he obtained from it formed a small lake. He therefore invited all the animals and fowls to a

---

*The tuft feathers of the red-headed woodpecker are used to ornament the stems of the Indian pipe, and are symbolic of valour.

banquet, and he made the order in which they partook of this repast the measure of their fatness. As fast as they arrived, he told them to plunge in. The bear came first, and was followed by the deer, opossum, and such other animals as are noted for their peculiar fatness at certain seasons. The moose and bison came tardily. The partridge looked on till the reservoir was nearly exhausted. The hare and marten came last, and these animals have, consequently, no fat. When this ceremony was over, he told the assembled animals and birds to dance, taking up his drum and crying, "New songs from the south, come, brothers, dance." He directed them to pass in a circle around him, and to shut their eyes. They did so. When he saw a fat fowl pass by him, he adroitly wrung off its head, at the same time beating his drum and singing with greater vehemence to drown the noise of the fluttering, and crying out, in a tone of admiration, "That's the way, my brothers, *that's* the way." At last a small duck (the diver), thinking there was something wrong, opened one eye and saw what he was doing. Giving a spring, and crying "Ha-ha-a! Manabozho is killing us," he made for the water. Manabozho followed him, and, just as the duck was getting into the water, gave him a kick, which is the cause of his back being flattened and his legs being straightened out backward, so that when he gets on land he cannot walk, and his tail feathers are few. Meantime the other birds flew off, and the animals ran into the woods.

After this Manabozho set out to travel. He wished to outdo all others, and to see new countries. But after walking over America and encountering many adventures, he became satisfied as well as fatigued. He had heard of great feats in hunting, and felt a desire to try his power in that way. One evening, as he was walking along the shores of a great lake, weary and hungry, he encountered a great magician in the form of an old wolf, with six young ones, coming towards him. The wolf, as soon as he saw him, told his whelps to keep out of the way of Manabozho, "for I know," continued he, "that it is him that we see yonder." The young wolves were in the act of running off when Manabozho cried out, "My grandchildren, where are you going? Stop, and I will go with you." He appeared rejoiced to see the old wolf, and asked him whither he was journeying. Being told that they were looking out for a place where they could find most game to pass the winter, he said he should like to go with them, and addressed the old wolf in the following words. "Brother, I have a passion for the chase; are you willing to change me into a wolf?" He was answered favourably, and his transformation immediately effected.

Manabozho was fond of novelty. He found himself a wolf corresponding in size with the others, but he was not quite satisfied with the change, crying out, "Oh, make me a little larger." They did so. "A little larger still," he exclaimed. They said, "Let us humour him," and granted his request. "Well," said he, "*that* will do." He looked at his tail. "Oh!" cried he, "do make my tail a little longer and more bushy." They did so. They then all started off in company, dashing up a ravine. After getting into the woods some distance, they fell in with the tracks of moose. The young ones went after them, Manabozho and the old wolf following at their leisure. "Well," said the wolf, "who do you think is the fastest of the boys? Can you tell by the jumps they take?" "Why," he replied, "that one that takes such long jumps, he is the fastest, to be sure." "Ha! ha! you are mistaken," said the old wolf. "He makes a good start, but he will be the first to tire out; this one, who appears to be behind, will be the one to kill the game." They then came to the place where the boys had started in chase. One had dropped his small bundle. "Take that, Manabozho," said the old wolf. "Esa," he replied, "what will I do with a dirty dogskin?" The wolf took it up; it was a beautiful robe. "Oh, I will carry it now," said Manabozho. "Oh no," replied the wolf, who at the moment exerted his magic power; "it is a robe of pearls!" And from this moment he omitted no occasion to display his superiority, both in the hunter's and magician's art, above his conceited companion. Coming to a place where the moose had lain down, they saw that the young wolves had made a fresh start after their prey. "Why," said the wolf, "this moose is poor. I know by the tracks, for I can always tell whether they are fat or not." They next came to a place where one of the wolves had bit at the moose, and had broken one of his teeth on a tree. "Manabozho," said the wolf, "one of your grandchildren has shot at the game. Take his arrow; there it is." "No," he replied; "what will I do with a dirty dog's tooth?" The old man took it up, and behold! it was a beautiful silver arrow. When they overtook the youngsters, they had killed a very fat moose. Manabozho was very hungry; but, alas! such is the power of enchantment, he saw nothing but the bones picked quite clean. He thought to himself, "Just as I expected, dirty, greedy fellows!" However, he sat down without saying a word. At length the old wolf spoke to one of the young ones, saying, "Give some meat to your grandfather." One of them obeyed, and, coming near to Manabozho, opened his mouth as if he was about to vomit. He jumped up, saying, "You filthy dog, you have eaten so much that your stomach refuses to hold it. Get you gone into some other place." The old wolf, hearing the abuse, went a little to one side to see, and behold, a heap of fresh ruddy meat, with the fat, lying all ready prepared. He was followed by Manabozho, who, having the enchantment instantly removed, put on a smiling face. "Amazement!" said he; "how fine the meat is." "Yes," replied the wolf; "it is always so with us; we know our work, and always get the best. It is not a long tail that makes a hunter." Manabozho bit his lip.

They then commenced fixing their winter quarters, while the youngsters went out in search of game, and soon brought in a large supply. One day, during the absence of the young wolves, the old one amused himself in cracking the large bones of a moose. "Manabozho," said he, "cover your head with the robe, and do not look at me while I am at these bones, for a piece may fly in your eye." He did as he was told; but, looking through a rent that was in the robe, he saw what the other was about. Just at that moment a piece flew off and hit him in the eye. He cried out, "Tyau, why do you strike me, you old dog?" The wolf said, "You must have been looking at me." But deception commonly leads to falsehood. "No, no," he said, "why should I want to look at you?" "Manabozho," said the wolf, "you *must* have been looking, or you would not have got hurt." "No, no," he replied again, "I was not. I will repay the saucy wolf this," thought he to himself. So, next day, taking up a bone to obtain the marrow, he said to the wolf, "Cover your head and don't look at me, for I fear a piece may fly in your eye." The wolf did so. He then took the leg-bone of the moose, and looking first to see if the wolf was well covered, he hit him a blow with all his might. The wolf jumped up, cried out, and fell prostrate from the effects of the blow. "Why," said he, "do you strike me so?" "Strike you!" he replied; "no, you must have been looking at me." "No," answered the wolf, "I say I have not." But he persisted in the assertion, and the poor magician had to give up.

Manabozho was an expert hunter when he earnestly undertook it. He went out one day and killed a fat moose. He was very hungry, and sat down to eat. But immediately he fell into great doubts as to the proper point to begin. "Well," said he, "I do not know where to commence. At the head? No! People will laugh, and say 'he ate him backward.'" He went to the side. "No!" said he, "they will say I ate him sideways." He then went to the hind-quarter. "No!" said he, "they will say I ate him forward. I will commence *here,* say what they will." He took a delicate piece from the rump, and was just ready to put it in his mouth, when a tree close by made a creaking noise, caused by the rubbing of one large branch against another. This annoyed him. "Why!" he exclaimed, "I cannot eat when I hear such a noise. Stop! stop!" said he to the tree. He was putting the morsel again to his mouth, when the noise was repeated. He put it down, exclaiming, "*I cannot eat* with such a noise"; and immediately left the meat, although he was very hungry, to go and put a stop to the noise. He climbed the tree and was pulling at the limb, when his arm was caught between the two branches so that he could not extricate himself. While thus held fast, he saw a pack of wolves coming in the direction towards his meat. "Go that way! go that way!" he cried out; "what would you come to get here?" The wolves talked among themselves and said, "Manabozho must have something there, or he would not tell us to go another way." "I begin to know him," said an old wolf, "and all his tricks. Let us go forward and see." They came on, and finding the moose, soon made way with the whole carcass. Manabozho looked on wishfully to see them eat till they were fully satisfied, and they left him nothing but the bare bones. The next heavy blast of wind opened the branches and liberated him. He went home, thinking to himself, "See the effect of meddling with frivolous things when I had certain good in my possession."

Next day the old wolf addressed him thus: "My brother, I am

going to separate from you, but I will leave behind me one of the young wolves to be your hunter." He then departed. In the act Manabozho was disenchanted, and again resumed his mortal shape. He was sorrowful and dejected, but soon resumed his wonted air of cheerfulness. The young wolf who was left with him was a good hunter, and never failed to keep the lodge well supplied with meat. One day he addressed him as follows: "My grandson, I had a dream last night, and it does not portend good. It is of the large lake which lies in *that* direction (pointing). You must be careful never to cross it, even if the ice should appear good. If you should come to it at night weary or hungry, you must make the circuit of it." Spring commenced, and the snow was melting fast before the rays of the sun, when one evening the wolf came to this lake, weary with the day's chase. He disliked to go so far to make the circuit of it. "Hwooh!" he exclaimed, "there can be no great harm in trying the ice, as it appears to be sound. Nesho* is overcautious on this point." But he had not got halfway across when the ice gave way and he fell in, and was immediately seized by the serpents, who knew it was Manabozho's grandson and were thirsting for revenge upon him. Manabozho sat pensively in his lodge.

Night came on, but no son returned. The second and third night passed, but he did not appear. He became very desolate and sorrowful. "Ah!" said he, "he must have disobeyed me, and has lost his life in that lake I told him of. Well!" said he at last, "I must mourn for him." So he took coal and blackened his face. But he was much perplexed as to the right mode. "I wonder," said he, "how I must do it? I will cry 'Oh! my grandson! Oh! my grandson!" He burst out a-laughing. "No! no! that won't do. I will try so—'Oh! my heart! Oh! my heart! ha! ha! ha!' That won't do either. I will cry 'Oh my grandson *obiquadj!*'"† This satisfied him, and he remained in his lodge and fasted, till his days of mourning were over. "Now," said he, "I will go in search of him." He set out and travelled some time. At last he came to a great

---

*Abbreviated from *Neshomiss,* my grandfather.
†That part of the intestines of a fish, which, by its expansion from air in the first stage of decomposition, causes the body to rise and float. The expression here means float.

lake. He then raised the same cries of lamentation for his grandson which had pleased him. He sat down near a small brook that emptied itself into the lake, and repeated his cries. Soon a bird called *Ke-ske-mun-i-see** came near to him. The bird inquired, "What are you doing here?" "Nothing," he replied; "but can you tell me whether any one lives in this lake, and what brings you here yourself?" "Yes!" responded the bird; "the Prince of Serpents lives here, and I am watching to see whether the obiquadj of Manabozho's grandson will not drift ashore, for he was killed by the serpents last spring. But are you not Manabozho himself?" "No," he answered, with his usual deceit; "how do you think *he* could get to this place? But tell me, do the serpents ever appear? when? and where? Tell me all about their habits." "Do you see that beautiful white sandy beach?" said the bird. "Yes!" he answered. "It is there," continued the Kingfisher, "that they bask in the sun. Before they come out, the lake will appear perfectly calm; not even a ripple will appear. After midday (na-wi-qua) you will see them."

"Thank you," he replied; "I am Manabozho himself. I have come in search of the body of my son, and to seek my revenge. Come near me that I may put a medal round your neck as a reward for your information." The bird unsuspectingly came near, and received a white medal, which can be seen to this day.†

While bestowing the medal, he attempted slyly to wring the bird's head off, but it escaped him, with only a disturbance of the crown feathers of its head, which are rumpled backward. He had found out all he wanted to know, and then desired to conceal the knowledge of his purposes by killing his informant.

He went to the sandy beach indicated, and transformed himself into an oak stump. He had not been there long before he saw the lake perfectly calm. Soon hundreds of monstrous serpents came crawling on the beach. One of the number was beautifully white. He was the prince. The others were red and yellow. The prince spoke to those about him as follows: "I never saw that

---

*The Alcedo or Kingfisher.
†This bird has a white spot on the breast, and a tufted head.

black stump standing there before. It may be Manabozho. There is no knowing but he may be somewhere about here. He has the power of an evil genius, and we should be on our guard against his wiles." One of the large serpents immediately went and twisted himself around it to the top, and pressed it very hard. The greatest pressure happened to be on his throat; he was just ready to cry out when the serpent let go. Eight of them went in succession and did the like, but always let go at the moment he was ready to cry out. "It cannot be him," they said. "He is too great a weak-heart* for that." They then coiled themselves in a circle about their prince. It was a long time before they fell asleep. When they did so, Manabozho took his bow and arrows, and cautiously stepping over the serpents till he came to the prince, drew up his arrow with the full strength of his arm, and shot him in the left side. He then gave a saw-saw-quan,† and ran off at full speed. The sound uttered by the snakes on seeing their prince mortally wounded was horrible. They cried, "Manabozho has killed our prince; go in chase of him." Meantime he ran over hill and valley, to gain the interior of the country, with all his strength and speed, treading a mile at a step. But his pursuers were also spirits, and he could hear that something was approaching him fast. He made for the highest mountain, and climbed the highest tree on its summit, when, dreadful to behold, the whole lower country was seen to be overflowed, and the water was gaining rapidly on the high lands. He saw it reach to the foot of the mountain, and at length it came up to the foot of the tree, but there was no abatement. The flood rose steadily and perceptibly. He soon felt the lower part of his body to be immersed in it. He addressed the tree: "Grandfather, stretch yourself." The tree did so. But the waters still rose. He repeated his request, and was again obeyed. He asked a third time, and was again obeyed; but the tree replied, "It is the last time; I cannot get any higher." The waters continued to rise till they reached up to his chin, at which point they stood, and soon began to abate. Hope revived in his heart. He then cast

---

*Shau-go-dai-a, i. e., a coward.
†The war-cry.

his eyes around the illimitable expanse, and spied a loon. "Dive down, my brother," he said to him, "and fetch up some earth, so that I can make a new earth." The bird obeyed, but rose up to the surface a lifeless form. He then saw a muskrat. "Dive!" said he, "and if you succeed, you may hereafter live either on land or water, as you please; or I will give you a chain of beautiful little lakes, surrounded with rushes, to inhabit." He dove down, but he floated up senseless. He took the body and breathed in his nostrils, which restored him to life. "Try again," said he. The muskrat did so. He came up senseless the second time, but clutched a little earth in one of his paws, from which, together with the carcass of the dead loon, he created a new earth as large as the former had been, with all living animals, fowls, and plants.

As he was walking to survey the new earth, he heard some one singing. He went to the place, and found a female spirit, in the disguise of an old woman, singing these words, and crying at every pause:

LITERAL TRANSLATION

Ma nau bo sho,	*Manabosho.*
O do´ zheem un,	*His nephew.*
Ogeem´ au wun,	*The king (or chief).*
Onis´ sa waun,	*He killed him.*
Hee-Ub bub ub bub,	*(crying).*

"Noko," said he, "what is the matter?" "Matter!" said she, "where have you been, not to have heard how Manabozho shot my son, the prince of serpents, in revenge for the loss of his nephew, and how the earth was overflowed, and created anew? So I brought my son here, that he might kill and destroy the inhabitants, as he did on the former earth. But," she continued, casting a scrutinizing glance, "N'yau! indego Manabozho! hub! ub! ub! ub! Oh, I am afraid you are Manabozho!" He burst out into a laugh to quiet her fears. "Ha! ha! ha! how can that be? Has not the old earth perished, and all that was in it?" "Impossible! impossible!" "But, Noko," he continued, "what do you intend doing with all that cedar cord on your back?" "Why," said she, "I am fixing a snare for Manabozho, if he should be on this earth; and, in the mean time, I am looking for herbs to heal my son. I am the only person that can do him any good. He always gets better when I sing,

> "'Manabozho a ne we guawk,
> Koan dan mau wah, ne we guawk,
> Koan dan mau wah, ne we guawk.'"

> *Manabozho's dart,*
> *I try to get his dart,*
> *I try to get his dart.*

Having found out, by conversation with her, all he wished, he put her to death. He then took off her skin, and assuming this disguise, took the cedar cord on his back, and limped away singing her songs. He completely aped the gait and voice of the old woman. He was met by one who told him to make haste; that the prince was worse. At the lodge, limping and muttering, he took notice that they had his grandson's hide to hang over the door. "Oh, dogs!" said he; "the evil dogs!" He sat down near the door and commenced sobbing like an aged woman. One observed, "Why don't you attend the sick, and not set there making such a noise?" He took up the poker and laid it on them, mimicking the voice of the old woman. "Dogs that you are! why do you laugh at me? You know very well that I am so sorry that I am nearly out of my head." With that he approached the prince, singing the songs of the old woman, without exciting any suspicion. He saw that his arrow had gone in about one half its length. He pretended to make preparations for extracting it, but only made ready to finish his victim; and giving the dart a sudden thrust, he put a period to the prince's life. He performed this act with the power of a giant, bursting the old woman's skin, and at the same moment rushing through the door. The serpents followed him, hissing and crying out, "Perfidy! murder! vengeance! it is Manabozho." He immediately transformed himself into a wolf, and ran over the plain with all his speed, aided by his father the West wind. When he got to the mountains he saw a badger. "Brother," said he, "make a hole quick, for the serpents are after me." The badger obeyed. They both went in, and the badger threw all the earth backward, so that it filled up the way behind.

The serpents came to the badger's wauzh,* and decided to watch. "We will starve him out," said they; so they continued watching. Manabozho told the badger to make an opening on the other side of the mountain, from which he could go out and hunt, and bring meat in. Thus they lived some time. One day the badger came in his way and displeased him. He immediately put him to death, and threw out his carcass, saying, "I don't like you to be getting in my way so often."

After living in this confinement for some time alone, he decided to go out. He immediately did so; and after making the circuit of the mountain, came to the corpse of the prince, who had been deserted by the serpents to pursue his destroyer. He went to work and skinned him. He then drew on his skin, in which there were great virtues, took up his war-club, and set out for the place where he first went in the ground. He found the serpents still watching. When they saw the form of their dead prince advancing towards them, fear and dread took hold of them. Some fled. Those who remained Manabozho killed. Those who fled went towards the South.

Having accomplished the victory over the reptiles, Manabozho returned to his former place of dwelling, and married the arrow-maker's daughter.

Concluding Note.—The story of this northern Hercules is dropped at this point of his triumph over the strongest of the reptile race. But his feats and adventures, by land and sea, do not terminate here. There is scarcely a prominent lake, mountain, precipice, or stream in the northern part of America which is not hallowed in Indian story by his fabled deeds. Further accounts will be found in several of the subsequent tales, which are narrated by the Indians in an independent form, and may be now appropriately left as they are found, as episodes, detached from the original story. To collect all these and arrange them in order would be an arduous labour; and, after all, such an arrangement would lack consistency and keeping, unless much of the thread necessary to present

---

*A burrow.

them in English dress were supplied by invention, alteration, and transposition. The portions above narrated present a beginning and an end, which could hardly be said of the loose and disjointed fragmentary tales referred to. How long Manabozho lived on earth is not related. We hear nothing more of his grandmother; every mouth is filled with his queer adventures, tricks, and sufferings. He was everywhere present where danger presented itself, power was required, or mischief was going forward. Nothing was too low or trivial for him to engage in, nor too high or difficult for him to attempt. He affected to be influenced by the spirit of a god, and was really actuated by the malignity of a devil. The period of his labours and adventures having expired, he withdrew to dwell with his brother in the North, where he is understood to direct those storms which proceed from points west of the pole. He is regarded as the spirit of the northwest tempests, but receives no worship from the present race of Indians. It is believed by them that he is again to appear, and to exercise an important power in the final disposition of the human race.

In this singular tissue of incongruities will be perceived several ideas probably derived from Asiatic sources. It will be found, in the tale of the visiters to the Sun and Moon, that Manabozho was met on the way, and he is represented as expressing a deep repentance for the sins he had committed while on earth. He is, however, found exercising the vocation of a necromancer; has a pointed lodge, from which utters oracles; and finally transforms on the spot two of the party who had consulted him and asked the gift of immortality, the one into a cedar-tree, and the other into a block of granite.

Manabozho is regarded by the Indians as a god and a benefactor, and is admired and extolled as the personification of strength and wisdom. Yet he constantly presents the paradox of being a mere mortal; is driven to low and common expedients; and never utters a sentiment wiser or better than the people among whom he appears. The conception of a divinity, pure, changeless, and just, as well as benevolent in the distribution of its providences, has not been reached by any traits exhibited in the character of this personage. And if such notions had ever been conceived by the ancestors of the present race of Indians in the East, they have been obscured, if not obliterated, in the course of their long, dark, and hopeless pilgrimage in the forests of America. That the tribes themselves are of Oriental origin is probable from the grammatical structure of their languages and their mode of expressing thought. But it is apparent that their separation took place at a very ancient period. Whether this event is of a date prior to the organization

of the Hebrew theocracy, or whether the American tribes have origi-
nated, as some writers suppose, in a separation from the latter sub-stock,
there is not, at this time, sufficient data, stamped with the character
of sound investigation, to determine; but is rendered manifest, by the
present investigation into Indian opinions, that, although they probably
had, at the epoch of their expatriation, a knowledge of the Creator and
a tradition of the creation, and also of the subsequent destruction of
men by the deluge, this knowledge was already corrupted and mixed
with notions of materialism and carnality, somewhat after the comparatively recent and grosser manner exhibited in the existing legend
of Manabozho.

BOKWEWA

or

THE HUMPBACK

From the Odjibwa

BOKWEWA AND his brother lived in a secluded part of the country. They were considered as Manitoes, who had assumed mortal shapes. Bokwewa was the more gifted in supernatural endowments, although he was deformed in person. His brother partook more of the nature of the present race of beings. They lived retired from the world, and undisturbed by its cares, and passed their time in contentment and happiness.

Bokwewa,* owing to his deformity, was very domestic in his habits, and gave his attention to household affairs. He instructed his brother in the manner of pursuing game, and made him acquainted with all the accomplishments of a sagacious and expert hunter. His brother possessed a fine form, and an active and robust constitution; and felt a disposition to show himself off among men. He was restiff in his seclusion, and showed a fondness for visiting remote places.

One day he told his brother that he was going to leave him; that he wished to visit the habitations of men, and procure a wife. Bokwewa objected to his going; but his brother overruled all that he said, and he finally departed on his travels. He travelled a long time. At length he fell in with the footsteps of men. They were moving by encampments, for he saw several places where they

---

*i.e., the sudden stopping of a voice.

75

had encamped. It was in the winter. He came to a place where one of their number had died. They had placed the corpse on a scaffold. He went to it and took it down. He saw that it was the corpse of a beautiful young woman. "She shall be my wife!" he exclaimed.

He took her up, and placing her on his back, returned to his brother. "Brother," he said, "cannot you restore her to life? Oh, do me that favour!" Bokwewa said he would try. He performed numerous ceremonies, and at last succeeded in restoring her to life. They lived very happily for some time. Bokwewa was extremely kind to his brother, and did everything to render his life happy. Being deformed and crippled, he always remained at home, while his brother went out to hunt. And it was by following his directions, which were those of a skilful hunter, that he always succeeded in returning with a good store of meat.

One day he had gone out as usual, and Bokwewa was sitting in his lodge, on the opposite side of his brother's wife, when a tall, fine young man entered, and immediately took the woman by the hand and drew her to the door. She resisted and called on Bokwewa, who jumped up to her assistance. But their joint resistance was unavailing; the man succeeded in carrying her away. In the scuffle, Bokwewa had his hump back much bruised on the stones near the door. He crawled into the lodge and wept very sorely, for he knew that it was a powerful Manito who had taken the woman.

When his brother returned he related all to him exactly as it had happened. He would not taste food for several days. Sometimes he would fall to weeping for a long time, and appeared almost beside himself. At last he said he would go in search of her. Bokwewa tried to dissuade him from it, but he insisted.

"Well!" said he, "since you are bent on going, listen to my advice. You will have to go south. It is a long distance to the residence of your captive wife, and there are so many charms and temptations in the way, I am afraid you will be led astray by them, and forget your errand. For the people whom you will see in that country do nothing but amuse themselves. They are very idle, gay, and effeminate, and I am fearful they will lead you astray. Your journey is beset with difficulties. I will mention one or two things, which you must be on your guard against. In the course of your journey, you will come to a large grapevine lying across your way. You must not even taste its fruit, for it is poisonous. Step over it. It is a snake. You will next come to something that looks like bear's fat, transparent and tremulous. Don't taste it, or you will be overcome by the pleasures of those people. It is frog's eggs. These are snares laid by the way for you."

He said he would follow the advice, and bid farewell to his brother. After travelling a long time, he came to the enchanted grapevine. It looked so tempting, he forgot his brother's advice and tasted the fruit. He went on till he came to the frog's eggs. The substance so much resembled bear's fat that he tasted it. He still went on. At length he came to a very extensive plain. As he emerged from the forest the sun was setting, and cast its scarlet and golden shades over all the plain. The air was perfectly calm, and the whole prospect had the air of an enchanted land. The most inviting fruits and flowers spread out before the eye. At a distance he beheld a large village, filled with people without number, and as he drew near he saw women beating corn in silver mortars. When they saw him approaching, they cried out, "Bokwewa's brother has come to see us." Throngs of men and women, gayly dressed, came out to meet him. He was soon overcome by their flatteries and pleasures, and he was not long afterward seen beating corn with their women (the strongest proof of effeminacy), although his wife, for whom he had mourned so much, was in that Indian metropolis.

Meantime Bokwewa waited patiently for the return of his brother. At length, after the lapse of several years, he set out in search of him, and arrived in safety among the luxuriant people of the South. He met with the same allurements on the road, and the same flattering reception that his brother did. But he was above all temptations. The pleasures he saw had no other effect upon him than to make him regret the weakness of mind of those who were led away by them. He shed tears of pity to see that his brother had laid aside the arms of a hunter, and was seen beating corn with the women.

He ascertained where his brother's wife remained. After deliberating some time, he went to the river where she usually came to draw water. He there changed himself into one of those hair-snakes which are sometimes seen in running water. When she came down, he spoke to her, saying, "Take me up; I am Bokwewa." She then scooped him out and went home. In a short time the Manito who had taken her away asked her for water to drink. The lodge in which they lived was partitioned. He occupied a secret place, and was never seen by any one but the woman. She handed him the water containing the hair-snake, which he drank, with the snake, and soon after was a dead Manito.

Bokwewa then resumed his former shape. He went to his brother, and used every means to reclaim him. But he would not listen. He was so much taken up with the pleasures and dissipations into which he had fallen, that he refused to give them up, although Bokwewa, with tears, tried to convince him of his foolishness, and to show him that those pleasures could not endure for a long time. Finding that he was past reclaiming, Bokwewa left him, and disappeared for ever.

IENA

or

THE MAGIC BUNDLE

A Maskego Allegory

THERE WAS once a poor man called Iena,* who was in the habit of wandering about from place to place, forlorn, without relations and almost helpless. One day, as he went on a hunting excursion, he hung up his bundle on the branch of a tree, to relieve himself from the burden of carrying it, and then went in quest of game. On returning to the spot in the evening, he was surprised to find a small but neat lodge built in the place where he had left his bundle; and on looking in, he beheld a beautiful female sitting in the lodge, with his blanket lying beside her. During the day he had been fortunate in killing a deer, which he laid down at the lodge door. But, to his surprise, the woman, in her attempt to bring it in, broke both her legs. He looked at her in astonishment, and thought to himself, "I supposed I was blessed, but I find my mistake. Gweengweeshee,"† said he, "I will leave my game with you, that you may feast on it."

He then took up his bundle and departed. After walking some time he came to another tree, on which he suspended his bundle as before, and went in search of game. Success again rewarded his efforts, and he returned bringing a deer, but found, as before, that a lodge had sprung up in the place where he had suspended his

---

*From *Ienawdizzi,* a wanderer.
†The night-hawk.

bundle. He looked in, and saw, as before, a beautiful female sitting alone, with his bundle by her side. She arose, and came out to bring in the deer, which he had deposited at the door, and he immediately went into the lodge and sat by the fire, as he felt fatigued with the day's labours. Wondering, at last, at the delay of the woman, he arose, and peeping through the door of the lodge, beheld her eating all the fat of the deer. He exclaimed, "I thought I was blessed, but I find I am mistaken." Then addressing the woman, "Poor Wabizhas,"* said he, "feast on the game that I have brought." He again took up his bundle and departed, and, as usual, hung it up on the branch of a tree, and wandered off in quest of game. In the evening he returned with his customary good luck, bringing in a fine deer, and again found a lodge occupying the place of his bundle. He gazed through an aperture in the side of the lodge, and saw a beautiful woman sitting alone, with a bundle by her side. As soon as he entered the lodge, she arose with alacrity, brought in the carcass, cut it up, and hung up the meat to dry. After this, she prepared a portion of it for the supper of the weary hunter. The man thought to himself, "Now I am certainly blessed." He continued his practice of hunting every day, and the woman, on his return, always readily took care of the meat, and prepared his meals for him. One thing, however, astonished him; he had never, as yet, seen her eat anything, and kindly said to her, "Why do you not eat?" She replied, "I have food of my own, which I eat."

On the fourth day he brought home with him a branch of uzadi† as a cane, which he placed, with his game, at the door of the lodge. His wife, as usual, went out to prepare and bring in the meat. While thus engaged, he heard her laughing to herself, and saying, "This is very acceptable." The man, in peeping out to see the cause of her joy, saw her, with astonishment, eating the bark of the poplar cane in the same manner that beavers gnaw. He then exclaimed, "Ho, ho! Ho, ho! this is Amik";‡ and ever afterward he was careful at evening to bring in a bough of the poplar

---

*A marten.
†The common poplar, or *P. tremuloides.*
‡The beaver.

or the red willow, when she would exclaim, "Oh, this is very acceptable; this is a change, for one gets tired eating white fish always (meaning the poplar); but the carp (meaning the red willow) is a pleasant change."

On the whole, Iena was much pleased with his wife for her neatness and attention to the things in the lodge, and he lived a contented and happy man. Being industrious, she made him beautiful bags from the bark of trees, and dressed the skins of the animals he killed in the most skilful manner. When spring opened, they found themselves blessed with two children, one of them resembling the father and the other the mother. One day the father made a bow and arrows for the child that resembled him, who was a son, saying, "My son, you will use these arrows to shoot at the little beavers when they begin to swim about the rivers." The mother, as soon as she heard this, was highly displeased; and taking her children, unknown to her husband, left the lodge in the night. A small river ran near the lodge, which the woman approached with her children. She built a dam across the stream, erected a lodge of earth, and lived after the manner of the beavers.

When the hunter awoke, he found himself alone in his lodge, and his wife and children absent. He immediately made diligent search after them, and at last discovered their retreat on the river. He approached the place of their habitation, and throwing himself prostrate on the top of the lodge, exclaimed, "Shingisshenaun tshee neeboyaun."* The woman allowed the children to go close to their father, but not to touch him; for, as soon as they came very near, she would draw them away again, and in this manner she continued to torment him a long time. The husband laid in this situation until he was almost starved, when a young female approached him, and thus accosted him: "Look here; why are you keeping yourself in misery, and thus starving yourself? Eat this," reaching him a little mokuk containing fresh raspberries which she had just gathered. As soon as the beaveress, his former wife, beheld this, she began to abuse the young woman, and said

---

*"Here I will lie until I die."

to her, "Why do you wish to show any kindness to that *animal* that has but two legs? You will soon repent it." She also made sport of the young woman, saying, "Look at her; she has a long nose, and she is just like a bear." The young woman, who was all the time a bear in disguise, hearing herself thus reproached, broke down the dam of the beaver, let the water run out, and nearly killed the beaver herself. Then turning to the man, she thus addressed him: "Follow me; I will be kind to you. Follow me closely. You must be courageous, for there are three persons who are desirous of marrying me, and will oppose you. Be careful of yourself. Follow me nimbly, and, just as we approach the lodge, put your feet in the prints of mine, for I have eight sisters who will do their utmost to divert your attention and make you lose the way. Look neither to the right nor to the left, but enter the lodge just as I do, and take your seat where I do." As they proceeded they came in sight of a large lodge, when he did as he had been directed, stepping in her tracks. As they entered the lodge, the eight sisters clamorously addressed him. "Oh, Ogidahkumigo* has lost his way," and each one invited him to take his seat with her, desiring to draw him from their sister. The old people also addressed him as he entered, and said, "Oh, make room for our son-in-law." The man, however, took his seat by the side of his protectress, and was not farther importuned.

As they sat in the lodge, a great rushing of waters, as of a swollen river, came through the centre of it, which also brought in its course a large stone, and left it before the man. When the water subsided, a large white bear came in, and taking up the stone, bit it, and scratched it with his paws, saying, "This is the manner in which I would handle Ogidahkumigo if I was jealous." A yellow bear also entered the lodge and did the same. A black bear followed and did the same. At length the man took up his bow and arrows, and prepared to shoot at the stone, saying, "This is the way I would treat ODANAMEKUMIGO† if I was jealous." He then drew up his bow and drove his arrow into the

---

*This term means a man that lives on the surface of the earth, as contradistinguished from beings living under ground.
†He who lives in the city under ground.

stone. Seeing this, the bears turned around, and with their eyes fixed on him, stepped backward and left the lodge, which highly delighted the woman. She exulted to think that her husband had conquered them.

Finally, one of the old folks made a cry, and said, "Come, come! there must be a gathering of provisions for the winter." So they all took their *cossoes,* or bark dishes, and departed to gather acorns for the winter. As they departed, the old man said to his daughter, "Tell Ogidahkumigo to go to the place where your sisters have gone, and let him select one of them, so that, through her aid, he may have some food for himself during the winter; but be sure to caution him to be very careful, when he is taking the skin from the animal, that he does not cut the flesh." No sooner had the man heard this message than he selected one of his sisters-in-law; and when he was taking the skin from her, for she was all the while an enchanted female bear, although careful, he cut her a little upon one of her arms, when she jumped up, assumed her natural form, and ran home. The man also went home, and found her with her arm bound up, and quite unwell.

A second cry was then made by the master of the lodge: "Come, come! seek for winter quarters"; and they all got ready to separate for the season. By this time the man had two children, one resembling himself and the other his wife. When the cry was made, the little boy who resembled his father was in such a hurry in putting on his moccasins, that he misplaced them, putting the moccasin of the right foot upon the left. And this is the reason why the foot of the bear is turned in.

They proceeded to seek their winter quarters, the wife going before to point the way. She always selected the *thickest* part of the forest, where the child resembling the father found it difficult to get along; and he never failed to cry out and complain. Iena then went in the advance, and sought the open plain, whereupon the child resembling the mother would cry out and complain, because she disliked an *open* path. As they were encamping, the woman said to her husband, "Go and break branches for the lodge for the night." He did so; but when she looked at the *manner* in which her husband broke the branches, she was very much offended, for he broke them *upward* instead of *downward*. "It is not only very awkward," said she, "but we will be found out; for the Ogidahkumigoes will see where we have passed by the branches we have broken." To avoid this, they agreed to change their route, and were finally well established in their winter quarters. The wife had sufficient food for her child, and would now and then give the dry berries she had gathered in the summer to her husband.

One day, as spring drew on, she said to her husband, "I must boil you some meat," meaning her own paws, which bears suck in the month of April. She had all along told him, during the winter, that she meant to resume her real shape of a female bear, and to give herself up to the Ogidahkumigoes, to be killed by them, and that the time of their coming was near at hand. It came to pass, soon afterward, that a hunter discovered her retreat. She told her husband to move aside, "for," she added, "I am now giving myself up." The hunter fired and killed her.

Iena then came out from his hiding-place, and went home with the hunter. As they went, he instructed him what he must hereafter do when he killed bears. "You must," said he, "never cut the flesh in taking off the skin, nor hang up the feet with the flesh when drying it. But you must take the head and feet, and decorate them handsomely, and place tobacco on the head, for these animals are very fond of this article, and on the *fourth day* they come to life again."

SHEEM*

or

THE FORSAKEN BOY

From the Odjibwa

A SOLITARY LODGE stood on the banks of a remote lake. It was near the hour of sunset. Silence reigned within and without. Not a sound was heard but the low breathing of the dying inmate and head of this poor family. His wife and three children surrounded his bed. Two of the latter were almost grown up; the other was a mere child. All their simple skill in medicine had been exhausted to no effect. They moved about the lodge in whispers, and were waiting the departure of the spirit. As one of the last acts of kindness, the skin door of the lodge had been thrown back to admit the fresh air. The poor man felt a momentary return of strength, and, raising himself a little, addressed his family.

"I leave you in a world of care, in which it has required all my strength and skill to supply you food, and protect you from the storms and cold of a severe climate. For you, my partner in life, I have less sorrow in parting, because I am persuaded you will not remain long behind me, and will therefore find the period of your sufferings shortened. But you, my children! my poor and forsaken children, who have just commenced the career of life, who will protect you from its evils? Listen to my words! Unkindness,

---

*Abbreviated from *Nee Sheema,* my younger brother or younger sister.

ingratitude, and every wickedness is in the scene before you. It is for this cause that, years ago, I withdrew from my kindred and my tribe, to spend my days in this lonely spot. I have contented myself with the company of your mother and yourselves during seasons of very frequent scarcity and want, while your kindred, feasting in a scene where food is plenty, have caused the forests to echo with the shouts of successful war. I gave up these things for the enjoyment of peace. I wished to shield you from the bad examples you would inevitably have followed. I have seen you, thus far, grow up in innocence. If we have sometimes suffered bodily want, we have escaped pain of mind.* We have been kept from scenes of rioting and bloodshed.

"My career is now at its close. I will shut my eyes in peace, if you, my children, will promise me to cherish each other. Let not your mother suffer during the few days that are left to her; and I charge you, on no account, to forsake your youngest brother. Of him I give you both my dying charge to take a tender care." He sank exhausted on his pallet. The family waited a moment, as if expecting to hear something further; but, when they came to his side, the spirit had taken its flight.

The mother and daughter gave vent to their feelings in lamentations. The elder son witnessed the scene in silence. He soon exerted himself to supply, with the bow and net, his father's place. Time, however, wore away heavily. Five moons had filled and waned, and the sixth was near its full, when the mother also died. In her last moments she pressed the fulfilment of their promise to their father, which the children readily renewed, because they were yet free from selfish motives.

The winter passed; and the spring, with its enlivening effects in a northern hemisphere, cheered the drooping spirits of the bereft little family. The girl, being the eldest, dictated to her brothers, and seemed to feel a tender and sisterly affection for the youngest, who was rather sickly and delicate. The other boy soon showed symptoms of restlessness and ambition, and addressed the sister

---

* *Wesugaindum,* meaning pain or bitterness of mind, is a single expression in the original. It is a trinary compound.

as follows: "My sister, are we always to live as if there were no other human beings in the world? Must I deprive myself of the pleasure of associating with my own kind? I have determined this question for myself. I shall seek the villages of men, and you cannot prevent me."

The sister replied: "I do not say no, my brother, to what you desire. We are not prohibited the society of our fellow-mortals; but we are told to cherish each other, and to do nothing independent of each other. Neither pleasure nor pain ought, therefore, to separate us, especially from our younger brother, who, being but a child, and weakly withal, is entitled to a double share of our affection. If we follow our separate gratifications, it will surely make us neglect him, whom we are bound by vows, both to our father and mother, to support." The young man received this address in silence. He appeared daily to grow more restiff and moody, and one day, taking his bow and arrows, left the lodge and never returned.

Affection nerved the sister's arm. She was not so ignorant of the forest arts as to let her brother want. For a long time she administered to his necessities, and supplied a mother's cares. At length, however, she began to be weary of solitude and of her charge. No one came to be a witness of her assiduity, or to let fall a single word in her native language. Years, which added to her strength and capability of directing the affairs of the household, brought with them the irrepressible desire of society, and made solitude irksome. At this point, selfishness gained the ascendency of her heart; for, in meditating a change in her mode of life, she lost sight of her younger brother, and left him to be provided for by contingencies.

One day, after collecting all the provisions she had been able to save for emergencies, after bringing a quantity of wood to the door, she said to her little brother: "My brother, you must not stray from the lodge. I am going to seek our elder brother. I shall be back soon." Then, taking her bundle, she set off in search of habitations. She soon found them, and was so much taken up with the pleasures and amusements of social life, that the thought of her brother was almost entirely obliterated. She accepted proposals of marriage; and, after that, thought still less of her hapless and abandoned relative.

Meantime her elder brother had also married, and lived on the shores of the same lake whose ample circuit contained the abandoned lodge of his father and his forsaken brother. The latter was soon brought to the pinching turn of his fate. As soon as he had eaten all the food left by his sister, he was obliged to pick berries and dig up roots. These were finally covered by snow. Winter came on with all its rigours. He was obliged to quit the lodge in search of other food. Sometimes he passed the night in the clefts of old trees or caverns, and ate the refuse meals of the wolves. The latter, at last, became his only resource; and he became so fearless of these animals that he would sit close by them while they devoured their prey. The wolves, on the other hand, became so familiar with his face and form that they were undisturbed by his approach; and, appearing to sympathize with him in his outcast condition, would always leave something for his repast. In this way he lived till spring. As soon as the lake was free from ice, he followed his new-found friends to the shore. It happened, the same day, that his elder brother was fishing in his canoe, a considerable distance out in the lake, when he thought he heard the cries of a child on the shore, and wondered how any could exist on so bleak and barren a part of the coast. He listened again attentively, and distinctly heard the cry repeated. He made for shore as quickly as possible, and, as he approached land, discovered and recognised his little brother, and heard him singing, in a plaintive voice,

> Neesia—neesia,
> Shyegwuh goosuh!
> Ni my een gwun iewh!
> Ni my een gwun iewh!
> > Heo hwooh.

> Ke ge wai bin im
> She gwuh dush
> Ni my een gwun iewh!
> Ni my een gwun iewh!
> > Heo hwooh.

Tyau, tyau! sunnagud,
Nin dininee wun aubun
She gwuh dush
Ni my een gwun iewh!
   Heo hwooh.

Listen, brother—elder brother!
 Now my fate is near its close;
Soon my state shall be another,
 Soon shall cease my day of woes.

Left by friends I loved the dearest,
 All who knew and loved me most;
Woes the darkest and severest,
 Bide me on this barren coast.

Pity! ah, that manly feeling,
 Fled from hearts where once it grew,
Now in wolfish forms revealing,
 Glows more warmly than in you.

Stony hearts! that saw me languish,
 Deaf to all a father said,
Deaf to all a mother's anguish,
 All a brother's feelings fled.

Ah, ye wolves, in all your ranging,
 I have found you kind and true;
More than man—and now I'm changing,
 And will soon be one of you.

At the termination of his song, which was drawn out with a peculiar cadence, he howled like a wolf. The elder brother was still more astonished, when, getting nearer shore, he perceived his poor brother partly transformed into that animal. He immediately leaped on shore, and strove to catch him in his arms, soothingly saying, "My brother, my brother, come to me." But the boy eluded his grasp, crying as he fled, "Neesia, neesia," &c., and howling in the intervals.

The elder brother, conscience-stricken, and feeling his brotherly affection strongly return, with redoubled force exclaimed, in great anguish, "My brother! my brother! my brother!"

But, the nearer he approached, the more rapidly the transformation went on; the boy alternately singing and howling, and calling out the name, first of his brother, and then of his sister, till the change was completely accomplished, when he exclaimed, "I am a wolf!" and bounded out of sight.

The moral of this tale may be said to rebuke a species of cruelty, which is not peculiar to the tribe from whose traditions it has been obtained. The truth it indicates is impressed upon the minds of the young, to warn them against the perpetration of similar barbarities— barbarities which claim pity even from wild animals.

But while we know of no recorded instance of abandonment of *children of either sex* by any North American tribes, it is attested by travellers that *the very aged and helplessly superannuated,* among some of the more northerly tribes, have been thus left. This remark was made at an early day, and has been repeated in modern times, as practised among bands on the borders of the Arctic Ocean. Certainly no practice of this kind has been found to prevail among the Odjibwas, Ottowas, and other more well-known existing branches of the Algic stock.

PAUP-PUK-KEEWISS

From the Algic

A MAN of large stature, and great activity of mind and body, found himself standing alone on a prairie. He thought to himself, "How came I here? Are there no beings on this earth but myself? I must travel and see. I must walk till I find the abodes of men." So soon as his mind was made up, he set out, he knew not where, in search of habitations. No obstacles could divert him from his purpose. Neither prairies, rivers, woods, nor storms had the effect to daunt his courage or turn him back. After travelling a long time he came to a wood, in which he saw decayed stumps of trees, as if they had been cut in ancient times, but no other traces of men. Pursuing his journey, he found more recent marks of the same kind; and after this, he came to fresh traces of human beings; first their footsteps, and then the wood they had cut, lying in heaps. Continuing on, he emerged towards dusk from the forest, and beheld at a distance a large village of high lodges, standing on rising ground. He said to himself, "I will arrive there on a run." Off he started with all his speed; on coming to the first large lodge, he jumped over it. Those within saw something pass over the opening, and then heard a thump on the ground.

"What is that?" they all said.

One came out to see, and invited him in. He found himself in company with an old chief and several men, who were seated in the lodge. Meat was set before him, after which the chief asked him where he was going and what his name was. He answered that he was in search of adventures, and his name was Paup-Puk-Keewiss. A stare followed.

"Paup-Puk-Keewiss!"* said one to another, and a general titter went round.

He was not easy in his new position; the village was too small to give him full scope for his powers, and after a short stay he made up his mind to go farther, taking with him a young man who had formed a strong attachment for him, and might serve him as his mesh-in-au-wa.† They set out together, and when his companion was fatigued with walking, he would show him a few tricks, such as leaping over trees, and turning round on one leg till he made the dust fly, by which he was mightily pleased, although it sometimes happened that the character of these tricks frightened him.

One day they came to a very large village, where they were well received. After staying in it some time, they were informed of a number of Manitoes who lived at a distance, and who made it a practice to kill all who came to their lodge. Attempts had been made to extirpate them, but the war-parties who went out for this purpose were always unsuccessful. Paup-Puk-Keewiss determined to visit them, although he was advised not to do so. The chief warned him of the danger of the visit; but, finding him resolved, "Well," said he, "if you will go, being my guest, I will send twenty warriors to serve you."

He thanked him for the offer. Twenty young men were ready at the instant, and they went forward, and in due time descried the lodge of the Manitoes. He placed his friend and the warriors near enough to see all that passed, while he went alone to the lodge. As he entered he saw five horrid-looking Manitoes in the act of eating. It was the father and his four sons. They looked hideous; their eyes were swimming low in their heads, as if half starved. They offered him something to eat, which he refused.

"What have you come for?" said the old one.

"Nothing," Paup-Puk-Keewiss answered.

---

*This word appears to be derived from the same root as *Paup-puk-ke-nay,* a grasshopper, the inflection *iss* making it personal. The Indian idea is that of harum scarum. He is regarded as a foil to Manabozho, with whom he is frequently brought in contact in aboriginal story craft.

†This is an official who bears the pipe for the ruling chief, and is an inferior dignitary in councils.

They all stared at him.

"Do you not wish to wrestle?" they all asked.

"Yes," he replied.

A hideous smile came over their faces.

"*You* go," they said to the eldest brother.

They got ready, and were soon clinched in each other's arms for a deadly throw. He knew their object—his death—his *flesh* was all they wanted, but he was prepared for them.

"Haw! haw!"* they cried, and soon the dust and dry leaves flew about as if driven by a strong wind.

The Manito was strong, but Paup-Puk-Keewiss soon found that he could master him; and, giving him a trip, he threw him with a giant's force head foremost on a stone, and he fell like a puffed thing.

The brothers stepped up in quick succession, but he put a number of tricks in force, and soon the whole four lay bleeding on the ground. The old Manito got frightened and ran for his life. Paup-Puk-Keewiss pursued him for sport; sometimes he was before him, sometimes flying over his head. He would now give him a kick, then a push or a trip, till he was almost exhausted. Meantime his friend and the warriors cried out, "Ha! ha! a! ha! ha! a! Paup-Puk-Keewiss is driving him before him." The Manito only turned his head now and then to look back; at last, Paup-Puk-Keewiss gave him a kick on his back, and broke his back bone; down he fell, and the blood gushing out of his mouth prevented him from saying a word. The warriors piled all the bodies together in the lodge, and then took fire and burned them. They all looked with deep interest at the quantity of human bones scattered around.

Paup-Puk-Keewiss then took three arrows, and, after having performed a ceremony to the Great Spirit, he shot one into the air, crying, with a loud voice,

"*You* who are lying down, rise up, or you will be hit!" The bones all moved to one place. He shot the second arrow, repeating the same words, when each bone drew towards its fellow-bone; the third arrow brought forth to life the whole multitude of people who

---

*This is a studied perversion of the interjection *Ho.* In another instance [*vide* Wassamo] it is rendered *Hoke.*

had been killed by the Manitoes. Paup-Puk-Keewiss then led them to the chief of the village who had proved his friend, and gave them up to him. Soon after the chief came with his counsellors.

"Who is more worthy," said he, "to rule than you? *You* alone can defend them."

Paup-Puk-Keewiss thanked him, and told him he was in search of more adventures. The chief insisted. Paup-Puk-Keewiss told him to confer the chieftainship on his friend, who, he said, would remain while he went on his travels. He told them that he would, some time or other, come back and see them.

"Ho! ho! ho!" they all cried, "come back again and see us," insisting on it. He promised them he would, and then set out alone.

After travelling some time he came to a large lake; on looking about, he discovered a very large otter on an island. He thought to himself, "His skin will make me a fine pouch," and immediately drew up, at long shots, and drove an arrow into his side. He waded into the lake, and with some difficulty dragged him ashore. He took out the entrails, and even then the carcass was so heavy that it was as much as he could do to drag it up a hill overlooking the lake. As soon as he got him up into the sunshine, where it was warm, he skinned him, and threw the carcass some distance, thinking the war-eagle would come, and he should have a chance to get his skin and feathers as head ornaments. He soon heard a rushing noise in the air, but could see nothing; by-and-by, a large eagle dropped, as if from the air, on the otter's carcass. He drew his bow, and the arrow passed through under both his wings. The bird made a convulsive flight upward with such force that the heavy carcass (which was nearly as big as a moose) was borne up several feet. Fortunately, both claws were fastened deeply into the meat, the weight of which soon brought the bird down. He skinned him, crowned his head with the trophy, and next day was on his way, on the lookout for something new.

After walking a while he came to a lake, which flooded the trees on its banks; he found it was only a lake made by beavers. He took his station on the elevated dam, where the stream escaped, to see whether any of the beavers would show themselves. He soon saw the head of one peeping out of the water to see who disturbed him.

"My friend," said Paup-Puk-Keewiss, "could you not turn me into a beaver like yourself?" for he thought, if he could become a beaver, he would see and know how these animals lived.

"I do not know," replied the beaver; "I will go and ask the others."

Soon all the beavers showed their heads above the water, and looked to see if he was armed; but he had left his bow and arrows in a hollow tree at a short distance. When they were satisfied, they all came near.

"Can you not, with all your united power"; said he, "turn me into a beaver? I wish to live among you."

"Yes," answered their chief, "lay down"; and he soon found himself changed into one of them.

"You must make me *large*," said he; "*larger* than any of you."

"Yes, yes!" said they. "By-and-by, when we get into the lodge, it shall be done."

In they all dove into the lake; and, in passing large heaps of limbs and logs at the bottom, he asked the use of them; they answered, "It is for our winter's provisions."* When they all got into the lodge, their number was about one hundred. The lodge was large and warm.

"Now we will make you large," said they. "Will *that* do?" exerting their power.

"Yes," he answered, for he found he was ten times the size of the largest.

"You need not go out," said they. "We will bring your food into the lodge, and you will be our chief."

"Very well," Paup-Puk-Keewiss answered. He thought, "I will stay here and grow fat at their expense. But, soon after, one ran into the lodge out of breath, saying, "We are visited by Indians." All huddled together in great fear. The water began to *lower,* for the hunters had broken down the dam, and they soon heard them on the roof of the lodge, breaking it up. Out jumped all the beavers into the water, and so escaped. Paup-Puk-Keewiss tried to follow them; but, alas! they had made him so large that he could not creep out of the hole. He tried to call them back, but

---

*We may mention, for the youth who may read these tales, that beavers live by gnawing the bark of trees.

to no effect; he worried himself so much in trying to escape that he looked like a bladder. He could not turn himself back into a man, although he heard and understood all the hunters said. One of them put his head in at the top of the lodge.

"*Ty-au!*" cried he; "*Tut Ty-au!* Me-shau-mik—king of the beavers is in." They all got at him, and knocked his skull till it was as soft as his brains. He thought, as well as ever he did, although he was a beaver. Seven or eight of them then placed his body on poles and carried him home. As they went, he reflected in this manner: "What will become of me? My ghost or shadow will not die after they get me to their lodges." Invitations were immediately sent out for a grand feast. The women took him out into the snow to skin him; but, as soon as his flesh got cold, his *Jee-bi* went off.

Paup-Puk-Keewiss found himself standing near a prairie, having reassumed his mortal shape. After walking a distance, he saw a herd of elk feeding. He admired the apparent ease and enjoyment of their life, and thought there could be nothing pleasanter than the liberty of running about and feeding on the prairies. He asked them if they could not turn him into their shape.

"Yes," they answered, after a pause. "Get down on your hands and feet." And he soon found himself an elk.

"I want big horns, big feet," said he; "I wish to be very large."

"Yes! yes!" they said.

"There!" exerting their power; "are you big enough?"

"Yes!" he answered, for he saw that he was very large. They spent a good time in grazing and running. Being rather cold one day, he went into a thick wood for shelter, and was followed by most of the herd. They had not been there long before some elks from behind passed the others like a strong wind. All took the alarm, and off they ran, he with the rest.

"Keep out on the plains," they said.

But he found it was too late, as they had already got entangled in the thick woods. Paup-Puk-Keewiss soon smelled the hunters, who were closely following his trail, for they had left all the others and followed him. He jumped furiously, and broke down saplings in his flight, but it only served to retard his progress. He soon felt an arrow in his side; he jumped over trees in his agony, but the arrows clattered thicker and thicker upon his sides, and at last one entered his heart. He fell to the ground, and heard the whoop of triumph sounded by the hunters. On coming up, they looked on the carcass with astonishment, and with their hands up to their mouths exclaimed *Ty-au! Ty-au!* There were about sixty in the party, who had come out on a special hunt, as one of their number had, the day before, observed his *large tracks* on the plains. After skinning him and his flesh getting cold, his *Jee-bi* took its flight from the carcass, and he again found himself in human shape, with a bow and arrows.

But his passion for adventure was not yet cooled; for, on coming to a large lake with a sandy beach, he saw a large flock of brant, and, speaking to them, asked them to turn him into a brant.

"Yes," they replied.

"But I want to be very large," he said.

"Very well," they answered; and he soon found himself a large brant, all the others standing gazing in astonishment at his large size.

"You must fly as leader," they said.

"No," answered Paup-Puk-Keewiss, "I will fly behind."

"Very well," they said. "One thing more we have to say to you. You must be careful, in flying, not to look *down,* for something may happen to you."

"Well! it is so," said he; and soon the flock rose up into the air, for they were bound north. They flew very fast, he behind. One day, while going with a strong wind, and as swift as their wings could flap, while passing over a large village, the Indians raised a great shout on seeing them, particularly on Paup-Puk-Keewiss's account, for his wings were broader than two large aupukwa.* They made such a noise that he forgot what had been told him about looking down. They were now going as swift as arrows; and, as soon as he brought his neck in and stretched it down to look at the shouters, his tail was caught by the wind, and over and over he was blown. He tried to right himself, but without success. Down, down he went, making more turns than he wished

---

*Mats.

for, from a height of several miles. The first thing he knew was
that he was jammed into a large hollow tree. To get back or forward was out of the question, and there he remained till his brant
life was ended by starvation. His *Jee-bi* again left the carcass, and
he once more found himself in the shape of a human being.

Travelling was still his passion; and, while travelling, he came
to a lodge in which were two old men with heads white from age.
They treated him well, and he told them that he was going back
to his village to see his friends and people. They said they would
aid him, and pointed out the direction he should go; but they
were deceivers. After walking all day, he came to a lodge looking
very much like the first, with two old men in it with white heads.
It was, in fact, the very same lodge, and he had been walking in
a circle; but they did not undeceive him, pretending to be
strangers, and saying, in a kind voice, "We will show you the
way." After walking the third day, and coming back to the same
place, he found them out in their tricks, for he had cut a notch on
the doorpost.

"Who are you," said he to them, "to treat me so?" and he gave
one a kick and the other a slap, which killed them. Their blood flew
against the rocks near the lodge, and this is the reason there are red
streaks in them to this day. He then burned their lodge down, and
freed the earth of two pretended good men, who were Manitoes.

He then continued his journey, not knowing exactly which way
to go. At last he came to a big lake. He got on the highest hill to
try and see the opposite side, but he could not. He then made a
canoe, and took a sail into the lake. On looking into the water,
which was very clear, before he got to the abrupt depth, he saw
the bottom covered with dark fishes, numbers of which he
caught. This inspired him with a wish to return to his village and
bring his people to live near this lake. He went on, and towards
evening came to a large island, where he encamped and ate the
fish he had speared.

Next day he returned to the main land, and, in wandering
along the shore, he encountered a more powerful Manito than
himself, called Manabozho. He thought best, after playing him a
trick, to keep out of his way. He again thought of returning to
his village; and, transforming himself into a partridge, took his

flight towards it. In a short time he reached it, and his return was welcomed with feasting and songs. He told them of the lake and the fish, and persuaded them all to remove to it, as it would be easier for them to live there. He immediately began to remove them by short encampments, and all things turned out as he had said. They caught abundance of fish. After this, a messenger came for him in the shape of a bear, who said that their king wished to see him immediately at his village. Paup-Puk-Keewiss was ready in an instant; and, getting on to the messenger's back, off he ran. Towards evening they went up a high mountain, and came to a cave where the bear-king lived. He was a very large person, and made him welcome by inviting him into his lodge. As soon as propriety allowed, he spoke, and said that he had sent for him on hearing that he was the chief who was moving a large party towards his hunting-grounds.

"You must know," said he, "that you have no right there. And I wish you would leave the country with your party, or else the strongest force will take possession."

"Very well," replied Paup-Puk-Keewiss. "So be it." He did not wish to do anything without consulting his people; and besides, he saw that the bear-king was raising a war-party. He then told him he would go back that night. The bear-king left him to do as he wished, but told him that one of his young men was ready at his command; and, immediately jumping on his back, Paup-Puk-Keewiss rode home. He assembled the village, and told the young men to kill the bear, make a feast of it, and hang the head outside the village, for he knew the bear spies would soon see it, and carry the news to their chief.

Next morning Paup-Puk-Keewiss got all his young warriors ready for a fight. After waiting one day the bear war-party came in sight, making a tremendous noise. The bear-chief advanced, and said that he did not wish to shed the blood of the young warriors; but that if he, Paup-Puk-Keewiss, consented, the two would have a race, and the winner should kill the losing chief, and all his young men should be slaves to the other. Paup-Puk-Keewiss agreed, and they ran before all the warriors. He was victor, and came in first; but, not to terminate the race too soon, he gave the bear-chief some specimens of his skill and swiftness by forming eddies and whirlwinds with the sand, as he leaped and turned about him. As the bear-chief came up, he drove an arrow through him, and a great chief fell. Having done this, he told his young men to take all those blackfish (meaning the bears), and tie them at the door of each lodge, that they might remain in future to serve as servants.

After seeing that all was quiet and prosperous in the village, Paup-Puk-Keewiss felt his desire for adventure returning. He took a kind leave of his friends and people, and started off again. After wandering a long time, he came to the lodge of Manabozho, who was absent. He thought he would play him a trick, and so turned everything in the lodge upside down, and killed his chickens. Now Manabozho calls all the fowls of the air his chickens; and among the number was a raven, the meanest of birds, which Paup-Puk-Keewiss killed and hung up by the neck to insult him. He then went on till he came to a very high point of rocks running out into the lake, from the top of which he could see the country back as far as the eye could reach. While sitting there, Manabozho's mountain chickens flew round and past him in great numbers. So, out of spite, he shot them in great numbers, for his arrows were sure and the birds very plenty, and he amused himself by throwing the birds down the rocky precipice. At length a wary bird cried out, "Paup-Puk-Keewiss is killing us. Go and tell our father." Away flew a delegation of them, and Manabozho soon made his appearance on the plains below. Paup-Puk-Keewiss made his escape on the opposite side. Manabozho cried out from the mountain,

"The earth is not so large but I can get up to you." Off Paup-Puk-Keewiss ran, and Manabozho after him. He ran over hills and prairies with all his speed, but still saw his pursuer hard after him. He thought of this expedient. He stopped and climbed a large pine-tree, stripped it of all its green foliage, and threw it to the winds, and then went on. When Manabozho reached the spot, the tree addressed him.

"Great chief," said the tree, "will you give me my life again? Paup-Puk-Keewiss has killed me."

"Yes," replied Manabozho; and it took him some time to gather the scattered foliage, and then renewed the pursuit. Paup-Puk-

Keewiss repeated the same thing with the hemlock, and with various other trees, for Manabozho would always stop to restore what he had destroyed. By this means he got in advance; but Manabozho persevered, and was fast overtaking him, when Paup-Puk-Keewiss happened to see an elk. He asked him to take him on his back, which the elk did, and for some time he made great progress, but still Manabozho was in sight. Paup-Puk-Keewiss dismounted, and, coming to a large sandstone rock, he broke it in pieces and scattered the grains. Manabozho was so close upon him at this place that he had almost caught him; but the foundation of the rock cried out,

"Haye! Ne-me-sho, Paup-Puk-Keewiss has spoiled me. Will you not restore me to life?"

"Yes," replied Manabozho; and he restored the rock to its previous shape. He then pushed on in the pursuit of Paup-Puk-Keewiss, and had got so near as to put out his arm to seize him; but Paup-Puk-Keewiss dodged him, and immediately raised such a dust and commotion by whirlwinds as made the trees break, and the sand and leaves dance in the air. Again and again Manabozho's hand was put out to catch him; but he dodged him at every turn, and kept up such a tumult of dust, that in the thickest of it, he dashed into a hollow tree which had been blown down, and changed himself into a snake, and crept out at the roots. Well that he did; for at the moment he had got out, Manabozho, who is Ogee-bau-ge-mon,* struck it with his power, and it was in fragments. Paup-Puk-Keewiss was again in human shape; and Manabozho pressed him hard. At a distance he saw a very high bluff of rock jutting out into the lake, and ran for the foot of the precipice, which was abrupt and elevated. As he came near, the local Manito of the rock opened his door and told him to come in. The door was no sooner closed than Manabozho knocked.

"Open it!" he cried, with a loud voice.

The Manito was afraid of him, but he said to his guest,

"Since I have sheltered you, I would sooner die with you than open the door."

---

*A species of lightning.

"Open it!" Manabozho again cried.

The Manito kept silent. Manabozho, however, made no attempt to open it by force. He waited a few moments. "Very well," he said; "I give you only till night to live." The Manito trembled, for he knew he would be shut up under the earth.

Night came. The clouds hung low and black, and every moment the forked lightning would flash from them. The black clouds advanced slowly, and threw their dark shadows afar, and behind there was heard the rumbling noise of the coming thunder. As they came near to the precipice, the thunders broke, the lightning flashed, the ground shook, and the solid rocks split, tottered, and fell. And under their ruins were crushed the mortal bodies of Paup-Puk-Keewiss and the Manito.

It was only then that Paup-Puk-Keewiss found he was really dead. He had been killed in different animal shapes; but now his body, in human shape, was crushed. Manabozho came and took their *Jee-bi-ug* or spirits.

"You," said he to Paup-Puk-Keewiss, "shall not be again permitted to live on the earth. I will give you the shape of the war-eagle, and you will be the chief of all fowls, and your duty shall be to watch over their destinies."

IADILLA

or

THE ORIGIN OF THE ROBIN

From the Odjibwa

A N OLD man had an only son named *Iadilla,* who had come to that age which is thought to be most proper to make the long and final fast that is to secure through life a guardian genius or spirit. In the influence of this choice, it is well known, our people have relied for their prosperity in after life; it was, therefore, an event of deep importance.

The old man was ambitious that his son should surpass all others in whatever was deemed most wise and great among his tribe; and, to fulfil his wishes, he thought it necessary that he should fast a much longer time than any of those persons, renowned for their prowess or wisdom, whose fame he coveted. He therefore directed his son to prepare, with great ceremony, for the important event. After he had been in the sweating lodge and bath several times, he ordered him to lie down upon a clean mat, in a little lodge expressly prepared for him; telling him, at the same time, to endure his fast like a man, and that, at the expiration of *twelve* days, he should receive food and the blessing of his father.

The lad carefully observed this injunction, lying with perfect composure, with his face covered, awaiting those mystic visitations which were to seal his good or evil fortune. His father visited him regularly every morning, to encourage him to perseverance, expatiating at length on the honour and renown that would attend him through life if he accomplished the full term prescribed. To these admonitions and encouragements the boy never replied, but lay, without the least sign of discontent or murmuring, until the ninth day, when he addressed his father as follows:

"My father, my dreams forbode evil. May I break my fast now, and at a more propitious time make a new fast?" The father answered,

"My son, you know not what you ask. If you get up now, all your glory will depart. Wait patiently a little longer. You have but three days yet to accomplish your desire. You know it is for your own good, and I encourage you to persevere."

The son assented; and, covering himself closer, he lay till the eleventh day, when he repeated his request. Very nearly the same answer was given him by his father, who added that the next day he would himself prepare his first meal, and bring it to him. The boy remained silent, but lay as motionless as a corpse. No one would have known he was living but by the gentle heaving of his breast.

The next morning, the father, elated at having gained his end, prepared a repast for his son, and hastened to set it before him. On coming to the door, he was surprised to hear his son talking to himself. He stooped to listen; and, looking through a small aperture, was more astonished when he beheld his son painted with vermilion over all his breast, and in the act of finishing his work by laying on the paint as far back on his shoulders as he could reach with his hands, saying, at the same time, to himself, "My father has destroyed my fortune as a man. He would not listen to my requests. He will be the loser. I shall be for ever happy in my new state, for I have been obedient to my parent; he alone will be the sufferer, for my guardian spirit is a just one; though not propitious to me in the manner I desired, he has shown me pity in another way; he has given me another shape; and now I must go."

At this moment the old man broke in, exclaiming, "My son! my son! I pray you leave me not." But the young man, with the quickness of a bird, had flown to the top of the lodge, and perched himself on the highest pole, having been changed into a beautiful robin redbreast.

He looked down upon his father with pity beaming in his eyes, and addressed him as follows: "Regret not, my father, the change you behold. I shall be happier in my present state than I could have been as a man. I shall always be the friend of men, and keep near their dwellings. I shall ever be happy and contented; and although I could not gratify your wishes as a warrior, it will be my daily aim to make you amends for it as a harbinger of peace and joy. I will cheer you by my songs, and strive to inspire in others the joy and lightsomeness I feel in my present state. This will be some compensation to you for the loss of the glory you expected. I am now free from the cares and pains of human life. My food is spontaneously furnished by the mountains and fields, and my pathway of life is in the bright air." Then stretching himself on his toes, as if delighted with the gift of wings, he carolled one of his sweetest songs, and flew away into a neighbouring grove.

IADILLA'S SONG.

In the boundless woods there are berries of red,
    And fruits of a beautiful blue,
Where, by nature's own hand, the sweet singers are fed,
    And to nature they ever are true.

We go not with arrow and bow to the field,
    Like men of the fierce ruddy race,
To take away lives which they never can give,
    And revel the lords of the chase.

If danger approaches, with instant alarm
    We fly to our own leafy woods,
And there, with an innocent carol and charm,
    We sing to our dear little broods.

At morning we sally in quest of the grain
    Kind nature in plenty supplies,
We skip o'er the beautiful wide-stretching plain,
    And sport in the vault of the skies.

At evening we perch in some neighbouring tree
    To carol our evening adieu,
And feel, although man may assert he is free,
    We only have liberty true.

We sing out our praises to God and to man,
  We live as heaven taught us to live,
And I would not change back to mortality's plan
  For all that the mortal can give.

Here ceased the sweet singer; then pluming his breast,
  He winged the blue firmament free,
Repeating, as homeward he flew to his rest,
  Tshee-ree-lee—Tshee-ree-lee—Tshee-ree-lee!

THE ENCHANTED MOCCASINS

A Maskego Tale

<hr/>

THERE ONCE lived a little boy with his sister, entirely alone, in an uninhabited country. He was called the Boy that Carries the Ball on His Back, from an idea of his having supernatural powers. This boy was constantly in the habit of meditating, and asking within himself whether there were other and similar beings to themselves on the earth. When he grew up to manhood, he asked his sister if she knew of any human beings besides themselves. She replied that she did; and that there was, at a great distance, a large village. As soon as he heard this, he said to his sister, "I am now a young man, and very much in want of a partner"; and he asked his sister to make him several pairs of moccasins. She complied with his request; and, as soon as he received the moccasins, he took up his war-club and set out in quest of the distant village. He travelled on, till at length he came to a small wigwam, and, on looking into it, discovered a very old woman setting alone by the fire. As soon as she saw the stranger, she invited him in, and thus addressed him: "My poor grand-child, I suppose you are one of those who seek for the distant village, from which no person has ever yet returned. Unless your guardian is more powerful than the guardian of your predecessors, you too will share a similar fate to theirs. Be careful to provide yourself with the Ozhebahguhnun—the bones they use in the medicine dance,* without which you cannot succeed." After she had thus spoken, she gave him the following directions for his journey. "When you come near to the village which you seek, you

<hr/>

*The idea attached to the use of these bones in the medicine dance is that, by their magical influence, the actor can penetrate and go through any substance.

will see in the centre a large lodge, in which the chief of the village, who has two daughters, resides. Before the door you will see a great tree, which is smooth and destitute of bark. On this tree, about the height of a man from the ground, a small lodge is suspended, in which these two daughters dwell. It is here so many have been destroyed. Be wise, my grandchild, and abide strictly by my directions." The old woman then gave him the Ozhebahguhnun, which would cause his success. Placing them in his bosom, he continued on his journey, till at length he arrived at the sought-for village; and, as he was gazing around him, he saw both the tree and the lodge which the old woman had mentioned. Immediately he bent his steps for the tree, and approaching, he endeavoured to reach the suspended lodge. But all his efforts were vain; for as often as he attempted to reach it, the tree began to tremble, and soon shot up so that the lodge could hardly be perceived. Foiled as he was in all his attempts, he thought of his guardian, and changed himself into a small squirrel, that he might more easily accomplish his design. He then mounted the tree in quest of the lodge. After climbing for some time, he became fatigued and panted for breath; but, remembering the instructions which the old woman had given him, he took from his bosom one of the bones, and thrust it into the trunk of the tree on which he sat. In this way he quickly found relief; and, as often as he became fatigued, he repeated this; but whenever he came near the lodge and attempted to touch it, the tree would shoot up as before, and place the lodge beyond his reach. At length, the bones being exhausted, he began to despair, for the earth had long since vanished from his sight. Summoning all resolution, he determined to make another effort to reach the object of his wishes. On he went; yet, as soon as he came near the lodge and attempted to touch it, the tree again shook, but it had reached the arch of heaven, and could go no higher; so now he entered the lodge, and beheld the two sisters sitting opposite each other. He asked their names. The one on his left hand called herself Azhabee,* and the one on the right Negahnahbee.† Whenever he

---

*One who sits behind.
†One who sits before.

addressed the one on his left hand, the tree would tremble as before, and settle down to its former position. But when he addressed the one on his right hand, it would again shoot upward as before. When he thus discovered that, by addressing the one on his left hand, the tree would descend, he continued to do so until it had resumed its former position; then seizing his war-club, he thus addressed the sisters: "You, who have caused the death of so many of my brothers, I will now put an end to, and thus have revenge for the numbers you have destroyed." As he said this he raised the club and laid them dead at his feet. He then descended, and learning that these sisters had a brother living with their father, who would pursue him for the deed he had done, he set off at random, not knowing whither he went. Soon after, the father and mother of the young women visited their residence and found their remains. They immediately told their son Mudjikewis that his sisters had been slain. He replied, "The person who has done this must be the Boy that Carries the Ball on His Back. I will pursue him, and have revenge for the blood of my sisters." "It is well, my son," replied the father. "The spirit of your life grant you success. I counsel you to be wary in the pursuit. It is a strong spirit who has done this injury to us, and he will try to deceive you in every way. Above all, avoid tasting food till you succeed; for if you break your fast before you see his blood, your power will be destroyed." So saying, they parted.

His son instantly set out in search of the murderer, who, finding he was closely pursued by the brother of the slain, climbed up into one of the tallest trees and shot forth his magic arrows. Finding that his pursuer was not turned back by his arrows, he renewed his flight; and when he found himself hard pressed, and his enemy close behind him, he transformed himself into the skeleton of a moose that had been killed, whose flesh had come off from his bones. He then remembered the moccasins which his sister had given him, which were enchanted. Taking a pair of them, he placed them near the skeleton. "Go," said he to them, "to the end of the earth."

The moccasins then left him and their tracks remained. Mudjikewis at length came to the skeleton of the moose, when he perceived that the track he had long been pursuing did not end there, so he continued to follow it up, till he came to the end of the earth, where he found only a pair of moccasins. Mortified that he had been outwitted by following a pair of moccasins instead of the object of his revenge, he bitterly complained, resolving not to give up the pursuit, and to be more wary and wise in scrutinizing signs. He then called to mind the skeleton he met with on his way, an concluded that *it* must be the object of his search. He retraced his steps towards the skeleton, but found, to his surprise, that it had disappeared, and that the tracks of *Onwee Bahmondung,* or He Who Carries the Ball, were in another direction. He now became faint with hunger, and resolved to give up the pursuit; but when he remembered the blood of his sisters, he determined again to pursue.

The other, finding he was closely pursued, now changed himself into a very old man, with two daughters, who lived in a large lodge in the centre of a beautiful garden, which was filled with everything that could delight the eye or was pleasant to the taste. He made himself appear so very old as to be unable to leave his lodge, and had his daughters to bring him food and wait on him. The garden also had the appearance of ancient occupancy, and was highly cultivated.

His pursuer continued on till he was nearly starved and ready to sink. He exclaimed, "Oh! I will forget the blood of my sisters, for I am starving." But again he thought of the blood of his sisters, and again he resolved to pursue, and be satisfied with nothing but the attainment of his right to revenge.

He went on till he came to the beautiful garden. He approached the lodge. As soon as the daughters of the owner perceived him, they ran and told their father that a stranger approached the lodge. Their father replied, "Invite him in, my children, invite him in." They quickly did so; and, by the command of their father, they boiled some corn and prepared other savoury food. Mudjikewis had no suspicion of the deception. He was faint and weary with travel, and felt that he could endure fasting no longer. Without hesitancy, he partook heartily of the meal, and in so doing was overcome. All at once he seemed to forget the blood of his sisters, and even the village of his nativity. He ate so heartily as to produce drowsiness, and soon fell into a profound sleep. Onwee Bahmondung watched his opportunity, and, as soon as he found his slumbers sound, resumed his youthful form. He then drew the magic ball from his back, which turned out to be a heavy war-club, with one blow of which he put an end to his pursuer, and thus vindicated his title as the Wearer of the Ball.

THE BROKEN WING

An Allegory

THERE WERE six young falcons living in a nest, all but one of whom, were still unable to fly, when it so happened that both the parent birds were shot by the hunters in one day. The young brood waited with impatience for their return; but night came, and they were left without parents and without food. Meeji-geeg-wona, or the Gray Eagle, the eldest, and the only one whose feathers had become stout enough to enable him to leave the nest, assumed the duty of stilling their cries and providing them with food, in which he was very successful. But, after a short time had passed, he, by an unlucky mischance, got one of his wings broken in pouncing upon a swan. This was the more unlucky because the season had arrived when they were soon to go off to a southern climate to pass the winter, and they were only waiting to become a little stouter and more expert for the journey. Finding that he did not return, they resolved to go in search of him, and found him sorely wounded and unable to fly.

"Brothers," he said, "an accident has befallen me, but let not this prevent your going to a warmer climate. Winter is rapidly approaching, and you cannot remain here. It is better that I alone should die than for you all to suffer miserably on my account." "No! no!" they replied, with one voice, "we will not forsake you; we will share your sufferings; we will abandon our journey, and take care of you, as you did of us, before we were able to take care of ourselves. If the climate kills you, it shall kill us. Do you think we can so soon forget your brotherly care, which has sur-passed a father's, and even a mother's kindness? Whether you live or die, we will live or die with you."

They sought out a hollow tree to winter in, and contrived to

112

carry their wounded nestmate there; and, before the rigours of winter set in, they had stored up food enough to carry them through its severities. To make it last the better, two of the number went off south, leaving the other three to watch over, feed, and protect the wounded bird. Meeji-geeg-wona in due time recovered from his wound, and he repaid their kindness by giving them such advice and instruction in the art of hunting as his experience had qualified him to impart. As spring advanced, they began to venture out of their hiding-place, and were all successful in getting food to eke out their winter's stock, except the youngest, who was called Peepi-geewi-zains, or the Pigeon Hawk. Being small and foolish, flying hither and yon, he always came back without anything. At last the Gray Eagle spoke to him, and demanded the cause of his ill luck. "It is not my smallness or weakness of body," said he, "that prevents my bringing home flesh as well as my brothers. I kill ducks and other birds every time I go out; but, just as I get to the woods, a large Ko-ko-ko-ho* robs me of my prey." "Well! don't despair, brother," said Meeji-geeg-wona. "I now feel my strength perfectly recovered, and I will go out with you to-morrow," for he was the most courageous and warlike of them all.

Next day they went forth in company, the elder seating himself near the lake. Peepi-geewi-zains started out, and soon pounced upon a duck.

"Well done!" thought his brother, who saw his success; but, just as he was getting to land with his prize, up came a large white owl from a tree, where he had been watching, and laid claim to it. He was about wresting it from him when Meeji-geeg-wona came up, and, fixing his talons in both sides of the owl, flew home with him.

The little pigeon hawk followed him closely, and was rejoiced and happy to think he had brought home something at last. He then flew in the owl's face, and wanted to tear out his eyes, and vented his passion in an abundance of reproachful terms. "Softly," said the Gray Eagle; "do not be in such a passion, or exhibit so

*Owl.

revengeful a disposition; for this will be a lesson to him not to tyrannize over any one who is weaker than himself for the future." So, after giving him good advice, and telling him what kind of herbs would cure his wounds, they let the owl go.

While this act was taking place, and before the liberated owl had yet got out of view, two visiters appeared at the hollow tree. They were the two nestmates, who had just returned from the south after passing the winter there, and they were thus all happily reunited, and each one soon chose a mate and flew off to the woods. Spring had now revisited the north. The cold winds had ceased, the ice had melted, the streams were open, and the forest began rapidly to put on its vernal hue. "But it is in vain," said the old man who related this story, "it is in vain that spring returns, if we are not thankful to the Master of Life who has preserved us through the winter. Nor does that man answer the end for which he was made who does not show a kind and charitable feeling to all who are in want or sickness, especially to his blood relations. These six birds only represent one of our empoverished northern families of children, who had been deprived of both their parents and the aid of their elder brother nearly at the same time."

THE THREE CRANBERRIES

A Chippewa Fable

THREE CRANBERRIES were living in a lodge together. One was green, one was white, and one red. They were sisters. There was snow on the ground; and as the men were absent, they felt afraid, and began to say to each other, "What shall we do if the wolf comes?" "I," said the green one, "will climb up a shingoub* tree." "I," said the white one, "will hide myself in the kettle of boiled hommony"; "And I," said the red one, "will conceal myself under the snow." Presently the wolves came, and each one did as she had said. But only one of the three had judged wisely. The wolves immediately ran to the kettle and ate up the corn, and, with it, the white cranberry. The red one was trampled to pieces by their feet, and her blood spotted the snow. But she who had climbed the thick spruce-tree escaped notice, and was saved.

---

*Spruce.

PARADISE OPENED
TO THE INDIANS

Pontiac's Tale

Historical Note.—The following is a literal translation of the story related by the noted Algic chief Pontiac to the Indian tribes whom he wished to bring into his views in forming his general confederacy against the Anglo-Saxon race in the last century. It is taken from an ancient manuscript journal now in the possession of the Michigan Historical Society. This journal, the preservation of which is due to one of the French families at Detroit, appears to have been kept by a person holding an official station, or intimate with the affairs of the day, during the siege of the fort of Detroit by the confederate Indians in 1763. It is minute in its details of the transactions of every day, from the investment of the fort until the disaster of the sortie made by the English garrison in the direction of Bloody Run. And its authenticity has never been brought into question. There is no air of exaggeration in the narrative. There is nothing recorded in the process of the negotiations, the siege, or the disclosure of the plot preceding it, which was not perfectly reasonable under the circumstances, and in keeping with the character of the tribes and their means of action.

That a document of so much historical interest might be the better preserved, the society took measures, about a twelvemonth since, for its translation; and the tale here furnished is a transcript of this particular portion of the journal. The only addition to the text consists of the insertion of four or five words of ordinary use in the narrative, which appear to have been obliterated by a chemical change in the ink in a few places.

Without entering into the moral bearing of this curious specimen of Indian fiction, it may be regarded as no equivocal testimony of the sagacity and foresight of its celebrated author. To turn the mythology and superstitious belief of his auditors to political account was certainly a capital stroke of policy. And no stronger proof could, perhaps, be adduced of the existence of the popular belief on this head, and the prevalence, at that time, of oral tales and fanciful legends among the tribes.

A N Indian of the Lenapee* tribe, anxious to know the Master of Life, resolved, without mentioning his design to any one, to undertake a journey to Paradise, which he knew to be God's residence. But, to succeed in his project, it was necessary for him to know the way to the celestial regions. Not knowing any person who, having been there himself, might aid him in finding the road, he commenced juggling, in the hope of drawing a good augury from his dream.

The Indian, in his dream, imagined that he had only to commence his journey, and that a continued walk would take him to the celestial abode. The next morning very early, he equipped himself as a hunter, taking a gun, powder-horn, ammunition, and a boiler to cook his provisions. The first part of his journey was pretty favourable; he walked a long time without being discouraged, having always a firm conviction that he should attain his aim. Eight days had already elapsed without his meeting with any one to oppose his desire. On the evening of the eighth day, at sunset, he stopped as usual on the bank of a brook, at the entrance of a little prairie, a place which he thought favourable for his night's encampment. As he was preparing his lodging, he perceived at the other end of the prairie three very wide and well-beaten paths; he thought this somewhat singular; he, however, continued to prepare his wigwam, that he might shelter himself from the weather. He also lighted a fire. While cooking, he found that, the darker it grew, the more distinct were those paths. This surprised, nay, even frightened him; he hesitated a few moments. Was it better for him to remain in his camp, or seek another at some distance? While in this incertitude, he remembered his juggling, or rather his dream. He thought that his only aim in undertaking

*Delawares.—H. R. S.

his journey was to see the Master of Life. This restored him to his senses. He thought it probable that one of those three roads led to the place which he wished to visit. He therefore resolved upon remaining in his camp until the morrow, when he would, at random, take one of them. His curiosity, however, scarcely allowed him time to take his meal; he left his encampment and fire, and took the widest of the paths. He followed it until the middle of the day without seeing anything to impede his progress; but, as he was resting a little to take breath, he suddenly perceived a large fire coming from under ground. It excited his curiosity; he went towards it to see what it might be; but, as the fire appeared to increase as he drew nearer, he was so overcome with fear, that he turned back and took the widest of the other two paths. Having followed it for the same space of time as he had the first, he perceived a similar spectacle. His fright, which had been lulled by the change of road, awoke, and he was obliged to take the third path, in which he walked a whole day without seeing anything. All at once, a mountain of a marvellous whiteness burst upon his sight. This filled him with astonishment; nevertheless, he took courage and advanced to examine it. Having arrived at the foot, he saw no signs of a road. He became very sad, not knowing how to continue his journey. In this conjuncture, he looked on all sides and perceived a female seated upon the mountain; her beauty was dazzling, and the whiteness of her garments surpassed that of snow. The woman said to him in his own language, "You appear surprised to find no longer a path to reach your wishes. I know that you have for a long time longed to see and speak to the Master of Life; and that you have undertaken this journey purposely to see him. The way which leads to his abode is upon this mountain. To ascend it, you must undress yourself completely, and leave all your accoutrements and clothing at the foot. No person shall injure them. You will then go and wash yourself in the river which I am now showing you, and afterward ascend the mountain."

The Indian obeyed punctually the woman's words; but one difficulty remained. How could he arrive at the top of the mountain, which was steep, without a path, and as smooth as glass? He asked the woman how he was to accomplish it. She replied, that if he really wished to see the Master of Life, he must, in mounting, only use his left hand and foot. This appeared almost impossible to the Indian. Encouraged, however, by the female, he commenced ascending, and succeeded after much trouble. When at the top, he was astonished to see no person, the woman having disappeared. He found himself alone, and without a guide. Three unknown villages were in sight; they were constructed on a different plan from his own, much handsomer, and more regular. After a few moments' reflection, he took his way towards the handsomest. When about half way from the top of the mountain, he recollected that he was naked, and was afraid to proceed; but a voice told him to advance, and have no apprehensions; that, as he had washed himself, he might walk in confidence. He proceeded without hesitation to a place which appeared to be the gate of the village, and stopped until some one came to open it. While he was considering the exterior of the village, the gate opened, and the Indian saw coming towards him a handsome man dressed all in white, who took him by the hand, and said he was going to satisfy his wishes by leading him to the presence of the Master of Life.

The Indian suffered himself to be conducted, and they arrived at a place of unequalled beauty. The Indian was lost in admiration. He there saw the Master of Life, who took him by the hand, and gave him for a seat a hat bordered with gold. The Indian, afraid of spoiling the hat, hesitated to sit down; but, being again ordered to do so, he obeyed without reply.

The Indian being seated, God said to him, "I am the Master of Life, whom thou wishest to see, and to whom thou wishest to speak. Listen to that which I will tell thee for thyself and for all the Indians. I am the Maker of Heaven and earth, the trees, lakes, rivers, men, and all that thou seest or hast seen on the earth or in the heavens; and because I love you, you must do my will; you must also avoid that which I hate; I hate you to drink as you do, until you lose your reason; I wish you not to fight one another; you take two wives, or run after other people's wives; you do wrong; I hate such conduct; you should have but one wife, and keep her until death. When you go to war, you juggle, you sing the medicine song, thinking you speak to me; you deceive yourselves; it is to the Manito that you speak; he is a wicked spirit who induces you to evil, and, for want of knowing me, you listen to him.

"The land on which you are, I have made for you, not for others: wherefore do you suffer the whites to dwell upon your lands? Can you not do without them? I know that those whom you call the children of your great Father supply your wants. But, were you not wicked as you are, you would not need them. You might live as you did before you knew them. Before those whom you call your brothers had arrived, did not your bow and arrow maintain you? You needed neither gun, powder, nor any other object. The flesh of animals was your food, their skins your raiment. But when I saw you inclined to evil, I removed the animals into the depths of the forest, that you might depend on your brothers for your necessaries, for your clothing. Again become good and do my will, and I will send animals for your sustenance. I do not, however, forbid suffering among you your Father's children; I love them, they know me, they pray to me; I supply their own wants, and give them that which they bring to you. Not so with those who are come to trouble your possessions. Drive them away; wage war against them. I love them not. They know me not. They are my enemies, they are your brothers' enemies. Send them back to the lands I have made for them. Let them remain there.

"Here is a written prayer which I give thee; learn it by heart, and teach it to all the Indians and children." (The Indian observing here that he could not read, the Master of Life told him that, on his return upon earth, he should give it to the chief of his village, who would read it, and also teach it to him, as also to all the Indians.) "It must be repeated," said the Master of Life, "morning and evening. Do all that I have told thee, and announce it to all the Indians as coming from the Master of Life. Let them drink but one draught, or two at most, in one day. Let them have but one wife, and discontinue running after other people's wives and daughters. Let them not fight one another. Let them not sing the medicine song, for in singing the medicine song they speak to the evil spirit. Drive from your lands," added the Master of Life, "those dogs in red clothing; they are only an injury to you. When you want anything, apply to me, as your brothers do, and I will give to both. Do not sell to your brothers that which I have placed on the earth as food. In short, become good, and you shall want nothing. When you meet one another, bow, and give one another the . . . hand of the heart. Above all, I command thee to repeat, morning and evening, the prayer which I have given thee."

The Indian promised to do the will of the Master of Life, and also to recommend it strongly to the Indians; adding that the Master of Life should be satisfied with them.

His conductor then came, and, leading him to the foot of the mountain, told him to take his garments and return to his village; which was immediately done by the Indian.

His return much surprised the inhabitants of the village, who did not know what had become of him. They asked him whence he came; but, as he had been enjoined to speak to no one until he saw the chief of the village, he motioned to them with his hand that he came from above. Having entered the village, he went immediately to the chief's wigwam, and delivered to him the prayer and laws intrusted to his care by the Master of Life.

VOLUME II

THE RED SWAN

From the Algic

T HREE BROTHERS were left destitute, by the death of their parents, at an early age. The eldest was not yet able to provide fully for their support, but did all he could in hunting, and with his aid, and the stock of provisions left by their father, they were preserved and kept alive, rather, it seems, by miraculous interposition, than the adequacy of their own exertions. For the father had been a hermit,* having removed far away from the body of the tribe, so that when he and his wife died they left their children without neighbours and friends, and the lads had no idea that there was a human being near them. They did not even know who their parents had been, for the eldest was too young, at the time of their death, to remember it. Forlorn as they were, they did not, however, give up to despondency, but made use of every exertion they could, and in process of time, learned the art of hunting and killing animals. The eldest soon became an expert hunter, and was very successful in procuring food. He was noted for his skill in killing buffalo, elk, and moose, and he instructed his brothers in the arts of the forest as soon as they become old enough to follow him. After they had become able to hunt and take care of themselves, the elder proposed to leave them, and go in search of habitations, promising to return as soon as he could procure them wives. In this project he was overruled by his brothers, who said they could not part with him. Maujeekewis, the second eldest, was loud in his disapproval, saying, "What will you do with *those you propose to get*—we have lived so long without

---

*Pai-gwud-aw-diz-zid.

them, and we can still do without them." His words prevailed, and the three brothers continued together for a time.

One day they agreed to kill, each, a male of those kind of animals each was most expert in hunting, for the purpose of making quivers from their skins. They did so, and immediately commenced making arrows to fill their quivers, that they might be prepared for any emergency. Soon after, they hunted on a wager, to see who should come in first with game, and prepare it so as to regale the others. They were to shoot no other animal but such as each was in the habit of killing. They set out different ways; Odjibwa, the youngest, had not gone far before he saw a bear, an animal he was not to kill, by the agreement. He followed him close and drove an arrow through him, which brought him to the ground. Although contrary to the bet, he immediately commenced skinning him, when suddenly something red tinged all the air around him. He rubbed his eyes, thinking he was perhaps deceived, but without effect, for the red hue continued. At length he heard a strange noise at a distance. It first appeared like a human voice, but after following the sound for some distance, he reached the shores of a lake, and soon saw the object he was looking for. At a distance out in the lake, sat a most beautiful Red Swan, whose plumage glittered in the sun, and who would, now and then, make the same noise he had heard. He was within long bow shot; and pulling the arrow from the bow-string up to his ear, took deliberate aim and shot. The arrow took no effect; and he shot and shot again till his quiver was empty. Still the swan remained, moving round and round, stretching its long neck and dipping its bill into the water, as if heedless of the arrows shot at it. Odjibwa ran home, and got all his own and his brothers' arrows, and shot them all away. He then stood and gazed at the beautiful bird. While standing, he remembered his brother's saying that in their deceased father's medicine sack were three magic arrows. Off he started, his anxiety to kill the swan overcoming all scruples. At any other time, he would have deemed it sacrilege to open his father's medicine sack, but now he hastily seized the three arrows and ran back, leaving the other contents of the sack scattered over the lodge. The swan was still there. He shot the first arrow with great precision, and came very near to it. The second came still closer; as he took the last arrow, he felt his arm firmer, and drawing it up with vigour, saw it pass through the neck of the swan a little above the breast. Still it did not prevent the bird from flying off, which it did, however, at first slowly, flapping its wings and rising gradually into the air, and then flying off toward the sinking of the sun.* Odjibwa was disappointed; he knew that his brothers would be displeased with him; he rushed into the water and rescued the two magic arrows, the third was carried off by the swan; but he thought that it could not fly very far with it, and let the consequences be what they might, he was bent on following it.

Off he started on the run; he was noted for speed, for he would shoot an arrow, and then run so fast that the arrow always fell behind him. I can run fast, he thought, and I can get up with the swan some time or other. He thus ran over hills and prairies, toward the west, till near night, and was only going to take one more run, and then seek a place to sleep for the night, when suddenly he heard noises at a distance, which he knew were from people; for some were cutting trees, and the strokes of their axes echoed through the woods. When he emerged from the forest, the sun was just falling below the horizon, and he felt pleased to find a place to sleep in, and get something to eat, as he had left home without a mouthful. All these circumstances could not damp his ardour for the accomplishment of his object, and he felt that if he only persevered, he would succeed. At a distance, on a rising piece of ground, he could see an extensive town. He went toward it, but soon heard the watchman, MUDJEE-KOKOKOHO, who was placed on some height, to overlook the place, and give notice of the approach of friends or foes—crying out, "We are visited"; and a loud holla indicated that they all heard it. The young man advanced, and was pointed by the watchman to the lodge of the chief, "It is there you must go in," he said, and left him. "Come in, come in," said the chief, take a seat there," pointing to the side where his daughter sat. "It is there you must sit." Soon they gave him something to eat, and very few questions were asked him,

---

*Pungish-e-moo: falling or sinking to a position of repose.

being a stranger. It was only when he spoke, that the others answered him. "Daughter," said the chief, after dark, "take our son-in-law's moccasins, and see if they be torn; if so, mend them for him, and bring in his bundle." The young man thought it strange that he should be so warmly received, and married instantly, without his wishing it, although the young girl was pretty. It was some time before she would take his moccasins, which he had taken off. It displeased him to see her so reluctant to do so, and when she did reach them, he snatched them out of her hand and hung them up himself. He laid down and thought of the swan, and made up his mind to be off by dawn. He awoke early, and spoke to the young woman, but she gave no answer. He slightly touched her. "What do you want?" she said, and turned her back toward him. "Tell me," he said, "what time the swan passed—I am following it—and come out and point the direction." "Do you think you can catch up to it?" she said. "Yes," he answered. "Naubesah," (foolishness) she said. She, however, went out and pointed in the direction he should go. The young man went slowly till the sun arose, when he commenced traveling at his accustomed speed. He passed the day in running, and when night came, he was unexpectedly pleased to find himself near another town; and when at a distance, he heard the watchman crying out, "We are visited"; and soon the men of the village stood out to see the stranger. He was again told to enter the lodge of the chief, and his reception was, in every respect, the same as he met the previous night; only that the young woman was more beautiful, and received him very kindly, and although urged to stay, his mind was fixed on the object of his journey. Before daylight he asked the young woman what time the Red Swan passed, and to point out the way. She did so, and said it passed yesterday when the sun was between midday and *pungishemoo*—its falling place. He again set out rather slowly, but when the sun had arisen he tried his speed by shooting an arrow ahead, and running after it; but it fell behind him. Nothing remarkable happened in the course of the day, and he went on leisurely. Toward night, he came to the lodge of an old man. Some time after dark he saw a light emitted from a small low lodge. He went up to it very slyly, and peeping through the door, saw an old man alone, warming his back before the fire, with his head down on his breast. He thought the old man did not know that he was standing near the door, but in this he was disappointed; for so soon as he looked in, "Walk in, Nosis,"* he said, "take a seat opposite to me, and take off your things and dry them, for you must be fatigued; and I will prepare you something to eat." Odjibwa did as he was requested. The old man, whom he perceived to be a magician, then said; "My kettle with water stands near the fire"; and immediately a small earthen or a kind of metallic pot with legs appeared by the fire. He then took one grain of corn, also one whortleberry, and put them in the pot. As the young man was very hungry, he thought that his chance for a supper was but small. Not a word or a look, however, revealed his feelings. The pot soon boiled, when the old man spoke, commanding it to stand some distance from the fire; "Nosis," said he, "feed yourself," and he handed him a dish and ladle made out of the same metal as the pot. The young man helped himself to all that was in the pot; he felt ashamed to think of his having done so, but before he could speak, the old man said, "Nosis, eat, eat"; and soon after he again said, "help yourself from the pot." Odjibwa was surprised on looking into it to see it full, he kept on taking *all out,* and as soon as it was done, it was again filled, till he had amply satisfied his hunger. The magician then spoke, and the pot occupied its accustomed place in one part of the lodge. The young man then leisurely reclined back, and listened to the predictions of his entertainer who told him to keep on, and he would obtain his object. "To tell you more," said he, "I am not permitted; but go on as you have commenced, and you will not be disappointed; to-morrow you will again reach one of my fellow old men; but the one you will see after him will tell you all, and the manner in which you will proceed to accomplish your journey. Often has this Red Swan passed, and those who have followed it have never returned: but you must be firm in your resolution, and be pre-pared for all events." "So will it be," answered Odjibwa, and they both laid down to sleep. Early in the morning, the old man had

*"My grandchild."

his magic kettle prepared, so that his guest should eat before leaving. When leaving, the old man gave him his parting advice.

Odjibwa set out in better spirits than he had done since leaving home. Night again found him in company with an old man, who received him kindly, and directed him on his way in the morning. He travelled with a light heart, expecting to meet the one who was to give him directions how to proceed to get the Red Swan. Toward nightfall, he reached the third old man's lodge. Before coming to the door, he heard him saying, "Nosis, come in," and going in immediately, he felt quite at home. The old man prepared him something to eat, acting as the other magicians had done, and his kettle was of the same dimensions and material. The old man waited till he had done eating, when he commenced addressing him. "Young man, the errand you are on is very difficult. Numbers of young men have passed with the same purpose, but never returned. Be careful, and if your guardian spirits are powerful, you may succeed. This Red Swan you are following, is the daughter of a magician, who has plenty of every thing, but he values his daughter but little less than wampum. He wore a cap of wampum, which was attached to his scalp; but powerful Indians—warriors of a distant chief—came and told him that their chief's daughter was on the brink of the grave, and she herself requested his scalp of wampum to effect a cure. If I can only see it, I will recover, she said, and it was for this reason they came, and after long urging the magician, he at last consented to part with it, only from the idea of restoring the young woman to health; although when he took it off, it left his head bare and bloody. Several years have passed since, and it has not healed. The warriors' coming for it was only a cheat, and they are now constantly making sport of it, dancing it about from village to village; and on every insult it receives the old man groans from pain. Those Indians are too powerful for the magician, and numbers have sacrificed themselves to recover it for him, but without success. The Red Swan has enticed many a young man, as she has done you, in order to get them to procure it, and whoever is the fortunate one that succeeds will receive the Red Swan as his reward. In the morning you will proceed on your way, and toward evening you will come to the magician's lodge, but before you enter you will hear his groans; he will immediately ask you in, and you will see no one but himself; he will make inquiries of you, as regards your dreams, and the powers of your guardian spirits; he will then ask you to attempt the recovery of his scalp; he will show you the direction, and if you feel inclined, as I dare say you do, go forward, my son, with a strong heart, persevere, and I have a presentiment you will succeed." The young man answered, "I will try." Early next morning, after having eaten from the magic kettle, he started off on his journey. Toward evening he came to the lodge as he was told, and soon heard the groans of the magician. "Come in," he said, even before the young man reached the door. On entering he saw his head all bloody, and he was groaning most terribly. "Sit down, sit down," he said, "while I prepare you something to eat," at the same time doing as the other magicians had done in preparing food—"You see," he said, "how poor I am; I have to attend to all my wants." He said this to conceal the fact that the Red Swan was there, but Odjibwa perceived that the lodge was partitioned, and he heard a rustling noise, now and then, in that quarter, which satisfied him that it was occupied. After having taken his leggings and moccasins off, and eaten, the old magician commenced telling him how he had lost his scalp—the insults it was receiving—the pain he was suffering in consequence—his wishes to regain it— the unsuccessful attempts that had already been made, and the numbers and power of those who detained it; stated the best and most probable way of getting it; touching the young man on his pride and ambition, by the proposed adventure, and last, he spoke of such things as would make an Indian rich. He would interrupt his discourse by now and then groaning, and saying, "Oh, how shamefully they are treating it." Odjibwa listened with solemn attention. The old man then asked him about his dreams, his dreams (or *as he saw when asleep**) at the particular time he had fasted and blackened his face to procure guardian spirits.

The young man then told him one dream; the magician groaned; "No, that is not it," he said. The young man told him

---

*Enaw-bandum.

another. He groaned again; "That is not it," he said. The young man told him of two or three others. The magician groaned at each recital, and said, rather peevishly, "No, those are not them." The young man then thought to himself, Who are you? you may groan as much as you please; I am inclined not to tell you any more dreams. The magician then spoke in rather a supplicating tone. "Have you no more dreams of another kind?" "Yes," said the young man, and told him one. "That is it, that is it," he cried; "you will cause me to live. That was what I was wishing you to say"; and he rejoiced greatly. "Will you then go and see if you cannot procure my scalp?" "Yes," said the young man. "I will go; and the day after to-morrow,* when you hear the cries of the Kakak,† you will know, by this sign, that I am successful, and you must prepare your head, and lean it out through the door, so that the moment I arrive, I may place your scalp on." "Yes, yes," said the magician; "as you say, it will be done." Early next morning, he set out on his perilous adventure, and about the time that the sun hangs toward home (afternoon), he heard the shouts of a great many people. He was in a wood at the time, and saw, as he thought, only a few men; but the farther he went, the more numerous they appeared. On emerging into a plain, their heads appeared like the hanging leaves for number. In the centre he perceived a post, and something waving on it, which was the scalp. Now and then the air was rent with the *Sau-sau-quan,* for they were dancing the war dance around it. Before he could be perceived, he turned himself into a No-noskau-see (humming bird), and flew toward the scalp.

As he passed some of those who were standing by, he flew close to their ears, making the humming noise which this bird does when it flies. They jumped on one side and asked each other what it could be. By this time he had nearly reached the scalp, but fearing he should be perceived while untying it, he changed himself into a Me-sau-be-wau-aun (the down of anything that floats lightly on the air), and then floated slowly and lightly on to the scalp. He untied it, and moved off slowly, as the weight was

---

*The Indian expression is Awuss-Waubung—the day *beyond* to-morrow.
†A species of hawk.

almost too great. It was as much as he could do to keep it up, and
prevent the Indians from snatching it away. The moment they
saw it was moving, they filled the air with their cries of "It is
taken from us; it is taken from us." He continued moving a few
feet above them: the rush and hum of the people was like the
dead beating surges after a storm. He soon gained on them, and
they gave up the pursuit. After going a little farther he changed
himself into a Kakak, and flew off with his prize, making that
peculiar noise which this bird makes.

In the meantime, the magician had followed his instructions,
placing his head outside of the lodge, as soon as he heard the cry
of the Kakak, and soon after he heard the rustling of its wings.
In a moment Odjibwa stood before him. He immediately gave the
magician a severe blow on the head with the wampum scalp: his
limbs extended and quivered in agony from the effects of the
blow: the scalp adhered, and the young man walked in and sat
down, feeling perfectly at home. The magician was so long in
recovering from the stunning blow that the young man feared he
had killed him. He was, however, pleased to see him show signs
of life; he first commenced moving, and soon sat up. But how
surprised was Odjibwa to see, not an aged man, far in years and
decrepitude, but one of the handsomest young men he ever saw
stand up before him.

"Thank you, my *friend*," he said; "you see that your kindness
and bravery has restored me to my former shape. It was so
ordained, and you have now accomplished the victory." The young
magician urged the stay of his deliverer for a few days; and they
soon formed a warm attachment for each other. The magician
never alluded to the Red Swan in their conversations.

At last, the day arrived when Odjibwa made preparations to
return. The young magician amply repaid him for his kindness
and bravery by various kinds of wampum, robes, and all such
things as he had need of to make him an influential man. But
though the young man's curiosity was at its height about the Red
Swan, he controlled his feelings, and never so much as even
hinted of her; feeling that he would surrender a point of propriety
in so doing; while the one he had rendered such service to, whose
hospitality he was now enjoying, and who had richly rewarded

him, had never so much as even mentioned anything about her, but studiously concealed her.

Odjibwa's pack for travelling was ready, and he was taking his farewell smoke, when the young magician thus addressed him: "Friend, you know for what cause you came thus far. You have accomplished your object, and conferred a lasting obligation on me. Your perseverance shall not go unrewarded; and if you undertake other things with the same spirit you have this, you will never fail to accomplish them. My duty renders it necessary for me to remain where I am, although I should feel happy to go with you. I have given you all you will need as long as you live; but I see you feel backward to speak about the Red Swan. I vowed that whoever procured me my scalp should be rewarded by possessing the Red Swan." He then spoke, and knocked on the partition. The door immediately opened, and the Red Swan met his eager gaze. She was a most beautiful female, and as she stood majestically before him, it would be impossible to describe her charms, for she looked as if she did not belong to earth. "Take her," the young magician said; "she is my sister, treat her well; she is worthy of you, and what you have done for me merits more. She is ready to go with you to your kindred and friends, and has been so ever since your arrival, and my good wishes go with you both." She then looked very kindly on her husband, who now bid farewell to his friend indeed, and accompanied by the object of his wishes, he commenced retracing his footsteps.

They travelled slowly, and after two or three days reached the lodge of the third old man, who had fed him from his small magic pot. He was very kind, and said, "You see what your perseverance has procured you; do so always and you will succeed in all things you undertake."

On the following morning when they were going to start, he pulled from the side of the lodge a bag, which he presented to the young man, saying, "Nosis, I give you this; it contains a present for you; and I hope you will live happily till old age." They then bid farewell to him and proceeded on.

They soon reached the second old man's lodge. Their reception there was the same as at the first; he also gave them a present, with the old man's wishes that they would be happy. They went on and reached the first town, which the young man had passed in his pursuit. The watchman gave notice, and he was shown into the chief's lodge. "Sit down there, son-in-law," said the chief, pointing to a place near his daughter. "And you also," he said to the Red Swan.

The young woman of the lodge was busy in making something, but she tried to show her indifference about what was taking place, for she did not even raise her head to see who was come. Soon the chief said, "Let some one bring in the bundle of our son-in-law." When it was brought in, the young man opened one of the bags, which he had received from one of the old men; it contained wampum, robes, and various other articles; he presented them to his father-in-law, and all expressed their surprise at the value and richness of the gift. The chief's daughter then only stole a glance at the present, then at Odjibwa and his beautiful wife; she stopped working, and remained silent and thoughtful all the evening. They conversed about his adventures; after this the chief told him that he should take his daughter along with him in the morning;—the young man said "Yes." The chief then spoke out, saying, "Daughter, be ready to go with him in the morning."

There was a Maujeekewis in the lodge, who thought to have got the young woman to wife; he jumped up, saying, "Who is he (meaning the young man), that he should take her for a few presents. I will kill him," and he raised a knife which he had in his hand. But he only waited till some one held him back, and then sat down, for he was too great a coward to do as he had threatened. Early they took their departure, amid the greetings of their new friends, and toward evening reached the other town. The watchman gave the signal, and numbers of men, women, and children stood out to see them. They were again shown into the chief's lodge, who welcomed them by saying, "Son-in-law, you are welcome," and requested him to take a seat by his daughter; and the two women did the same.

After the usual formalities of smoking and eating, the chief requested the young man to relate his travels in the hearing of all the inmates of the lodge, and those who came to see. They looked with admiration and astonishment at the Red Swan, for she was so beautiful. Odjibwa gave them his whole history. The chief then told him that his brothers had been to their town in search of him, but had returned, and given up all hopes of ever seeing him again. He concluded by saying that since he had been so fortunate and so manly, he should take his daughter with him; "For although your brothers," said he, "were here, they were too timid to enter any of our lodges, and merely inquired for you and returned. You will take my daughter, treat her well, and that will bind us more closely together."

It is always the case in towns that some one in it is foolish or clownish. It happened to be so here; for a Maujeekewis was in the lodge; and after the young man had given his father-in-law presents, as he did to the first, this Maujeekewis jumped up in a passion, saying, "Who is this stranger, that he should have her? I want her myself." The chief told him to be quiet, and not to disturb or quarrel with one who was enjoying their hospitality. "No, no," he boisterously cried, and made an attempt to strike the stranger. Odjibwa was above fearing his threats, and paid no attention to him. He cried the louder, "I will have her; I will have her." In an instant he was laid flat on the ground from a blow of a war club given by the chief. After he came to himself, the chief upbraided him for his foolishness, and told him to go out and tell stories to the old women.

Their arrangements were then made, and the stranger invited a number of families to go and visit their hunting grounds, as there was plenty of game. They consented, and in the morning a large party were assembled to accompany the young man; and the chief with a large party of warriors escorted them a long distance. When ready to return the chief made a speech, and invoked the blessing of the great good Spirit on his son-in-law and party.

After a number of days' travel, Odjibwa and his party came in sight of his home. The party rested while he went alone in advance to see his brothers. When he entered the lodge he found it all dirty and covered with ashes: on one side was his eldest brother, with his face blackened, and sitting amid ashes, crying aloud. On the other side was Maujeekewis, his other brother; his face was also blackened, but his head was covered with feathers and swan's down; he looked so odd that the young man could not keep from laughing, for he appeared and pretended to be so absorbed with grief that he did not notice his brother's arrival. The eldest jumped up and shook hands with him and kissed him, and felt very happy to see him again.

Odjibwa, after seeing all things put to rights, told them that he had brought each of them a wife. When Maujeekewis heard about the wife, he jumped up and said, "Why, is it just now that you have come?" and made for the door and peeped out to see the women. He then commenced jumping and laughing, saying, "Women! women!" That was the only reception he gave his brother. Odjibwa then told them to wash themselves and prepare, for he would go and fetch them in. Maujeekewis jumped and washed himself, but would every now and then go and peep out to see the women. When they came near he said, I will have this one, and that one, he did not exactly know which—he would go and sit down for an instant, and then go and peep and laugh; he acted like a madman.

As soon as order was restored, and all seated, Odjibwa presented one of the women to his eldest brother, saying, "These women were given to me; I now give one to each; I intended so from the first." Maujeekewis spoke, and said, "I think three wives would have been *enough* for you. The young man led one to Maujeekewis, saying, "My brother, here is one for you, and live happily." Maujeekewis hung down his head as if he was ashamed, but would every now and then steal a glance at his wife, and also at the other women. By and by he turned toward his wife, and acted as if he had been married for years. "Wife," he said, "I will go and hunt," and off he started.

All lived peaceably for some time, and their town prospered, the inhabitants increased, and everything was abundant among them. One day dissatisfaction was manifested in the conduct of the two elder brothers, on account of Odjibwa's having taken their deceased father's magic arrows: they upbraided and urged him to procure others if he could. Their object was to get him away, so that one of them might afterward get his wife. One day, after listening to them, he told them he would go. Maujeekewis and himself went together into a sweating lodge to purify themselves. Even there, although it was held sacred, Maujeekewis upbraided him for the arrows. He told him again he would go; and next day, true to his word, he left them. After travelling a long way he came to an opening in the earth, and descending, it led him to the abode of departed spirits. The country appeared beautiful, the extent of it was lost in the distance: he saw animals of various kinds in abundance. The first he came near to were buffalo; his surprise was great when these animals addressed him as human beings. They asked him what he came for, how he descended, why he was so bold as to visit the abode of the dead. He told them he was in search of magic arrows to appease his brothers. "Very well," said the leader of the buffaloes, whose whole form was nothing but bone. "Yes, we know it," and he and his followers moved off a little space as if they were afraid of him. "You have come," resumed the Buffalo Spirit, "to a place where a living man has never before been. You will return immediately to your tribe, for your brothers are trying to dishonour your wife; and you will live to a very old age, and live and die happily; you can go no farther in these abodes of ours." Odjibwa looked, as he thought, to the west, and saw a bright light, as if the sun was shining in its splendour, but he saw no sun. "What light is that I see yonder," he asked. The all-boned buffalo answered, "It is the place where those who were good dwell." "And that dark cloud," Odjibwa again asked. "Mudjee-izzhi-wabezewin," (wickedness) answered the buffalo. He asked no more questions, and with the aid of his guardian spirits, again stood on this earth and saw the sun giving light as usual, and breathed the pure air. All else he saw in the abodes of the dead and his travels and actions previous to his return are unknown. After wandering a long time in quest of information to make his people happy, he one evening drew near to his village or town. Passing all the other lodges and coming to his own, he heard his brothers at high words with each other; they were quarrelling for the possession of his wife. She had, however, remained constant and mourned the absence and probable loss of her husband; but she had mourned him with the dignity of virtue. The noble youth listened till he was satisfied of the base principles of his brothers. He then entered the lodge, with the stern air and conscious dignity of a brave and honest man. He spoke not a word, but placing the magic arrows to his bow, drew them to their length and laid the brothers dead at his feet. Thus ended the contest between the hermit's sons, and a firm and happy union was consummated between ODJIBWA,* or him of the primitive or gathered voice, and the Red Swan.

---

*This word may be a derivative from *Ojeebik,* a root, &c. and *maidwa,* voice, or from *odjeebwuh,* to gather, v.a.

AGGO DAH GAUDA

or

THE MAN WITH HIS LEG TIED UP

GGO DAH Gauda had one leg looped up to his thigh, so that he was obliged to get along by hopping. He had a beautiful daughter, and his chief care was to secure her from being carried off by the king of the buffaloes. It was a peculiarity in which he differed from other Indians, that he lived in a log house, and he advised his daughter to keep in doors and never go out into the neighbourhood for fear of being stolen away.

One sunshiny morning Aggo Dah Gauda prepared to go out a fishing, but before he left the lodge reminded his daughter of her strange and persecuting lover. "My daughter," said he, "I am going out to fish, and as the day will be a pleasant one, you must recollect that we have an enemy near, who is constantly going about, and do not expose yourself out of the lodge." When he had reached his fishing ground, he heard a voice singing at a distance the following strains, in derision of him.

Aggo Dah Gauda
Aggo Dah Gauda
Ke anne po—po—
Ko no gun a.

Aggo Dah Gauda
Aggo Dah Gauda
Ke anne po—po—
Ko gau da.

140

Man with the leg tied up,
Man with the leg tied up,
Broken hip—hip—
            Hipped.

Man with the leg tied up,
Man with the leg tied up,
Broken leg—leg—
            Legged.

He saw no one, but suspecting it to come from his enemies the buffaloes, he hastened his return.

Let us now see what happened to the daughter. Her father had not been long absent from the lodge when she thought in her mind [*ke in ain dum*], it is hard to be thus for ever kept in doors. The spring is now coming on, and the days are so sunny and warm, that it would be very pleasant to sit out doors. But my father says it would be dangerous. I know what I will do. I will get on the top of the house, and there I can comb and dress my hair. She accordingly got up on the roof of the small house, and busied herself in untying and combing her beautiful hair. For her hair was not only of a fine glossy quality, but was so long that it reached down on the ground, and hung over the eaves of the house, as she sat dressing it. She was so intent upon this, that she forgot all ideas of danger, till it was too late to escape. For, all of a sudden, the king* of the buffaloes came dashing on, with his herd of followers, and taking her between his horns, away he cantered over the plains, plunged into a river that bounded his land, and carried her safely to his lodge on the other side. Here he paid every attention to gain her affections, but all to no purpose, for she sat pensively and disconsolate in the lodge among the other females, and scarcely ever spoke, and took no part in the domestic cares of her lover the king. He, on the contrary, did every thing

---

*In our Indian languages the highest terms for men in power are KOSINAUN, our father, and OGIMAU, chief. Both admit of a prefixed adjective to indicate great, and of a diminutive inflection to denote inferiority in size, power, or excellence. The term "king" is retained here, from the verbal narration of the interpreters.

he could think of to please her and win her affections. He told
the others in his lodge to give her every thing she wanted, and to
be careful not to displease her. They set before her the choicest
food. They gave her the seat of honour in the lodge. The king
himself went out hunting to obtain the most dainty bits of meat,
both of animals and wild fowl. And not content with these
proofs of his attachment he fasted himself, and would often take
his pib be gwun,* and sit near the lodge indulging his mind in
repeating a few pensive notes.

> Ne ne moo sha
> Ne ne moo sha
> > We yea.

> Ma kow
> We au nin
> > We yea.

> Azhe—azhe
> Sau gee naun ih
> > We yea.

> Ka-go ka-go
> Dush ween e
> Shing gain—
> E me she kain
> > We yea.

> *My sweetheart,*
> *My sweetheart,*
> > *Ah me!*

> *When I think of you,*
> *When I think of you,*
> > *Ah me!*

> *How I love you,*
> *How I love you,*
> > *Ah me!*

---

*Indian flute.

Do not hate me,
Do not hate me,
Ah me!

In the meantime Aggo Dah Gauda came home, and finding his daughter had been stolen, determined to get her back. For this purpose he immediately set out. He could easily track the king, until he came to the banks of the river, and saw that he had plunged in and swam over. But there had been a frosty night or two since, and the water was so covered with thin ice so that he could not walk on it. He determined to encamp till it became solid, and then crossed over and pursued the trail. As he went along he saw branches broken off and strewed behind, for these had been purposely cast along by the daughter, that the way might be found. And the manner in which she had accomplished it, was this: Her hair was all untied when she was caught up, and being very long, it caught on the branches as they darted along, and it was these twigs that she broke off for signs to her father. When he came to the king's lodge it was evening. Carefully approaching it, he peeped through the sides and saw his daughter sitting disconsolately. She immediately caught his eye, and knowing that it was her father come for her, she all at once appeared to relent in her heart, and asking for the dipper, said to the king, "I will go and get you a drink of water." This token of submission delighted him, and he waited with impatience for her return. At last he went out with his followers, but nothing could be seen or heard of the captive daughter. They sallied out in the plains, but had not gone far, by the light of the moon, when a party of hunters, headed by the father-in-law of Aggo Dah Gauda, set up their yells in their rear, and a shower of arrows was poured in upon them. Many of their numbers fell, but the king being stronger and swifter than the rest, fled toward the west, and never again appeared in that part of the country.

While all this was passing Aggo Dah Gauda, who had met his daughter the moment she came out of the lodge, and being helped by his guardian spirit took her on his shoulders and hopped off, a hundred steps in one, till he reached the stream, crossed it, and brought back his daughter in triumph to his lodge.

IOSCO

or

A VISIT TO THE SUN AND MOON

A Tale of Indian Cosmogony, from the Ottowa

ONE DAY five young men and a boy of about ten years of age went out a-shooting with their bows and arrows. They left their lodges with the first appearance of daylight, and having passed through a long reach of woods, had ascended a lofty eminence before the sun arose. While standing there in a group, the sun suddenly burst forth in all the effulgence of a summer's morning. It appeared to them to be at no great distance from the position they occupied. "How very near it is," they all said. "It cannot be far," said Iosco, the eldest, "and if you will accompany me, we will see if we cannot reach it." "I will go! I will go!" burst from every lip. Even the boy said he would also go. They told him he was too young; but he replied, "If you do not permit me to go with you, I will mention your design to each of your parents." They then said to him, "You shall also go with us, so be quiet."

They then fell upon the following arrangement. It was resolved that each one should obtain from his parents as many pairs of moccasins as he could, and also new clothing of leather. They fixed on a spot where they would conceal all their articles, until they were ready to start on their journey, and which would serve, in the meantime, as a place of rendezvous, where they might secretly meet and consult. This being arranged, they returned home.

A long time passed before they could put their plans into execution. But they kept it a profound secret, even to the boy. They frequently met at the appointed place, and discussed the subject. At length every thing was in readiness, and they decided on a day to set out. That morning the boy shed tears for a pair of new leather leggings. "Don't you see," said he to his parents, "how my companions are dressed?" This appeal to their pride and envy prevailed. He obtained the leggings. Artifices were also resorted to by the others, under the plea of going out on a special hunt. They said to one another, but in a tone that they might be overheard, "We will see who will bring in the most game." They went out in different directions, but soon met at the appointed place, where they had hid the articles for their journey, and as many arrows as they had time to make. Each one took something on his back, and they began their march. They travelled day after day, through a thick forest, but the sun was always at the same distance. "We must," said they, "travel toward Waubunong,* and we shall get to the object, some time or other." No one was discouraged, although winter overtook them. They built a lodge and hunted, till they obtained as much dried meat as they could carry, and then continued on. This they did several times; season followed season. More than one winter overtook them. Yet none of them became discouraged, or expressed dissatisfaction.

One day the travellers came to the banks of a river, whose waters ran toward Waubunong. They followed it down many days. As they were walking, one day, they came to rising grounds, from which they saw something white or clear through the trees. They encamped on this elevation. Next morning they came, suddenly, in view of an immense body of water. No land could be seen as far as the eye could reach. One or two of them laid down on the beach to drink. As soon as they got the water into their mouths, they spit it out, and exclaimed with surprise, Shewetagon awbo! [salt water]. It was the sea. While looking on the water, the sun arose as if from the deep, and went on in its steady course through the heavens, enlivening the scene with his cheering and animating beams. They stood in fixed admiration, but the object appeared to be as distant from them as ever. They thought it best

---

*The East—i. e., place of light.

to encamp, and consult whether it were advisable to go on, or return. "We see," said the leader, "that the sun is still on the opposite side of this great water, but let us not be disheartened. We can walk around the shore." To this they all assented.

Next morning they took the northerly shore, to walk around it, but had only gone a short distance when they came to a large river. They again encamped, and while sitting before the fire, the question was put, whether any one of them had ever dreamed of water, or of walking on it. After a long silence, the eldest said he had. Soon after they laid down to sleep. When they arose the following morning, the eldest addressed them: "We have done wrong in coming north. Last night my spirit appeared to me, and told me to go south, and that but a short distance beyond the spot we left yesterday we should come to a river with high banks. That by looking off its mouth, we should see an island, which would approach to us. He directed that we should all get on it. He then told me to cast my eyes toward the water. I did so, and I saw all he had declared. He then informed me that we must return south, and wait at the river until the day after to-morrow. I believe all that was revealed to me in this dream, and that we shall do well to follow it."

The party immediately retraced their footsteps in exact obedience to these intimations. Toward the evening they came to the borders of the indicated river. It had high banks, behind which they encamped, and here they patiently awaited the fulfilment of the dream. The appointed day arrived. They said, we will see if that which has been said will be seen. Midday is the promised time. Early in the morning two had gone to the shore to keep a look out. They waited anxiously for the middle of the day, straining their eyes to see if they could discover any thing. Suddenly they raised a shout. Ewaddee suh neen! There it is! There it is! On rushing to the spot they beheld something like an *island* steadily advancing toward the shore. As it approached, they could discover that something was moving on it in various directions. They said, it is a Manito, let us be off into the woods. No, no, cried the eldest, let us stay and watch. It now became stationary, and lost much of its imagined height. They could only see *three* trees, as they thought, resembling trees in a pinery that had been burnt. The wind, which had been off the sea, now died away into a perfect calm. They saw something leaving the fancied island and approaching the shore, throwing and flapping its wings, like a loon when he attempts to fly in calm weather. It entered the mouth of the river. They were on the point of running away, but the eldest dissuaded them. Let us hide in this hollow, he said, and we will see what it can be. They did so. They soon heard the sounds of chopping, and quickly after they heard the falling of trees. Suddenly a man came up to their place of concealment. He stood still and gazed at them. They did the same in utter amazement. After looking at them for some time, the person advanced and extended his hand toward them. The eldest took it, and they shook hands. He then spoke, but they could not understand each other. He then cried out for his comrades. They came, and examined very minutely their dresses. They again tried to converse. Finding it impossible, the strangers then motioned to the Naubequon, and to the Naubequon-ais,* wishing them to embark. They consulted with each other for a short time. The eldest then motioned that they should go on board. They embarked on board the boat, which they found to be loaded with wood. When they reached the side of the supposed island, they were surprised to see a great number of people, who all came to the side and looked at them with open mouths. One spoke out, above the others, and appeared to be the leader. He motioned them to get on board. He looked and examined them, and took them down into the cabin, and set things before them to eat. He treated them very kindly.

When they came on deck again all the sails were spread, and they were fast losing sight of land. In the course of the night and the following day they were sick at the stomach, but soon recovered. When they had been out at sea ten days, they became sorrowful, as they could not converse with those who had hats on.†

The following night Iosco dreamed that his spirit appeared to

---

*Ship and boat. These terms exhibit the simple and the diminutive forms of the name for ship or vessel. It is also the term for a woman's needlework, and seems to imply a tangled thready mass, and was perhaps transferred in allusion to a ship's ropes.

† *Wewaquonidjig,* a term early and extensively applied to white man, by our Indians, and still frequently used.

him. He told him not to be discouraged, that he would open his ears, so as to be able to understand the people with hats. I will not permit you to understand much, said he, only sufficient to reveal your wants, and to know what is said to you. He repeated this dream to his friends, and they were satisfied and encouraged by it. When they had been out about thirty days, the master of the ship told them, and motioned them to change their dresses of leather for such as his people wore; for if they did not, his master would be displeased. It was on this occasion that the elder first understood a few words of the language. The first phrase he comprehended was *La que notte,* and from one word to another he was soon able to speak it.

One day the men cried out, land! and soon after they heard a noise resembling thunder, in repeated peals. When they had got over their fears, they were shown the large guns which made this noise. Soon after they saw a vessel smaller than their own, sailing out of a bay, in the direction toward them. She had flags on her masts, and when she came near she fired a gun. The large vessel also hoisted her flags, and the boat came alongside. The master told the person who came in it to tell his master or king that he had six strangers on board, such as had never been seen before, and that they were coming to visit him. It was some time after the departure of this messenger before the vessel got up to the town. It was then dark, but they could see people, and horses, and odawbons* ashore. They were landed and placed in a covered vehicle, and driven off. When they stopped, they were taken into a large and splendid room. They were here told that the great chief wished to see them. They were shown into another large room, filled with men and women. All the room was Shoneancauda.† The chief asked them their business, and the object of their journey. They told him where they were from, and where they were going, and the nature of the enterprise which they had undertaken. He tried to dissuade them from its execution, telling them of the many trials and difficulties they would

---

Odawbon comprehends all vehicles between a dog train and a coach, whether on wheels or runners. The term is nearest allied to *vehicle.*
†Massive silver.

have to undergo: that so many days' march from his country dwelt a bad spirit, or Manito, who foreknew and foretold the existence and arrival of all who entered into his country. It is impossible, he said, my children, for you ever to arrive at the object you are in search of.

Iosco replied; "Nosa,"* and they could see the chief blush in being called *father,* "we have come so far on our way, and we will continue it: we have resolved firmly that we will do so. We think our lives are of no value, for we have given them up for this object. Nosa," he repeated, "do not then prevent us from going on our journey." The chief then dismissed them with valuable presents, after having appointed the next day to speak to them again, and provided every thing that they needed or wished for.

Next day they were again summoned to appear before the king. He again tried to dissuade them. He said he would send them back to their country in one of his vessels: but all he said had no effect. "Well," said he, "if you will go, I will furnish you all that is needed for your journey." He had every thing provided accordingly. He told them that three days before they reached the Bad Spirit he had warned them of, they would hear his Shéshegwun.† He cautioned them to be wise, for he felt that he should never see them all again.

They resumed their journey, and travelled sometimes through villages, but they soon left them behind and passed over a region of forests and plains, without inhabitants. They found all the productions of a new country—trees, animals, birds—were entirely different from those they were accustomed to on the other side of the great waters. They travelled, and travelled, till they wore out all of the clothing that had been given to them, and had to take to their leather clothing again.

The three days the chief spoke of meant three years, for it was only at the end of the third year that they came within the sight of the spirit's Shéshegwun. The sound appeared to be near, but they continued walking on, day after day, without apparently getting any nearer to it. Suddenly they came to a very extensive

---

*"My father."
†A rattle.

plain; they could see the blue ridges of distant mountains rising on the horizon beyond it: they pushed on, thinking to get over the plain before night, but they were overtaken by darkness: they were now on a stony part of the plain, covered by about a foot's depth of water: they were weary and fatigued: some of them said, let us lie down; no, no, said the others, let us push on. Soon they stood on firm ground, but it was as much as they could do to stand, for they were very weary. They, however, made an effort to encamp, lighted up a fire, and refreshed themselves by eating. They then commenced conversing about the sound of the spirit's Shéshegwun, which they had heard for several days. Suddenly the instrument commenced; it sounded as if it was subterraneous, and it shook the ground: they tied up their bundles and went toward the spot. They soon came to a large building, which was illuminated. As soon as they came to the door, they were met by a rather elderly man. "How do ye do," said he, "my grandsons? Walk in, walk in; I am glad to see you: I knew when you started: I saw you encamp this evening: sit down, and tell me the news of the country you left, for I feel interested in it." They complied with his wishes, and when they had concluded, each one presented him with a piece of tobacco. He then revealed to them things that would happen in their journey, and predicted its successful accomplishment. "I do not say that all of you," said he, "will successfully go through it. You have passed over three-fourths of your way, and I will tell you how to proceed after you get to the edge of the earth. Soon after you leave this place, you will hear a deafening sound: it is the sky descending on the edge, but it keeps moving up and down; you will watch, and when it moves up, you will see a vacant space between it and the earth. You must not be afraid. A chasm of awful depth is there, which separates the unknown from this earth, and a veil of darkness conceals it. Fear not. You must leap through, and if you succeed you will find yourselves on a beautiful plain, and in a soft and mild light emitted by the moon." They thanked him for his advice. A pause ensued.

"I have told you the way," he said; "now tell me again of the country you have left; for I committed dreadful ravages while I was there: does not the country show marks of it? and do not the inhabitants tell of me to their children? I came to this place to mourn over my bad actions, and am trying, by my present course of life, to relieve my mind of the load that is on it." They told him that their fathers spoke often of a celebrated personage called Manabozho, who performed great exploits. "I am he," said the Spirit. They gazed with astonishment and fear. "Do you see this pointed house?" said he, pointing to one that resembled a sugar-loaf; "you can now each speak your wishes and will be answered from that house. Speak out, and ask what each wants, and it shall be granted." One of them, who was vain, asked with presumption that he might live for ever, and never be in want. He was answered, "Your wish shall be granted." The second made the same request, and received the same answer. The third asked to live longer than common people, and to be always successful in his war excursions, never losing any of his young men. He was told, "Your wishes are granted." The fourth joined in the same request, and received the same reply. The fifth made a humble request, asking to live as long as men generally do, and that he might be crowned with such success in hunting as to be able to provide for his parents and relatives. The sixth made the same request, and it was granted to both, in pleasing tones, from the pointed house.

After hearing these responses they prepared to depart. They were told by Manabozho, that they had been with him but one day, but they afterward found that they had remained there upward of a year. When they were on the point of setting out, Manabozho exclaimed, "Stop! you two, who asked me for eternal life, will receive the boon you wish immediately." He spake, and one was turned into a stone called Shingauba-wossin,* and the other into a cedar-tree. "Now," said he to the others, "you can go." They left him in fear, saying, we were fortunate to escape so, for the king told us he was wicked, and that we should not prob-ably escape from him. They had not proceeded far when they began to hear the sound of the beating sky. It appeared to be near at hand, but they had a long interval to travel before they

---

*A hard primitive stone, frequently found along the borders of the lakes and water-courses, generally fretted into image shapes. Hardness and indestructibility are regarded as its characteristics by the Indians. It is often granite.

came near, and the sound was then stunning to their senses; for when the sky came down, its pressure would force gusts of wind from the opening, so strong that it was with difficulty they could keep their feet, and the sun passed but a short distance above their heads. They, however, approached boldly, but had to wait some time before they could muster courage enough to leap through the dark veil that covered the passage. The sky would come down with violence, but it would rise slowly and gradually. The two who had made the humble request stood near the edge, and with no little exertion, succeeded, one after the other, in leaping through, and gaining a firm foothold. The remaining two were fearful and undecided: the others spoke to them through the darkness, saying, "Leap! leap! the sky is on its way down." These two looked up and saw it descending, but fear paralyzed their efforts; they made but a feeble attempt, so as to reach the opposite side with their hands; but the sky at the same time struck on the earth with great violence and a terrible sound, and forced them into the dreadful black chasm.

The two successful adventurers found themselves in a beautiful country, lighted by the moon, which shed around a mild and pleasant light. They could see the moon approaching as if it were from behind a hill. They advanced, and an aged woman spoke to them; she had a white face and pleasing air, and looked rather old, though she spoke to them very kindly: they knew from her first appearance that she was the moon: she asked them several questions: she told them that she knew of their coming, and was happy to see them: she informed them that they were half way to her brother's, and that from the earth to her abode was half the distance. "I will, by and by, have leisure," said she, "and will go and conduct you to my brother, for he is now absent on his daily course: you will succeed in your object, and return in safety to your country and friends, with the good wishes, I am sure, of my brother." While the travellers were with her, they received every attention. When the proper time arrived, she said to them, "My brother is now rising from below, and we shall see his light as he comes over the distant edge: come," said she, "I will lead you up." They went forward, but in some mysterious way they hardly knew how: they rose almost directly up, as if they had ascended steps. They then came upon an immense plain, declining in the direction of the sun's approach. When he came near, the moon spake—"I have brought you these persons, whom we knew were coming"; and with this she disappeared. The sun motioned with his hand for them to follow him. They did so, but found it rather difficult, as the way was steep: they found it particularly so from the edge of the earth till they got halfway between that point and midday: when they reached this spot, the sun stopped, and sat down to rest. "What, my children," said he, "has brought you here? I could not speak to you before: I could not stop at any place but this, for this is my first resting place—then at the centre, which is at midday, and then halfway from that to the western edge.* "Tell me," he continued, "the object of your undertaking this journey and all the circumstances which have happened to you on the way." They complied. Iosco told him their main object was to see him. They had lost four of their friends on the way, and they wished to know whether they could return in safety to the earth, that they might inform their friends and relatives of all that had befallen them. They concluded by requesting him to grant their wishes. He replied, "Yes, you shall certainly return in safety; but your companions were vain and presumptuous in their demands. They were Gug-ge-baw-diz-ze-wug.† They aspired to what Manitoes only could enjoy. But you two, as I said, shall get back to your country, and become as happy as the hunter's life can make you. You shall never be in want of the necessaries of life, as long as you are permitted to live; and you will have the satisfaction of relating your journey to your friends, and also of telling them of me. Follow me, follow me," he said, commencing his course again. The ascent was now gradual, and they soon came to a level plain. After travelling some time he again sat down to rest, for they had arrived at Nau-we-qua.‡ "You see," said he, "it is level at this place, but a short distance onwards, my way descends gradually to my last resting place, from which there is

---

*This computation of time separates the day into four portions of six hours each—two of which, from 1 to 6, and from 6 to 12, A.M., compose the *morning,* and the other two, from 1 to 6, and from 6 to 12, P.M., compose the *evening.*
†This is a verbal form, plural number, of the transitive adjective "foolish."
‡Midday, or middle line.

an abrupt descent." He repeated his assurance that they should be shielded from danger, if they relied firmly on his power. "Come here quickly," he said, placing something before them on which they could descend; "keep firm," said he, as they resumed the descent. They went downward as if they had been let down by ropes.

In the meantime the parents of these two young men dreamed that their sons were returning, and that they should soon see them. They placed the fullest confidence in their dreams. Early in the morning they left their lodges for a remote point in the forest, where they expected to meet them. They were not long at the place before they saw the adventurers returning, for they had descended not far from that place. The young men knew they were their fathers. They met, and were happy. They related all that had befallen them. They did not conceal any thing; and they expressed their gratitude to the different Manitoes who had preserved them, by feasting and gifts, and particularly to the sun and moon, who had received them as their children.

The foregoing tale was related by Chusco, an Ottowa chief, converted to Christianity a few years ago. He was born at L'arbre Croche, in Michigan, some years after the taking of Fort Mackinac, in 1763,—an event of such notoriety in Indian tradition that it is generally referred to by them as an era. He was present at the treaty of Greenville, in 1793, and received an annuity during the last few years of his life in consequence of a promise understood to have been made to him by General Wayne.

Chusco was a man of small stature; he appears to have possessed great bodily activity in his youth, united to a mind of quick observation. He embraced, at an early period of his life, the profession of seer, and practised it with the approbation of his tribe till within a few years. About 1827 his mind was arrested by the truths of revelation, which were first brought to his notice by his wife, who had been instructed at a mission on the island of Mackinac. He made a profession of religion within a year or two after, renounced his idolatry, gave up the use of ardent spirits and every species of fermented drink, and exhibited a consistent Christian life, to the period of his death, in 1837. He is buried at Round Island, in Lake Huron, where a neat paling has been placed over his grave. The story itself, so far as respects the object, is calculated to remind the reader of South American history, of the alleged descent of Manco Capac and the Children of the Sun. But I am not prepared to say that an examination of the traditional history of the Algics will sustain the comparison.

The tale does not appear to be of great comparative antiquity. The introduction of ships, and guns, and axes, is sufficient to indicate this. It is interesting, however, as revealing their notions of cosmogony, the division of the day into quartads, and their impressions of general geography. It would appear that they believe the earth to be *globular,* they speak of but a single sea. The tradition of Manabozho is attested, and he is here represented, as in all other known instances, to be a Bad, and not a Good Spirit, and there is no countenance given to the verbal opinion, sometimes expressed, that this personage partakes of any of the characters of a Saviour.

The moral bearing of the story is, perhaps, to indicate the danger of ambition. Ambition and presumption, in human wishes, are very clearly rebuked by the results of the oracular response, and by the immediate fulfilment of the predictions.

THE TWO JEEBI-UG*

or

A TRIAL OF FEELING

From the Odjibwa

THERE LIVED a hunter in the north who had a wife and one child. His lodge stood far off in the forest, several days' journey from any other. He spent his days in hunting, and his evenings in relating to his wife the incidents that had befallen him. As game was very abundant he found no difficulty in killing as much as they wanted. Just in all his acts, he lived a peaceful and happy life.

One evening during the winter season, it chanced that he remained out later than usual, and his wife began to feel uneasy, for fear some accident had befallen him. It was already dark. She listened attentively and at last heard the sound of approaching footsteps. Not doubting it was her husband, she went to the door and beheld two strange females. She bade them enter, and invited them to remain.

She observed that they were total strangers in the country. There was something so peculiar in their looks, air, and manner, that she was uneasy in their company. They would not come near the fire; they sat in a remote part of the lodge, were shy and taciturn, and drew their garments about them in such a manner as nearly to hide their faces. So far as she could judge, they were pale, hollow-eyed, and long-visaged, very thin and emaciated.

---

*Ghosts.

156

There was but little light in the lodge, as the fire was low, and served, by its fitful flashes, rather to increase than dispel their fears. "Merciful spirit!" cried a voice from the opposite part of the lodge, "there are two corpses clothed with garments." The hunter's wife turned around, but seeing nobody, she concluded the sounds were but gusts of wind. She trembled, and was ready to sink to the earth.

Her husband at this moment entered and dispelled her fears. He threw down the carcass of a large fat deer. "Behold what a fine and fat animal," cried the mysterious females, and they immediately ran and pulled off pieces of the whitest fat,* which they ate with greediness. The hunter and his wife looked on with astonishment, but remained silent. They supposed their guests might have been famished. Next day, however, the same unusual conduct was repeated. The strange females tore off the fat and devoured it with eagerness. The third day the hunter thought he would anticipate their wants by tying up a portion of the fattest pieces for them, which he placed on the top of his load. They accepted it, but still appeared dissatisfied, and went to the wife's portion and tore off more. The man and his wife felt surprised at such rude and unaccountable conduct, but they remained silent, for they respected their guests, and had observed that they had been attended with marked good luck during the residence of these mysterious visiters.

In other respects the deportment of the females was strictly unexceptionable. They were modest, distant, and silent. They never uttered a word during the day. At night they would occupy themselves in procuring wood, which they carried to the lodge, and then returning the implements exactly to the places in which they had found them, resume their places without speaking. They were never known to stay out until daylight. They never laughed or jested.

The winter had nearly passed away without anything uncommon happening when, one evening, the hunter stayed out very late. The moment he entered and laid down his day's hunt as usual

---

*The fat of animals is esteemed by the N. A. Indians as among the choicest parts.

before his wife, the two females began to tear off the fat, in so unceremonious a way that her anger was excited. She constrained herself, however, in a measure, but did not conceal her feelings, although she said but little. The guests observed the excited state of her mind, and became unusually reserved and uneasy. The good hunter saw the change, and carefully inquired into the cause, but his wife denied having used any hard words. They retired to their couches, and he tried to compose himself to sleep, but could not, for the sobs and sighs of the two females were incessant. He arose on his couch and addressed them as follows:

"Tell me," said he, "what is it that gives you pain of mind, and causes you to utter those sighs. Has my wife given you offence, or trespassed on the rights of hospitality?"

They replied in the negative. "We have been treated by you with kindness and affection. It is not for any slight we have received that we weep. Our mission is not to you only. We come from the land of the dead to test mankind, and to try the sincerity of the living. Often we have heard the bereaved by death say that if the dead could be restored, they would devote their lives to make them happy. We have been moved by the bitter lamentations which have reached the place of the dead, and have come to make proof of the sincerity of those who have lost friends. Three moons were allotted to us by the Master of Life to make the trial. More than half the time had been successfully past, when the angry feelings of your wife indicated the irksomeness you felt at our presence, and has made us resolve on our departure."

They continued to talk to the hunter and his wife, gave them instructions as to a future life, and pronounced a blessing upon them.

"There is one point," they added, "of which we wish to speak. You have thought our conduct very strange in rudely possessing ourselves of the choicest parts of your hunt. *That* was the point of trial selected to put you to. It is the wife's peculiar privilege. For another to usurp it, we knew to be the severest trial of her, and consequently of your temper and feelings. We know your manners and customs, but we came to prove you, not by a compliance with them, but a violation of them. Pardon us. We are the agents of him who sent us. Peace to your dwelling, adieu!"

When they ceased, total darkness filled the lodge. No object could be seen. The inmates heard the door open and shut, but they never saw more of the two JEEBI-UG.

The hunter found the success which they had promised. He became celebrated in the chase, and never wanted for any thing. He had many children, all of whom grew up to manhood, and health, peace, and long life were the rewards of his hospitality.

PAH-HAH-UNDOOTAH

or

THE RED HEAD

A Sioux Tale

AS SPRING approaches, the Indians return from their wintering ground to their villages, engage in feasting, soon exhaust their stock of provisions, and begin to suffer for the want of food. Such of the hunters as are of an active and enterprising cast of character take the occasion to separate from the mass of the population, and remove to some neighbouring locality in the forest, which promises the means of subsistence during this season of general lassitude and enjoyment.

Among the families who thus separated themselves, on a certain occasion, there was a man called ODSIIEDOPH* WAUCHEENTONGAH, or the Child of Strong Desires, who had a wife and one son. After a day's travel he reached an ample wood with his family, which was thought to be a suitable place to encamp. The wife fixed the lodge, while the husband went out to hunt. Early in the evening he returned with a deer. Being tired and thirsty he asked his son to go to the river for some water. The son replied that it was dark and he was afraid. He urged him to go, saying that his mother, as well as himself, was tired, and the distance to the water was very short. But no persuasion was of any avail. He refused to go. "Ah, my son," said the father, at last, "if you are afraid to go to the river you will never kill the Red Head."

---

*[possibly ODSHEDOPH].

The boy was deeply mortified by this observation. It seemed to call up all his latent energies. He mused in silence. He refused to eat, and made no reply when spoken to.

The next day he asked his mother to dress the skin of the deer, and make it into moccasins for him, while he busied himself in preparing a bow and arrows. As soon as these things were done, he left the lodge one morning at sunrise, without saying a word to his father or mother. He fired one of his arrows in the air, which fell westward. He took that course, and at night coming to the spot where the arrow had fallen, was rejoiced to find it piercing the heart of a deer. He refreshed himself with a meal of the venison, and the next morning fired another arrow. After travelling all day, he found it also in another deer. In this manner he fired four arrows, and every evening found that he had killed a deer. What was very singular, however, was that he left the arrows sticking in the carcass, and passed on without withdrawing them. In consequence of this, he had no arrow for the fifth day, and was in great distress at night for the want of food. At last he threw himself upon the ground in despair, concluding that he might as well perish there as go farther. But he had not lain long before he heard a hollow, rumbling noise in the ground beneath him. He sprang up, and discovered at a distance the figure of a human being, walking with a stick. He looked attentively and saw that the figure was walking in a wide beaten path, in a prairie, leading from a lodge to a lake. To his surprise this lodge was at no great distance. He approached a little nearer and concealed himself. He soon discovered that the figure was no other than that of the terrible witch, WOK-ON-KAHTOHN-ZOOEYAH´ PEE-KAH-HAITCHEE, or the Little Old Woman Who Makes War. Her path to the lake was perfectly smooth and solid, and the noise our adventurer had heard was caused by the striking of her walking staff upon the ground. The top of this staff was decorated with a string of the toes and bills of birds of every kind, who at every stroke of the stick, fluttered and sung their various notes in concert.

She entered her lodge and laid off her mantle, which was entirely composed of the scalps of women. Before folding it, she shook it several times, and at every shake the scalps uttered loud shouts of laughter, in which the old hag joined. Nothing could have frightened him more than this horrific exhibition. After laying by the cloak she came directly to him. She informed him that she had known him from the time he left his father's lodge, and watched his movements. She told him not to fear or despair, for she would be his friend and protector. She invited him into her lodge, and gave him a supper. During the repast, she inquired of him his motives for visiting her. He related his history, stated the manner in which he had been disgraced, and the difficulties he laboured under. She cheered him with the assurance of her friendship, and told him he would be a brave man yet.

She then commenced the exercise of her power upon him. His hair being very short she took a large leaden comb, and after drawing it through his hair several times, it became of a handsome feminine length. She then proceeded to dress him as a female, furnishing him with the necessary garments, and decorated his face with paints of the most beautiful dye. She gave him a bowl of shining metal. She directed him to put in his girdle a blade of scented sword-grass, and to proceed the next morning to the banks of the lake, which was no other than that over which the Red Head reigned. Now PAH-HAH-UNDOOTAH, or the Red Head, was a most powerful sorcerer and the terror of all the country, living upon an island in the centre of the lake.

She informed him that there would be many Indians on the island, who as soon as they saw him use the shining bowl to drink with, would come and solicit him to be their wife, and to take him over to the island. These offers he was to refuse, and say that he had come a great distance to be the wife of the Red Head, and that if the chief could not come for her in his own canoe, she should return to her village. She said that as soon as the Red Head heard of this, he would come for her in his own canoe, in which she must embark. On reaching the island he must consent to be his wife, and in the evening induce him to take a walk out of the village, when he was to take the first opportunity to cut off his head with the blade of grass. She also gave him general advice how he was to conduct himself to sustain his assumed character of a woman. His fear would scarcely permit him to accede to this plan, but the recollection of his father's words and looks decided him.

Early in the morning, he left the witch's lodge, and took the hard beaten path to the banks of the lake. He reached the water at a point directly opposite the Red Head's village. It was a beautiful day. The heavens were clear, and the sun shone out in the greatest effulgence. He had not been long there, having sauntered along the beach, when he displayed the glittering bowl, by dipping water from the lake. Very soon a number of canoes came off from the island. The men admired his dress, and were charmed by his beauty, and a great number made proposals of marriage. These he promptly declined, agreeably to the concerted plan. When the facts were reported to the Red Head, he ordered his canoe to be put in the water by his chosen men, and crossed over to see this wonderful girl. As he came near the shore, he saw that the ribs of the sorcerer's canoe were formed of living rattlesnakes, whose heads pointed outward to guard him from enemies. Our adventurer had no sooner stepped into the canoe then they began to hiss and rattle, which put him in a great fright. But the magician spoke to them, after which they became pacified and quiet, and all at once they were at the landing upon the island. The marriage immediately took place, and the bride made presents of various valuables which had been furnished by the old witch.

As they were sitting in the lodge surrounded by friends and relatives, the mother of the Red Head regarded the face of her new daughter-in-law for a long time with fixed attention. From this scrutiny she was convinced that this singular and hasty marriage augured no good to her son. She drew her husband aside and disclosed to him her suspicions: This can be no female, said she, the figure and manners, the countenance, and more especially the expression of the eyes, are, beyond a doubt, those of a man. Her husband immediately rejected her suspicions, and rebuked her severely for the indignity offered to her daughter-in-law. He became so angry, that seizing the first thing that came to hand, which happened to be his pipe stem, he beat her unmercifully. This act requiring to be explained to the spectators, the mock bride immediately rose up, and assuming an air of offended dignity, told the Red Head that after receiving so gross an insult from his relatives he could not think of remaining with him as his wife, but should forthwith return to his village and friends. He left the lodge followed by the Red Head, and walked until he came upon the beach of the island, near the spot where they had first landed. Red Head entreated him to remain. He pressed him by every motive which he thought might have weight, but they were all rejected. During this conference they had seated themselves upon the ground, and Red Head, in great affliction, reclined his head upon his fancied wife's lap. This was the opportunity ardently sought for, and it was improved to the best advantage. Every means was taken to lull him to sleep, and partly by a soothing manner, and partly by a seeming compliance with his request, the object was at last attained. Red Head fell into a sound sleep. Our aspirant, for the glory of a brave man, then drew his blade of grass, and drawing it once across the neck of the Red Head completely severed the head from the body.

He immediately stripped off his dress, seized the bleeding head, and plunging into the lake, swam safely over to the main shore. He had scarcely reached it, when looking back he saw amid the darkness, the torches of persons come out in search of the new-married couple. He listened till they had found the headless body, and he heard their piercing shrieks of sorrow, as he took his way to the lodge of his kind adviser.

She received him with rejoicing. She admired his prudence, and told him his bravery could never be questioned again. Lifting up the head, she said he need only have brought the scalp. She cut off a small piece for herself, and told him he might now return with the head, which would be evidence of an achievement that would cause the Indians to respect him. In your way home, she said, you will meet with but one difficulty. MAUNKAH KEESH WOCCAUNG, or the Spirit of the Earth, requires an offering from those who perform extraordinary achievements. As you walk along in a prairie, there will be an earthquake. The earth will open and divide the prairie in the middle. Take this partridge and throw it into the opening, and instantly spring over it. All this happened precisely as it had been foretold. He cast the partridge into the crevice and leapt over it. He then proceeded without obstruction to a place near his village, where he secreted his trophy. On entering the village he found his parents had returned from the place of their spring encampment, and were in great sorrow for their son, whom they supposed to be lost. One and another of the young men had presented themselves to the disconsolate parents, and said, "Look up, I am your son." Having been often deceived in this manner, when their own son actually presented himself, they sat with their heads down, and with their eyes nearly blinded with weeping. It was some time before they could be prevailed upon to bestow a glance upon him. It was still longer before they recognised him for their son; when he recounted his adventures they believed him mad. The young men laughed at him. He left the lodge and soon returned with his trophy. It was soon recognised. All doubts of the reality of his adventures now vanished. He was greeted with joy and placed among the first warriors of the nation. He finally became a chief, and his family were ever after respected and esteemed.

LEELINAU

or

THE LOST DAUGHTER

An Odjibwa Tale

L EELINAU WAS the favourite daughter of an able hunter who lived near the base of the lofty highlands called Kaug Wudjoo, on the shore of Lake Superior. From her earliest youth she was observed to be pensive and timid, and to spend much of her time in solitude and fasting. Whenever she could leave her father's lodge she would fly to remote haunts and recesses in the woods, or sit upon some high promontory of rock overlooking the lake. In such places she was supposed to invoke her guardian spirit. But amid all the sylvan haunts, so numerous in a highly picturesque section of country, none had so great attractions for her mind as a forest of pines, on the open shore, called Manitowak, or the Sacred Grove. It was one of those consecrated places which are supposed to be the residence of the PUK WUDJ ININEE, or Little Wild Men of the Woods, and MISHEN IMOKINAKOG, or Turtle-Spirits, two classes of minor spirits or fairies who love romantic scenes. Owing to this notion, it was seldom visited by Indians, who attribute to these imaginary beings a mischievous agency. And whenever they were compelled by stress of weather to make a landing on this part of the coast, they never failed to leave an offering of tobacco or some other article.

To this fearful spot Leelinau had made her way at an early age, gathering strange flowers or plants, which she would bring home to her parents, and relate to them all the little incidents that had

occurred in her rambles. Although they discountenanced her visits
to the place, they were unable to restrain them, for they did not
wish to lay any violent commands upon her. Her attachment to
the spot, therefore, increased with her age. If she wished to propi-
tiate her spirits to procure pleasant dreams, or any other favour,
she repaired to the Manitowok. If her father remained out later
than usual, and it was feared he had been overwhelmed by the tempest, or met with some other accident, she offered up her prayers
at the Manitowok. It was there that she fasted, supplicated, and
strolled. And she spent so much of her time there, that her parents
began to suspect some bad spirit had enticed her to its haunts,
and thrown a charm around her which she was unable to resist.
This conjecture was confirmed by her mother (who had secretly
followed her) overhearing her repeat sentiments like these.

> Spirit of the dancing leaves
> Hear a throbbing heart that grieves,
> Not for joys this world can give,
> But the life that spirits live:
> Spirits of the foaming billow,
> Visit thou my nightly pillow,
> Shedding o'er it silver dreams,
> Of the mountain brooks and streams,
> Sunny glades, and golden hours,
> Such as suit thy buoyant powers:
> Spirit of the starry night,
> Pencil out thy fleecy light,
> That my footprints still may lead
> To the blush-let Miscodeed,*
> Or the flower to passion true
> Yielding free its carmine hue:
> Spirit of the morning dawn,
> Waft thy fleecy columns on,
> Snowy white, or tender blue
> Such as brave men love to view.
> Spirit of the green wood plume
> Shed around thy leaf perfume

Claytonia Virginica.

Such as spring from buds of gold
Which thy tiny hands unfold.
Spirits hither quick repair,
Hear a maiden's evening prayer.

The effect of these visits was to render the daughter dissatisfied
with the realities of life, and to disqualify her for an active and
useful participation in its duties. She became melancholy and taciturn. She had permitted her mind to dwell so much on imaginary
scenes, that she at last mistook them for realities, and sighed for
an existence inconsistent with the accidents of mortality. The
consequence was, a disrelish for all the ordinary sources of amusement and employment, which engaged her equals in years. When
the girls of the neighbouring lodges assembled to play at the
favourite game of pappus-e-kowaun,* before the lodge door,
Leelinau would sit vacantly by, or enter so feebly into the spirit
of the play, as to show plainly that it was irksome to her. Again,
in the evening, when the youths and girls formed a social ring
around the lodge, and the piepeendjigun† passed rapidly from
hand to hand, she either handed it along without attempting to
play, or if she played, it was with no effort to swell her count. Her
parents saw that she was a prey to some secret power, and
attempted to divert her in every way they could. They favoured
the attentions paid to her by a man much her senior in years, but
who had the reputation of great activity, and was the eldest son
of a neighbouring chief. But she could not be persuaded to listen
to the proposal. Supposing her aversion merely the result of natural
timidity, her objections were not deemed of a serious character;
and in a state of society where matches are left very much in the
hands of the parents, they proceeded to make the customary
arrangements for the union. The young man was informed,
through his parents, that his offer had been favourably received.
The day was fixed for the marriage visit to the lodge, and the
persons who were to be present were invited. As the favourable

---

*A game played by females with sticks and two small blocks on a string.
†A game played with a piece of perforated leather and a bone.

expression of the will of the parents had been explicitly given, and compliance was as certainly expected, she saw no means of frustrating the object, but by a firm declaration of her sentiments. She told her parents that she could never consent to the match, and that her mind was unalterably made up.

It had been her custom to pass many of her hours in her favourite place of retirement, under a low, broad-topped young pine, whose leaves whispered in the wind. Thither she now went, and while leaning pensively against its trunk, she fancied she heard articulate sounds. Very soon they became more distinct, and appeared to address her.

> Maiden, think me not a tree
> But thine own dear lover free,
> Tall and youthful in my bloom
> With the bright green nodding plume.
> Thou art leaning on my breast,
> Lean for ever there, and rest!
> Fly from man, that bloody race,
> Pards, assassins, bold and base;
> Quit their din, and false parade
> For the quiet lonely shade.
> Leave the windy birchen cot
> For my own, light happy lot,
> O'er thee I my veil will fling,
> Light as beetle's silken wing;
> I will breathe perfume of flowers,
> O'er thy happy evening hours;
> I will in my shell canoe
> Waft thee o'er the waters blue;
> I will deck thy mantle fold,
> With the sun's last rays of gold.
> Come, and on the mountain free
> Rove a fairy bright with me.

Her fancy confirmed all she heard as the words of sober truth. She needed nothing more to settle her purpose.

On the evening preceding the day fixed for her marriage, she dressed herself in her best garments. She arranged her hair according to the fashion of her tribe, and put on the ornaments she possessed. Thus robed, she assumed an air of unwonted gayety, as she presented herself before her parents. I am going, said she, to meet my little lover, the chieftain of the green plume, who is waiting for me at the Spirit Grove; and her countenance expressed a buoyant delight, which she had seldom evinced. They were quite pleased with these evidences of restored cheerfulness, supposing she was going to act some harmless freak. "I am going," said she, to her mother, as she left the lodge, "from one who has watched my infancy, and guarded my youth. Who has given me medicine when I was sick, and prepared me food when I was well. I am going from a father who has ranged the forest to procure the choicest skins for my dress, and kept his lodge supplied with the best food of the chase. I am going from a lodge which has been my shelter from the storms of winter, and my shield from the heats of summer. Adieu! adieu!" she cried as she skipped lightly over the plain.

So saying she hastened to the confines of the fairy haunted grove. As it was her common resort, no alarm was entertained, and the parents confidently waited her return with the sunset hour. But as she did not arrive, they began to feel uneasy. Darkness approached, and no daughter returned. They now lighted torches of pine wood, and proceeded to the gloomy forest of pines, but were wholly unsuccessful in the search. They called aloud upon her name, but the echo was their only reply. Next day the search was renewed, but with no better success. Suns rose and set, but they rose and set upon a bereaved father and mother, who were never afterward permitted to behold a daughter whose manners and habits they had not sufficiently guarded, and whose inclinations they had, in the end, too violently thwarted.

One night a party of fishermen, who were spearing fish near the Spirit Grove, descried something resembling a female figure standing on the shore. As the evening was mild, and the waters calm, they cautiously paddled their canoe ashore, but the slight ripple of the water excited alarm. The figure fled, but they recognised, in the shape and dress, as she ascended the bank, the lost daughter, and they saw the green plumes of her lover waving over his forehead, as he glided lightly through the forest of young pines.

PUCK WUDJ ININEE

An Odjibwa Tale

T HERE WAS a time when all the inhabitants of the earth had
died, excepting two helpless children, a baby boy, and a
little girl. When their parents died, these children were
asleep. The little girl, who was the elder, was the first to awake.
She looked around her, but seeing nobody besides her little
brother, who lay asleep, she quietly resumed her bed. At the end
of ten days her brother moved without opening his eyes. At the end
of ten days more he changed his position, lying on the other side.

The girl soon grew up to woman's estate, but the boy increased
in stature very slowly. It was a long time before he could even
creep. When he was able to walk, his sister made him a little bow
and arrows, and suspended around his neck a small shell, saying,
you shall be called WA-DAIS-AIS-IMID, or He of the Little Shell.
Every day he would go out with his little bow shooting at the
small birds. The first bird he killed was a tomtit. His sister was
highly pleased when he took it to her. She carefully skinned and
stuffed it, and put it away for him. The next day he killed a red
squirrel. His sister preserved this too. The third day he killed a
partridge (Peéna), which she stuffed and set up. After this, he
acquired more courage, and would venture some distance from
home. His skill and success as a hunter daily increased, and he
killed the deer, bear, moose, and other large animals inhabiting
the forest. In time he became a great hunter.

He had now arrived to maturity of years, but remained a perfect infant in stature. One day walking about he came to a small
lake. It was in the winter season. He saw a man on the ice killing
beavers. He appeared to be a giant. Comparing himself to this

171

great man he appeared no bigger than an insect. He seated himself on the shore, and watched his movements. When the large man had killed many beavers, he put them on a hand sled, which he had, and pursued his way home. When he saw him retire, he followed him, and wielding his magic shell, cut off the tail of one of the beavers, and ran home with his trophy. When the tall stranger reached his lodge, with his sled load of beavers, he was surprised to find the tail of one of them gone, for he had not observed the movements of the little hero of the shell.

The next day WA-DAIS-AIS-IMID went to the same lake. The man had already fixed his load of beavers on his *odaw'bon* or sled, and commenced his return. But he nimbly ran forward, and overtaking him, succeeded, by the same means, in securing another of the beavers' tails. When the man saw that he had lost another of this most esteemed part of the animal, he was very angry. I wonder, said he, what dog it is, that has thus cheated me. Could I meet him, I would make his flesh quiver at the point of my lance. Next day he pursued his hunting at the beaver dam near the lake, and was followed again by the little man of the shell. On this occasion the hunter had used so much expedition, that he had accomplished his object, and nearly reached his home, before our tiny hero could overtake him. He nimbly drew his shell and cut off another beaver's tail. In all these pranks, he availed himself of his power of invisibility, and thus escaped observation. When the man saw that the trick had been so often repeated, his anger was greater than ever. He gave vent to his feelings in words. He looked carefully around to see whether he could discover any tracks. But he could find none. His unknown visiter had stepped so lightly as to leave no track.

Next day he resolved to disappoint him by going to his beaver pond very early. When WA-DAIS-AIS-IMID reached the place, he found the fresh traces of his work, but he had already returned. He followed his tracks, but failed to overtake him. When he came in sight of the lodge the stranger was in front of it, employed in skinning his beavers. As he stood looking at him, he thought, I will let him see me. Presently the man, who proved to be no less a personage than Manabozho, looked up and saw him. After regarding him with attention, "who are you, little

man," said Manabozho. "I have a mind to kill you." The little
hero of the shell replied, "If you were to try to kill me you could
not do it."

When he returned home he told his sister that they must separate. "I must go away," said he, "it is my fate. You too," he added,
"must go away soon. Tell me where you would wish to dwell."
She said, "I would like to go to the place of the breaking of daylight. I have always loved the east. The earliest glimpses of light
are from that quarter, and it is, to my mind, the most beautiful
part of the heavens. After I get there, my brother, whenever you
see the clouds in that direction of various colours, you may think
that your sister is painting her face."

"And I," said he, "my sister, shall live on the mountains and
rocks. There I can see you at the earliest hour, and there the streams
of water are clear, and the air pure. And I shall ever be called PUCK
WUDJ ININEE, or the little wild man of the mountains."

"But," he resumed, "before we part for ever, I must go and try
to find some Manitoes." He left her and travelled over the surface
of the globe, and then went far down into the earth. He had been
treated well wherever he went. At last he found a giant Manito,
who had a large kettle, which was for ever boiling. The giant
regarded him with a stern look, and then took him up in his
hand, and threw him unceremoniously into the kettle. But by the
protection of his personal spirit, he was shielded from harm, and
with much ado got out of it and escaped. He returned to his sister, and related his rovings and misadventures. He finished his
story by addressing her thus: "My sister, there is a Manito, at
each of the four corners of the earth.* There is also one above
them, far in the sky, and last," continued he, "there is another,
and wicked one, who lives deep down in the earth. We must now
separate. When the winds blow from the four corners of the earth
you must then go. They will carry you to the place you wish. I go
to the rocks and mountains, where my kindred will ever delight
to dwell." He then took his ball stick, and commenced running
up a high mountain, whooping as he went. Presently the winds

---

*The opinion that the earth is a square and level plain, and that the winds blow from its
four corners, is a very ancient eastern opinion.

blew, and as he predicted his sister was borne by them to the eastern sky, where she has ever since been, and her name is the Morning Star.

> Blow, winds, blow! my sister lingers
>   For her dwelling in the sky,
> Where the morn, with rosy fingers,
>   Shall her cheeks with vermil dye.
>
> There, my earliest views directed,
>   Shall from her their colour take,
> And her smiles, through clouds reflected,
>   Guide me on, by wood or lake.
>
> While I range the highest mountains,
>   Sport in valleys green and low,
> Or beside our Indian fountains
>   Raise my tiny hip holla.

MISHOSHA

or

THE MAGICIAN OF THE LAKES

I N AN early age of the world, when there were fewer inhabitants than there now are, there lived an Indian, in a remote place, who had a wife and two children. They seldom saw any one out of the circle of their own lodge. Animals were abundant in so secluded a situation, and the man found no difficulty in supplying his family with food.

In this way they lived in peace and happiness, which might have continued if the hunter had not found cause to suspect his wife. She secretly cherished an attachment for a young man whom she accidentally met one day in the woods. She even planned the death of her husband for his sake, for she knew if she did not kill her husband, her husband, the moment he detected her crime, would kill her.

The husband, however, eluded her project by his readiness and decision. He narrowly watched her movements. One day he secretly followed her footsteps into the forest, and having concealed himself behind a tree, he soon beheld a tall young man approach and lead away his wife. His arrows were in his hands, but he did not use them. He thought he would kill her the moment she returned.

Meantime, he went home and sat down to think. At last he came to the determination of quitting her for ever, thinking that her own conscience would punish her sufficiently, and relying on her maternal feelings to take care of the two children, who were boys, he immediately took up his arms and departed.

When the wife returned she was disappointed in not finding her husband, for she had now concerted her plan, and intended

175

to have despatched him. She waited several days, thinking he might have been led away by the chase, but finding he did not return, she suspected the true cause. Leaving her two children in the lodge, she told them she was going a short distance and would return. She then fled to her paramour and came back no more.

The children thus abandoned, soon made way with the food left in the lodge, and were compelled to quit it in search of more. The eldest boy, who was of an intrepid temper, was strongly attached to his brother, frequently carrying him when he became weary, and gathering all the wild fruit he saw. They wandered deeper and deeper into the forest, losing all traces of their former habitation, until they were completely lost in its mazes.

The eldest boy had a knife, with which he made a bow and arrows, and was thus enabled to kill a few birds for himself and brother. In this manner they continued to pass on, from one piece of forest to another, not knowing whither they were going. At length they saw an opening through the woods, and were shortly afterward delighted to find themselves on the borders of a large lake. Here the elder brother busied himself in picking the seed pods of the wild rose, which he preserved as food. In the meantime, the younger brother amused himself by shooting arrows in the sand, one of which happened to fall into the lake. PANIGWUN,* the elder brother, not willing to lose the arrow, waded in the water to reach it. Just as he was about to grasp the arrow, a canoe passed up to him with great rapidity. An old man, sitting in the centre, seized the affrighted youth and placed him in the canoe. In vain the boy addressed him—"My grandfather (a term of respect for old people), pray take my little brother also. Alone, I cannot go with you; he will starve if I leave him." Mishosha (the old man) only laughed at him. Then uttering the charm, CHEMAUN POLL, and giving his canoe a slap, it glided through the water with inconceivable swiftness. In a few moments they reached the habitation of the magician, standing on an island in the centre of the lake. Here he lived with his two daughters, who managed the affairs of his household. Leading the young

---

*The end wing feather.

man up to the lodge, he addressed his eldest daughter. "Here,"
said he, "my daughter, I have brought a young man to be your
husband." Husband! thought the young woman; rather another
victim of your bad arts, and your insatiate enmity to the human
race. But she made no reply, seeming thereby to acquiesce in her
father's will.

The young man thought he saw surprise depicted in the eyes of
the daughter, during the scene of this introduction, and determined to watch events narrowly. In the evening he overheard the
two daughters in conversation. "There," said the eldest daughter,
"I told you he would not be satisfied with his last sacrifice. He
has brought another victim, under the pretence of providing me
a husband. Husband, indeed! the poor youth will be in some horrible predicament before another sun has set. When shall we be
spared the scenes of vice and wickedness which are daily taking
place before our eyes."

Panigwun took the first opportunity of acquainting the
daughters how he had been carried off, and been compelled to
leave his little brother on the shore. They told him to wait until
their father was asleep, then to get up and take his canoe, and
using the charm he had obtained, it would carry him quickly to
his brother. That he could carry him food, prepare a lodge for
him, and be back before daybreak. He did, in every respect, as he
had been directed—the canoe obeyed the charm, and carried him
safely over, and after providing for the subsistence of his brother,
told him that in a short time he should come for him. Then
returning to the enchanted island, he resumed his place in the
lodge, before the magician awoke. Once, during the night,
Mishosha awoke, and not seeing his destined son-in-law, asked
his daughter what had become of him. She replied that he had
merely stepped out, and would be back soon. This satisfied him.
In the morning, finding the young man in the lodge, his suspicions were completely lulled. "I see, my daughter," said he, "you
have told the truth."

As soon as the sun arose, Mishosha thus addressed the young
man. "Come, my son, I have a mind to gather gulls' eggs. I know
an island where there are great quantities, and I wish your aid in
getting them." The young man saw no reasonable excuse; and

getting into the canoe, the magician gave it a slap, and uttering a command, they were in an instant at the island. They found the shores strown with gulls' eggs, and the island full of birds of this species. "Go, my son," said the old man, "and gather the eggs, while I remain in the canoe."

But Panigwun had no sooner got ashore, than Mishosha pushed his canoe a little from the land, and exclaimed—"Listen, ye gulls! you have long expected an offering from me. I now give you a victim. Fly down and devour him." Then striking his canoe, he left the young man to his fate.

The birds immediately came in clouds around their victim, darkening the air with their numbers. But the youth seizing the first that came near him, and drawing his knife, cut off its head. He immediately skinned the bird, and hung the feathers as a trophy on his breast. "Thus," he exclaimed, "will I treat every one of you who approaches me. Forbear, therefore, and listen to my words. It is not for you to eat human flesh. You have been given by the Great Spirit as food for man. Neither is it in the power of that old magician to do you any good. Take me on your backs and carry me to his lodge, and you shall see that I am not ungrateful." The gulls obeyed; collecting in a cloud for him to rest upon, and quickly flew to the lodge, where they arrived before the magician. The daughters were surprised at his return, but Mishosha, on entering the lodge, conducted himself as if nothing extraordinary had taken place.

The next day he again addressed the youth:—"Come, my son," said he, "I will take you to an island covered with the most beautiful stones and pebbles, looking like silver. I wish you to assist me in gathering some of them. They will make handsome ornaments, and possess great medicinal virtues." Entering the canoe, the magician made use of his charm, and they were carried in a few moments to a solitary bay in an island, where there was a smooth sandy beach. The young man went ashore as usual, and began to search. "A little farther, a little farther," cried the old man. "Upon that rock you will get some fine ones." Then pushing his canoe from land—"Come, thou great king of fishes," cried the old man; "you have long expected an offering from me. Come, and eat the stranger whom I have just put ashore on your island." So saying, he commanded his canoe to return, and it was soon out of sight.

Immediately, a monstrous fish thrust his long snout from the water, crawling partially on the beach, and opening wide his jaws to receive his victim. "When!" exclaimed the young man, drawing his knife and putting himself in a threatening attitude, "When did you ever taste human flesh? Have a care of yourself. You were given by the Great Spirit to man, and if you or any of your tribe eat human flesh, you will fall sick and die. Listen not to the words of that wicked man, but carry me back to his island, in return for which I will present you a piece of red cloth." The fish complied, raising his back out of the water to allow the young man to get on. Then taking his way through the lake, he landed his charge safely on the island before the return of the magician. The daughters were still more surprised to see that he had escaped the arts of their father the second time. But the old man on his return maintained his taciturnity and self-composure. He could not, however, help saying to himself—"What manner of boy is this, who is ever escaping from my power. But his spirit shall not save him. I will entrap him to-morrow. Ha, ha, ha!"

Next day the magician addressed the young man as follows: "Come, my son," said he, "you must go with me to procure some young eagles. I wish to tame them. I have discovered an island where they are in great abundance." When they had reached the island, Mishosha led him inland until they came to the foot of a tall pine, upon which the nests were. "Now, my son," said he, "climb up this tree and bring down the birds." The young man obeyed. When he had with great difficulty got near the nest, "Now," exclaimed the magician, addressing the tree, "stretch yourself up and be very tall." The tree rose up at the command. "Listen, ye eagles," continued the old man, "you have long expected a gift from me. I now present you this boy, who has had the presumption to molest your young. Stretch forth your claws and seize him." So saying he left the young man to his fate, and returned.

But the intrepid youth drawing his knife, and cutting off the head of the first eagle that menaced him, raised his voice and exclaimed, "Thus will I deal with all who come near me. What right have you, ye ravenous birds, who were made to feed on beasts, to eat human flesh? Is it because that cowardly old canoe-man has bid you do so? He is an old woman. He can neither do you good nor harm. See, I have already slain one of your number. Respect my bravery, and carry me back that I may show you how I shall treat you."

The eagles, pleased with his spirit, assented, and clustering thick around him formed a seat with their backs, and flew toward the enchanted island. As they crossed the water they passed over the magician, lying half asleep in his canoe.

The return of the young man was hailed with joy by the daughters, who now plainly saw that he was under the guidance of a strong spirit. But the ire of the old man was excited, although he kept his temper under subjection. He taxed his wits for some new mode of ridding himself of the youth, who had so success-fully baffled his skill. He next invited him to go a hunting.

Taking his canoe, they proceeded to an island and built a lodge to shelter themselves during the night. In the mean while the magician caused a deep fall of snow, with a storm of wind and severe cold. According to custom, the young man pulled off his moccasins and leggings and hung them before the fire to dry. After he had gone to sleep the magician, watching his opportunity, got up, and taking one moccasin and one legging, threw them into the fire. He then went to sleep. In the morning, stretching himself as he arose and uttering an exclamation of surprise, "My son," said he, "what has become of your moccasin and legging? I believe this is the moon in which fire attracts, and I fear they have been drawn in." The young man suspected the true cause of his loss, and rightly attributed it to a design of the magician to freeze him to death on the march. But he maintained the strictest silence, and drawing his conaus over his head thus communed with himself: "I have full faith in the Manito who has preserved me thus far, I do not fear that he will forsake me in this cruel and emergency. Great is his power, and I invoke it now that he may enable me to prevail over this wicked enemy of mankind."

He then drew on the remaining moccasin and legging, and taking a dead coal from the fireplace, invoked his spirit to give it efficacy, and blackened his foot and leg as far as the lost garment usually reached. He then got up and announced himself ready

for the march. In vain Mishosha led him through snows and
over morasses, hoping to see the lad sink at every moment. But
in this he was disappointed, and for the first time they returned
home together.

Taking courage from this success, the young man now determined to try his own power, having previously consulted with the
daughters. They all agreed that the life the old man led was
detestable, and that whoever would rid the world of him, would
entitle himself to the thanks of the human race.

On the following day the young man thus addressed his hoary
captor. "My grandfather, I have often gone with you on perilous
excursions and never murmured. I must now request that you
will accompany me. I wish to visit my little brother, and to bring
him home with me." They accordingly went on a visit to the main
land, and found the little lad in the spot where he had been left.
After taking him into the canoe, the young man again addressed
the magician: "My grandfather, will you go and cut me a few of
those red willows on the bank, I wish to prepare some smoking
mixture." "Certainly, my son," replied the old man, "what you
wish is not very hard. Ha, ha, ha! do you think me too old to get
up there?" No sooner was Mishosha ashore, than the young man,
placing himself in the proper position struck the canoe with his
hand, and pronouncing the charm, N'CHIMAUN POLL, the canoe
immediately flew through the water on its return to the island. It
was evening when the two brothers arrived, and carried the canoe
ashore. But the elder daughter informed the young man that unless
he sat up and watched the canoe, and kept his hand upon it, such
was the power of their father, it would slip off and return to him.
Panigwun watched faithfully till near the dawn of day, when he
could no longer resist the drowsiness which oppressed him, and
he fell into a short doze. In the meantime the canoe slipped off
and sought its master, who soon returned in high glee. "Ha, ha,
ha! my son," said he; "you thought to play me a trick. It was very
clever. But you see I am too old for you."

A short time after, the youth again addressed the magician.
"My grandfather, I wish to try my skill in hunting. It is said there
is plenty of game on an island not far off, and I have to request
that you will take me there in your canoe." They accordingly

went to the island and spent the day in hunting. Night coming on they put up a temporary lodge. When the magician had sunk into a profound sleep, the young man got up, and taking one of Mishosha's leggings and moccasins from the place where they hung, threw them into the fire, thus retaliating the artifice before played upon himself. He had discovered that the foot and leg were the only vulnerable parts of the magician's body. Having committed these articles to the fire, he besought his Manito that he would raise a great storm of snow, wind, and hail, and then laid himself down beside the old man. Consternation was depicted on the countenance of the latter, when he awoke in the morning and found his moccasin and legging missing. "I believe, my grandfather," said the young man, "that this is the moon in which fire attracts, and I fear your foot and leg garments have been drawn in." Then rising and bidding the old man follow him, he began the morning's hunt, frequently turning to see how Mishosha kept up. He saw him faltering at every step, and almost benumbed with cold, but encouraged him to follow, saying, we shall soon get through and reach the shore; although he took pains, at the same time, to lead him in roundabout ways, so as to let the frost take complete effect. At length the old man reached the brink of the island where the woods are succeeded by a border of smooth sand. But he could go no farther; his legs became stiff and refused motion, and he found himself fixed to the spot. But he still kept stretching out his arms and swinging his body to and fro. Every moment he found the numbness creeping higher. He felt his legs growing downward like roots, the feathers of his head turned to leaves, and in a few seconds he stood a tall and stiff sycamore, leaning toward the water.

Panigwun leaped into the canoe, and pronouncing the charm, was soon transported to the island, where he related his victory to the daughters. They applauded the deed, agreed to put on mortal shapes, become wives to the two young men, and for ever quit the enchanted island. And passing immediately over to the main land, they lived lives of happiness and peace.

THE WEENDIGOES*

A Saginaw Story

O NCE THERE lived in a lonely forest a man and his wife, who had a son. The father went out every day, according to the custom of the Indians, to hunt for food, to support his family. One day while he was absent, his wife, on going out of the lodge, looked toward the lake that was near, and saw a very large man walking on the water, and coming fast toward the lodge. He had already advanced so near that flight was useless. She thought to herself, what shall I say to the monster that will please him. As he came near, she ran in, and taking the hand of her son, a boy of three or four years old, led him out. Speaking very loud, "See, my son," said she, "your grandfather," and then added in a conciliatory tone, "he will have pity on us." The giant advanced, and said sneeringly, "Yes, my son." And then addressing the woman said, "Have you anything to eat?" Fortunately the lodge was filled with meat of various kinds. The woman thought to please him by handing him some cooked meat, but he pushed it away in a dissatisfied manner, and took up the raw carcass of a deer, which he *glutted* up, sucking the bones, and drinking the blood.

When the hunter came home, he was surprised to see the monster, for he looked very frightful. He had again brought home the whole carcass of a deer, which he had no sooner put down than the cannibal seized it, tore it to pieces, and devoured it, as if it had been a mere mouthful. The hunter looked at him with fear

---

*The radix of this word is not apparent. The term is used to signify cannibal, giant, monster. The plural termination in *es* is in accordance with the rule of number in English orthography, applied to originally foreign substantives ending in *o,* as in potatoes, mulattoes, &c., and previously applied in relation to Indian words, in Winnebagoes, Otoes, &c.

and astonishment, telling his wife that he was afraid for their lives, as this monster was one whom Indians called Weendigo. He did not even dare to speak to him, nor did the cannibal say a word, but as soon as he had finished his meal, he laid himself down and fell asleep.

Early next morning he told the hunter that he should also go out hunting, and they went together. Toward evening they returned, the man bringing a deer, but the Weendigo brought home the bodies of two Indians, whom he had killed. He very composedly sat down and commenced tearing the limbs apart, breaking the bones with his teeth, and despatching them as easily as if they had been soft pieces of flesh. He was not even satisfied with that, but again took up the deer which the hunter had brought, to finish his supper, while the hunter and his family had to live on their dried meat.

In this manner the hunter and the Weendigo lived for some time, and it is remarkable that the monster never made an attempt on their lives, although the ground outside the lodge was white with the human bones he had cast out. He was always still and gloomy, and seldom spake to them. One evening he told the hunter that the time had now arrived for him to take his leave, but before doing so he would give him a charm, that would always make him successful in killing moose. This charm consisted of two arrows, and after giving them to the hunter he thanked him and his wife for their kindness, and departed, saying that he had all the world to travel over.

The hunter and his wife felt happy when freed from his presence, for they had expected, at every mment, to have been devoured by him. He tried the virtues of his arrows, and never failed to be suc-cessful in their use. They had lived in this manner for a year, when a great evil befell them. The hunter was absent one day when his wife, on going out of the lodge, saw something like a black cloud approaching. She looked till it came near, when she perceived that it was another Weendigo. She apprehended no danger, thinking he would treat them as the first one had done. In this she was wholly mistaken. Unluckily they had but a small portion of moose meat in the lodge. The Weendigo looked around for something to eat, and being disappointed he took the lodge and threw it to the winds. He hardly seemed to notice the woman, for she was but a morsel to him. However, he grasped her by the waist. Her cries and entreaties, with those of her son, had no effect—the monster tore out her entrails, and taking her body at one mouthful, started off without noticing the boy, probably thinking it was not worth his while to take half a mouthful.

When the hunter returned from the forest, he did not know what to think. His lodge was gone, and he saw his son sitting near the spot where it had stood, shedding tears. On a nearer approach he saw a few remains of his wife, and his son related all the circumstances of her death. The man blackened his face and vowed in his heart he would have revenge. He built another lodge, and collecting the remains of his wife, placed them in the hollow part of a dry tree. He left his boy to take care of the lodge while he was absent, hunting, and would roam about from place to place, trying to forget his misfortune. He made a bow and arrows for his son, and did every thing in his power to please him.

One day, while he was absent, his son shot his arrows out, through the top of the lodge, but when he went out to look for them he could not find them. His father made him some more, and when he was again left alone, he shot one of them out, but although he paid particular attention to the spot where it fell, he could not find it. He shot another, and immediately ran out of the lodge to see where it fell. He was surprised to see a beautiful boy, just in the act of taking it up, and running with it toward a large tree, where he disappeared. He followed, and having come to the tree, he beheld the face of the boy, looking out through an opening in the hollow part. *Nha-ha** (oh dear), he said, my friend, come out and play with me. And he urged him till he consented. They played and shot their arrows by turns. Suddenly the younger boy said, "Your father is coming. We must stop. Promise me that you will not tell him." The elder promised, and the other disappeared in the tree. The elder boy then went home, and when his father returned from the chase, sat demurely by the fire. In the course of the evening he asked his father to make him a new bow.

---

*This phrase is peculiar to boys and girls, and is sung repeating it several times.

To an inquiry of his father as to the use he meant to make of two bows, he replied, that one might break, or get lost; he then consented. Next day, after his father had gone, he went to his friend, and invited him to come out and play, and at the same time presented him the new bow. They went and played in the lodge together, and raised the ashes all over it. Suddenly again the youngest said, "Your father is coming, I must leave." He again exacted a promise of secrecy, and went back to his tree. The eldest took his seat near the fire. When the hunter came in, he was surprised to see the ashes scattered about. "Why, my son," said he, "you must have played very hard to-day to raise such a dust, all alone." "Yes," said the boy, "I was lonesome, and ran round and round—*that* is the cause of it."

Next day the hunter made ready for the chase as usual. The boy said, "Father, try and hunt all day, and see what you can kill." As soon as he had gone, the boy called his friend, and they played and chased each other round the lodge. The man was returning and came to a rising piece of ground, when he heard his son laughing and making a noise, but the sounds appeared as if they arose from *two* persons playing. At the same instant the young boy of the tree stopped, and after saying, "Your father is coming," ran off to the tree, which stood near the lodge. The hunter, on entering, found his son sitting near the fire, very quiet, but he was much surprised to see all the articles of the lodge lying in various directions. "Why, my son," said he, "you must play *very* hard, every day, and what do you do all alone to throw about all our things in this manner, and cause the ashes to spread about the lodge?" The boy again made excuse. "Father," said he, "I play in *this* manner—I chase and drag my coat around the lodge, and that is the reason you see ashes spread about." The hunter was not satisfied until he saw his son play with the coat, which he did so adroitly as to deceive him. Next day the boy repeated his request that the father would be absent all day, and see if he could not kill *two* deer. He thought it strange for his son to make such a request, and rather suspected something. He, however, went into the forest, and when out of sight, his son went for his young companion to the tree, and they resumed their sports. The father, on coming home at evening, when he reached the rising ground, which almost overlooked the lodge, heard again the sounds of laughing and playing, and could not be mistaken; he was now certain there were two voices. The boy from the tree had barely time to escape, when he entered and found his son, sitting as usual, near the fire. When he was seated and cast his eyes around, he saw the lodge was in worse confusion than before. "My son," said he, "you must be very foolish, when alone, to play so. But tell me—I heard two voices, I am certain," and he looked closely on the prints of the footsteps in the ashes. "True," he said, "here is the print of a foot that is smaller than my son's," which satisfied him that his suspicions were well founded, and that some very young person had played with his son. The boy, at this time, thought best to tell his father all that had been done. "Why, father," said he, "I found a boy in the hollow of the tree, near the lodge, where you put my mother's bones." Strange thoughts came over the man; he thought that this little boy might have been created from the remains of his deceased wife. But as Indians are generally fearful of disturbing the dead, he did not dare to go near the place where he had placed her remains. He thought best to tell his son, and make him promise, that he would entice his friend to a dead tree, that was near their lodge, by telling him that they could kill many flying squirrels by setting fire to it. He said he would conceal himself near by, and take the boy. Next day the hunter went into the woods, and his son went and insisted on his friend's going with him to kill the squirrels. He objected that his father was near, but was, at length, persuaded to go, and, after they had set fire to the tree, and while they were busy in killing the squirrels, the father suddenly made his appearance and clasped the boy in his arms. He cried out, "Kago! Kago! (don't, don't) you will tear my clothes"—which appeared to have been made of a fine transparent skin. The father tried to reassure him by every means in his power. By long-continued kindness, he, at last, succeeded, and the boy was reconciled to his new situation; but it was owing principally to the society of his friend. The father now knew that it was the Great Spirit who had thus miraculously raised him a son from the remains of his wife; and he felt persuaded that the boy would, in time, become a great man, and aid him in his revenge on the Weendigoes.

The hunter was now more reconciled to the loss of his wife, and spent as much time as he could spare from the chase, in attending to his sons. But what was very remarkable, both his sons retained their low stature, although they were well formed and beautiful.

One day he advised his sons not to go near a certain lake, which, he said, was inhabited by foul birds, who were vicious and dangerous. In the course of one of their rambles, the boys had wandered near it, and they came out and stood on its banks. They saw, on one side, a mountain, rising precipitously from the water, and reaching apparently to the sky. They stood and looked for some time with astonishment at the sight. The youngest spoke and said, "I see no harm in climbing the rock to see what is to be discovered on its top." They ascended, and had got up, with difficulty, half way, when the rumbling noise of thunder was heard, and lightning began to play near them. But they were undaunted, and reached the top, where they beheld an enormous bird's nest, and in it two very large young birds. Although they had only the soft down, as yet, on their bodies, they appeared to be monsters, and when the young men put a stick near their eyes, which they opened and shut very quick, the flashes they emitted broke the stick in pieces. They, however, took the young birds, and with great difficulty reached the lodge with them. When their father came home, they told him what fine birds they had, and requested him to tame them, and bring them up as pets, "for," said they, "when we took them we intended them for you." They told him where they had procured them, saying, that he need not have given them the caution respecting the dangers of the lake. The father was now convinced that both his sons were gifted with supernatural powers. He, however, advised them not to go near another lake he told them of, which was inhabited by *Mishe-genabigoes.* * When he was again absent, the boys wandered near that lake, and as they were talking, they heard some one ordering them away, and telling them not to make so much noise. "Who are you?" they answered. "I am Mishegenabig," cried the same voice; "and who are you that dare to disobey me?" The youngest boy told his brother to sing some magic words, while he

---

*Monstrous serpents.

went in search of the one who had so insultingly spoken to them; and while he waded into the water, the other sang these words:

LITERAL TRANSLATION

O pau neence	*Little slave—*
In de go wish	*Bad monster—*
Se nau bun	*I spy him—*
Opunai sun	*His diminutive liver—*
Mau moke e sagin.	*Peeping out* (as a mushroom suddenly

shooting out of the ground, or a thing appearing from beneath the water, and applied generally to a person, or noun animate, unexpectedly appearing as a mushroom, &c.)

He continued singing as he was directed, and he soon saw pieces of liver floating on the water. Soon after his brother returned from under the water with a mishegenabig, whom he dragged by his horns. "Brother," said he, "this is the one who was so insolent to us. We will now go home and make a pet of him." When they reached home they told their father that they had brought him another pet. Their father was thoughtful. He was surprised to see his son overcome all manner of monsters; he, however, kept silent, and rejoiced in spirit to think that his sons were so fortunate in commencing life.

One day, after musing for a long time, he told his sons that his time was come, and that he should have to follow his forefathers to the land of the west. "But," he continued, "before I leave this earth, my sons, listen to my advice." He proceeded to speak to them, and when he had done, the youngest said, "Father, you must remember the Weendigoes, and the misery they brought on you. You will now leave earth, with your two feathered favourites; but first we will feed them with the flesh of the Mishegenabig." They did so, and their father departed amid thunder and lightnings, for the two birds were the offspring of thunder. He fixed his residence as directed by the Great Manito in the sky toward the north, and he retains his name to the present day, which is, The Thunder Commencing in the North, and Going South.*

---

*Thunder from this part of the heavens is called, by the Indians, the autumnal thunder. It is the last generally heard for the season, and they say, speaking of it in the plural, that "they are hollaing on their way home."

This story exhibits the mind of the Saginaws in a characteristic light. This tribe are emphatically the Seminoles of the North, consisting originally of individuals who were refugees from the great Odjibwa family. Their origin, as a distinct band, is comparatively recent, dating no farther back than the time of the flight of the Sauks from the district of country which is now, in allusion to them, denominated Saginaw. The principal town of that adventurous and warlike tribe, was, and is still, called by the natives SAUKINONG (i.e. Sauk-town), and the Chippewa refugees who succeed, took their denomination of Saginaws from the term. Without further allusion to their history, it may be observed, that the Saginaws have never made the least advances in education or religion. Cruelty, deception, intemperance, and a blind adherence to the idolatrous customs and superstitions of the nation from which they sprang, have been their characteristics. Up to this day, there is not a school, or teacher, or preacher, among them. There is not one individual of unmixed blood in the tribe who can read, or has any pretence to the knowledge of Christianity. Most of their lore is of murders and thefts committed, or vicious adventures of some sort. They have been, emphatically, a band of plunderers. They bore a conspicuous part in the depredations committed on the frontiers of Virginia and Pennsylvania, during the revolutionary, and Wayne's war. Their late leader and head chief, KISHKAKO, was a perfect Abællino in purpose, who spent a long life in iniquities, private and public, and would, at last, have paid the forfeit of his life on the gallows, had he not committed suicide in jail.

The tales of this tribe, of which there are three specimens furnished, partake strongly of the character of the tribe. They have less originality, less moral, and less adherence to the ancient manners and customs of the original stock, than any other of the traditionary fictions yet examined. There is also less purity of language in the original, and a strong dash of vulgarity, which it has required some care to keep out of the translation.

THE RACOON AND CRAWFISH

A Fable from the Odjibwa

THE RACOON searches the margins of streams for shell-fish, where he is generally sure of finding the AS-[?]HOG-AISH-I,* or crawfish. Indian story says, that the enmity between these two species, and the consequent wariness of each for the other, was such, that the poor racoon, with all his stealthiness, was at last put to great straits for a meal. The crawfish would no longer venture near the shore, and the racoon was on the point of starvation. At length he fixed on this expedient to decoy his enemy.

Knowing the crawfish to feed on worms, he procured a quantity of old rotten wood (filled with these worms) and stuffing it in his mouth and ears, and powdering it over his body, he lay down by the water's edge, to induce the belief that he was dead.

An old crawfish came out warily from the water, and crawled around and over his apparently deceased enemy. He rejoiced to find an end put to his murderous career, and cried out to his fellows, "Come up my brothers and sisters, Aissibun† is dead, come up and eat him." When a great multitude had gathered around, the racoon suddenly sprung up, and set to killing and devouring them in such a way that not one was left alive.

While he was still engaged with the broken limbs, a little female crawfish, carrying her infant sister on her back, came up, seeking her relations. Finding they had all been devoured by the Racoon, she resolved not to survive the destruction of her kindred, but went boldly up to the enemy and said, "Here, Aissibun, you behold

---

*[This spelling is unclear in the original edition. The third letter resembles the number 3.]
†The Racoon.

191

me and my little sister. We are all alone. You have eaten up our parents, and all our friends, eat us too." And she continued plaintively singing her chant.

> Racoon, racoon, monster thin!
> You have murdered all my kin:
> Leave not one to pine alone
> On those shores so late our own.
> You have glutted not a few,
> Stealthy monster, eat us too—
> Let the work be finished soon,
>   *Aissibun amoon.**

> Here, behold us! linger not,
> Sad and lone is now my lot:
> One poor sister, young and small,
> Now makes up my little all—
> She a baby—faint and weak,
> Who cannot yet "mother" speak—
> Come, you monster, eat us soon,
>   *Aissibun amoon.*

> Once my people, lodge and band,
> Stretched their numbers through the land;
> Roving brooks and limpid streams,
> By the moon's benignant beams.
> First in revel, dance, and play,
> Now, alas! ah! where are they?
> Clutch us, monster,—eat us soon,
>   *Aissibun amoon.*

The Racoon felt reproached by this act of courage and magnanimity. "No," said he, "I have banqueted on the largest and the fattest,—I will not dishonour myself by such little prey."

At this moment Manabozha happened to pass by. Seeing how things were, "Tyau!" said he to the Racoon, "thou art a thief and an unmerciful dog. Get thee up into the trees, lest I change thee

---

*"Racoon, eat us."

into one of these same worm-fish, for thou wast thyself originally a shell, and bearest in thy name the influence of my transforming hand."*

He then took up the little supplicant crawfish and her infant sister and cast them into the stream. "There," said he, "you may dwell. Hide yourselves under the stones, and hereafter you shall be playthings for little children."

---

*The name of the Racoon in the Chippewa language appears to be a derivation from *Ais,* a shell, with the inflection for the perfect past tense (bun) united with the copulative vowel *i*. But no tale of such transformation, as is here alluded to, has been met with.

LA POUDRE

or

THE STORM-FOOL

From the Odjibwa

THE VERNAL equinox in America, north of the 44° of north latitude, generally takes place while the ground is covered with snow, and winter still wears a polar aspect. Storms of wind and light drifting snow, expressively called *poudre* by the French of the upper Lakes, fill the atmosphere, and render it impossible to distinguish objects at a short distance. The fine powdery flakes of snow are driven into the smallest crannies of buildings and fixtures, and seem to be endowed with a subtile power of insinuation, which renders northern joinerwork but a poor defence. It is not uncommon for the sleeper on waking up in the morning, to find heaps of snow, where he had supposed himself quite secure on lying down.

Such seasons are, almost invariably, times of scarcity and hunger with the Indians, for the light snows have buried up the traps of the hunters, and the fishermen are deterred from exercising their customary skill in decoying fish through the ice. They are often reduced to the greatest straits, and compelled to exercise their utmost ingenuity to keep their children from starving. Abstinence, on the part of the elder members of the family, is regarded both as a duty and a merit. Every effort is made to satisfy the importunity of the little ones for food, and if there be a story-teller in the lodge, he is sure to draw upon his cabin lore, to amuse their minds, and beguile the time.

In these storms, when each inmate of the lodge has his *conaus,* or wrapper, tightly drawn around him, and all are cowering around the cabin fire, should some sudden puff of wind drive a volume of light snow into the lodge, it would scarcely happen, but that some one of the group would cry out "Ah, Pauppukeewiss is now gathering his harvest," an expression which has the effect to put them all into good humour.

Pauppukeewiss was a crazy brain who played many queer tricks, but took care, nevertheless, to supply his family and children with food. But, in this, he was not always successful. Many winters have passed since he was overtaken, at this very season of the year, with great want, and he, with his whole family, was on the point of starvation. Every resource seemed to have failed. The snow was so deep, and the storm continued so long, that he could not even find a partridge or a hare. And his usual resource of fish had entirely failed. His lodge stood in a point of woods, not far back from the shores of the Gitchiguma, or Great Water, where the autumnal storms had piled up the ice into high pinnacles, resembling castles.

"I will go," said he to his family one morning, "to these castles, and solicit the pity of the spirits who inhabit them, for I know that they are the residence of some of the spirits of Kabiboonoka." He did so, and found that his petition was not disregarded. They told him to fill his mushkemoots, or sacks, with the ice and snow, and pass on toward his lodge, without looking back, until he came to a certain hill. He must then drop his sacks, and leave them till morning, when he would find them filled with fish.

They cautioned him that he must by no means look back, although he would hear a great many voices crying out to him, in abusive terms, for these voices were nothing but the wind playing through the branches of the trees. He faithfully obeyed the injunction, although he found it hard to avoid turning round to see who was calling out to him. And when he visited his sacks in the morning, he found them filled with fish.

It chanced that Manabozho visited him on the morning that he brought home the sacks of fish. He was invited to partake of

a feast, which Pauppukeewiss ordered to be prepared for him.
While they were eating, Manabozho could not help asking him
by what means he had procured such an abundance of food at a
time when they were all in a state of starvation.

Pauppukeewiss frankly told him the secret, and repeated the
precautions which were necessary to ensure success. Manabozho
determined to profit by his information, and as soon as he could
he set out to visit the icy castles. All things happened as he had
been told. The spirits seemed propitious, and told him to fill and
carry. He accordingly filled his sacks with ice and snow, and proceeded rapidly toward the hill of transmutation. But as he ran he
heard voices calling out behind him, "Thief! thief! He has stolen
fish from Kabiboonoka," cried one. "Mukumik! mukumik! Take
it away! Take it away!"cried another.

In fine his ears were so assailed by all manner of opprobrious
terms that he could not avoid turning his head to see who it was
that thus abused him. But his curiosity dissolved the charm.
When he came to visit his bags next morning, he found them
filled with ice and snow.

In consequence, he is condemned every year, during the month
of March, to run over the hills, with Pauppukeewiss following
him, with the cries of "Mukumik! mukumik!"

This trick seems put, with allegoric justice, on Manabozho, on account of his vain-glorious boasting, and imitation of others; for there
was nothing done by anyone which he did not deem himself adequate
to, and immediately set about to perform. Story-tellers say he was once
rebuked for this spirit, by a little child who, picking up his foot, put his
great toe in his mouth, which Manabozho tried but could not do. The
Odjibwas apply the term PEEWUN to the kind of finely granulated
snow-storm above alluded to.

GIT-CHEE-GAU-ZINEE

or

THE TRANCE

The following story is related by the Odjibwas as semi-traditionary. Without attaching importance to it, in that light, it may be regarded as indicating Indian opinion on the temporary suspension of nervous action in trance, and on the (to them) great unknown void of a future state. The individual, whose name it bears, is vouched to have been an actual personage living on the shores of Lake Superior, where he exercised the authority of a village chief.

In former times, it is averred, the Chippewas followed the custom of interring many articles with the dead, including, if the deceased was a male, his gun, trap, pipe, kettle, war-club, clothes, wampum, ornaments, and even a portion of food. This practice has been gradually falling into disuse, until at present it is rare to see the Indians deposit any articles of value with adults. What effect tales like the following may have had, in bringing this ancient pagan custom into discredit, we will not undertake to decide. Much of the change of opinion which has supervened, within the last century, may be fairly attributable to the intercourse of the Indians with white men, and in some situations to the gradual and almost imperceptible influence of Christianity on their external manners and customs. Still, more is probably due to the keen observation of a people who have very little property, and may be naturally judged to have ascertained the folly of burying any valuable portion of it with the dead.

G IT-CHEE-GAU-ZINEE, after a few days' illness, suddenly expired in the presence of his friends, by whom he was beloved and lamented. He had been an expert hunter, and left, among other things, a fine gun, which he had requested

197

might be buried with his body. There were some who thought his death a suspension and not an extinction of the animal functions, and that he would again be restored. His widow was among the number, and she carefully watched the body for the space of four days. She thought that by laying her hand upon his breast she could discover remaining indications of vitality. Twenty-four hours had elapsed, and nearly every vestige of hope had departed, when the man came to life. He gave the following narration to his friends:

"After death, my Jeebi travelled in the broad road of the dead toward the happy land, which is the Indian paradise. I passed on many days without meeting with any thing of an extraordinary nature. Plains of large extent, and luxuriant herbage, began to pass before my eyes. I saw many beautiful groves, and heard the songs of innumerable birds. At length I began to suffer for the want of food. I reached the summit of an elevation. My eyes caught the glimpse of the city of the dead. But it appeared to be distant, and the intervening space, partly veiled in silvery mists, was spangled with glittering lakes and streams. At this spot I came in sight of numerous herds of stately deer, moose, and other animals, which walked near my path, and appeared to have lost their natural timidity. But having no gun I was unable to kill them. I thought of the request I had made to my friends, to put my gun in my grave, and resolved to go back and seek for it.

"I found I had the free use of my limbs and faculties, and I had no sooner made this resolution, than I turned back. But I now beheld an immense number of men, women, and children, travelling toward the city of the dead, every one of whom I had to face in going back. I saw, in this throng, persons of every age, from the little infant—the sweet and lovely *Penaisee**—to the feeble gray-headed man, stooping with the weight of years. All whom I met, however, were heavily laden with implements, guns, pipes, kettles, meats, and other articles. One man stopped me and complained of the great burdens he had to carry. He offered me his gun, which I however refused, having made up my mind to

---

*The term of endearment for a young son.

procure my own. Another offered me a kettle. I saw women who were carrying their basket work and painted paddles, and little boys, with their ornamented war-clubs and bows and arrows— the presents of their friends.

"After encountering this throng for two days and nights, I came to the place where I had died. But I could see nothing but a great fire, the flames of which rose up before me, and spread around me. Whichever way I turned to avoid them, the flames still barred my advance. I was in the utmost perplexity, and knew not what to do. At length I determined to make a desperate leap, thinking my friends were on the other side, and in this effort, I awoke from my trance." Here the chief paused, and after a few moments concluded his story with the following admonitory remarks:

"My chiefs and friends," said he, "I will tell you of one practice, in which our forefathers have been wrong. They have been accustomed to deposit too many things with the dead. These implements are burthensome to them. It requires a longer time for them to reach the peace of repose, and almost every one I have conversed with complained bitterly to me of the evil. It would be wiser to put such things only, in the grave, as the deceased was particularly attached to, or made a formal request to have deposited with him. If he has been successful in the chase, and has abundance of things in his lodge, it would be better that they should remain for his family, or for division among his friends and relatives."

Advice which comes in this pleasing form of story and allegory, can give offence to no one. And it is probably the mode which the northern Indians have employed, from the earliest times, to rebuke faults and instil instruction. The old men, upon whom the duty of giving advice uniformly falls, may have found this the most efficacious means of moulding opinion and forming character.

WASSAMO

or

THE FIRE PLUME

From the Ottowa

W ASSAMO WAS living with his parents on the shores of a large bay on the east coast of Lake Michigan. It was at a period when nature spontaneously furnished everything that was wanted, when the Indian used skins for clothing, and flints for arrow heads. It was long before the time that the flag of the white man had been first seen in these lakes, or the sound of an iron axe had been heard. The skill of our people supplied them with weapons to kill game, and instruments to procure bark for their canoes, and to dress and cook their victuals.

One day, when the season had commenced for fish to be plenty near the shore of the lake, Wassamo's mother said to him, "My son, I wish you would go to yonder point, and see if you cannot procure me some fish, and ask your cousin to accompany you." He did so. They set out, and in the course of the afternoon arrived at the fishing ground. His cousin attended to the nets, for he was grown up to manhood, but Wassamo had not quite reached that age. They put their nets in the water and encamped near them, using only a few pieces of birch bark for a lodge to shelter them at night. They lit up a fire, and while they sat conversing with each other, the moon arose. Not a breath of wind disturbed the smooth and bright surface of the lake. Not a cloud was seen. Wassamo looked out on the water toward their nets, and saw that almost all the floats had disappeared. "Cousin," he said, "let us visit our nets, perhaps we are fortunate." They did so, and were rejoiced, as they drew them up, to see the meshes white, here and there, with fish. They landed in fine spirits, and put away their canoe in safety from the winds. "Wassamo," said his cousin, "you cook, that we may eat." He set about it immediately, and soon got his kettle on the fire, while his cousin was lying at his ease on the opposite side of the fire. "Cousin," said Wassamo, "tell me stories, or sing me some love songs." The other obeyed and sung his plaintive songs. He would frequently break off, and tell parts of stories, and then sing again, as suited his feelings or fancy. While thus employed, he unconsciously fell asleep. Wassamo had scarcely noticed it, in his care to watch the kettle, and when the fish were done, he took the kettle off. He spoke to his cousin, but received no answer. He took the wooden ladle and skimmed off the oil, for the fish were very fat. He had a flambeau of twisted bark in one hand to give light, but when he came to take out the fish he did not know how to manage to hold the light. He took off his garters and tied them around his head, and then placed the lighted flambeau above his forehead, so that it was firmly held by the bandage, and threw its light brilliantly around him. Having both hands thus at liberty, he began to take out the fish, every now and then moving his head, as he blew off the oil from the broth. He again spoke to his cousin, but he now perceived by his breathing, that he was asleep. He hastened to finish the removal of the fish, and while he blew over the broth repeatedly, the plume of fire over his forehead waved brilliantly in the air. Suddenly he heard a laugh. There appeared to be one or two persons, at no great distance. "Cousin," he said, to the sleeping boy, "some person is near us. I hear a laugh; awake and let us look out." But his cousin was in a profound sleep. Again he heard the laughing. Looking out as far as the reflection of the fire threw light, he beheld two beautiful young females smiling on him. Their countenances appeared to be perfectly white, and were exceedingly beautiful. He crouched down and pushed his cousin, saying, in a low voice, "awake! awake! here are two young women." But he received no answer. His cousin seemed locked up in one of the deepest slumbers. He started up alone, and went toward the females. He was charmed with their looks, but just as he was about to speak to them, he suddenly fell senseless, and both he and they vanished together.

Some short time afterward the cousin awoke. He saw the kettle near him. Some of the fish were in the bowl. The fire still cast its glare faintly around, but he could discover no person. He waited and waited, but Wassamo did not appear. Perhaps, thought he, he is gone out again to visit the nets. He looked, but the canoe was still in the place where it had been left. He searched and found his footsteps on the ashes. He became uneasy—NETAWIS! NETAWIS! (cousin, cousin), he cried out, but there was no answer. He cried out louder and louder, NETAWIS, NETAWIS, where are you gone? but still no answer. He started for the edge of the woods, crying NETAWIS, NETAWIS. He ran in various directions repeating the same words. The dark woods echoed NETAWIS, NETAWIS. He burst into tears and sobbed aloud.

He returned to the fire and sat down, but he had no heart to eat. Various conjectures passed in his mind respecting his cousin. He thought he may have been playing a trick. No, impossible! or he may have become deranged and ran into the woods. He hoped the morning would bring with it some discovery. But he was oppressed by the thought that the Indians would consider him the murderer of the lost man. "Although," reasoned he, "his parents are my relations, and they know that we are inseparable friends, they will not believe me, if I go home with a report that he is lost. They will say I killed him, and will require blood for blood."

These thoughts weighed upon his mind. He could not sleep. Early in the morning he got up and took in the nets, and set out on foot for the village, running all the way. When they saw him coming, they said, "some accident has happened." When he got in, he told them how his cousin had disappeared. He stated all the circumstances. He kept back nothing. He declared all he knew. Some said, "he has killed him treacherously." Others said, "it is impossible, they were like brothers; sooner than do that they would have given up their lives for each other." He asserted his innocence, and asked them to go and look at the spot of their encampment. Many of the men accordingly went, and found all as he had stated. No footsteps showed that any scuffle had taken

place. There were no signs of blood. They came to the conclusion
that the young man had got deranged, and strayed away, and was
lost. With this belief they returned to the village. But the parents
still waited and hoped he would return. Spring came on and the
Indians assembled from various quarters. Among them was
Wassamo's cousin. He continued to say that he had done nothing to hurt his friend. Anxiety and fear had, however, produced
a visible change in his features. He was pale and emaciated. The
idea of the blood of his friend and relation being laid to his
charge, caused a continual pain of mind.

The parents of Wassamo now demanded the life of Netawis.
The village was in an uproar. Some sided with the parents, some
with the young man. All showed anxiety in the affair. They at
last, however, decided to give the young man's life to the parents.
They said they had waited long enough for the return of their son.
A day was appointed on which the young man should give his life
for his friend's. He still went at large. He said he was not afraid
to die, for he had never committed what they laid to his charge.
A day or two before the time set to take his life, he wandered in
a melancholy mood from the village, following the beach. His
feelings were wrought to such a pitch that he thought once or
twice to throw himself into the lake. But he reflected, "They will
say I was guilty, or I would not have done so. No, I will not, I
would prefer dying under their hands." He walked on, thinking
of his coming fate, till he reached the sand banks, a short distance
from the village. Here we will dismiss him for the present.

When Wassamo fell senseless before the two young women, it
must have been some minutes before he recovered, for when he
came to himself, he did not know where he was, and had been
removed to a distant scene. On recovering his senses he heard
persons conversing. One spoke in a tone of authority, saying,
"You foolish girls, is this the way you go about at nights, without
our knowing it? Put that person you brought on that bed of
yours, and let him not lie on the ground." After this Wassamo felt
himself moved and placed on a bed. Some time after he opened
his eyes fully, and was surprised to find himself in a spacious and
superb lodge, extending as far as the eye could reach. One spoke
to him, saying, "Stranger, awake, and take something to eat." He

arose and sat up. On each side of the lodge he beheld rows of people sitting in regular order. At a distance he could see two prominent persons who looked rather older than the rest, and who appeared to command obedience from all around them. One of them, the Old Spirit man, addressed him. "My son," said he, "those foolish girls brought you here. They saw you at the fishing ground. When you attempted to approach them, you fell senseless, and they conveyed you underground to this place. But be satisfied. We will make your stay with us pleasant. I am the guardian Spirit of Nagow Wudjoo.* I have wished frequently to get one of your race to intermarry with us. If you can make up your mind to remain, I will give you one of my daughters—the one who brought you away from your parents and friends."† The young man dropped his head and made no answer. His silence they construed into an assent to their wishes.

"Your wants," continued the Old Spirit, "will all be supplied, only be careful not to stray away far from this. I am afraid of that Spirit who rules all islands lying in the Lakes. For he demanded my daughter in marriage, and I refused him: when he hears that you are my guest, it may be an inducement for him to harm you. There is my daughter (he pointed). Take her, she shall be your wife." And forthwith they sat near each other in the lodge, and were considered as married.

"Son-in-law," said the Old Spirit, "I am in want of tobacco. You shall return to visit your parents, and can make known my wishes. For it is very seldom that those few who pass these Sand Hills, offer a piece of tobacco. When they do it, it immediately comes to me. Just so," he added, putting his hand out of the side of the lodge, and drawing in several pieces of tobacco, which some one at that moment happened to offer to the Spirit, for a smooth lake and prosperous voyage. "You see," he said, "every

---

*Sand mountains, usually called *La Grandes Sables,* a noted range of Sand Downs, of oceanic formation, on the south shores of Lake Superior.

†This speech was commenced by throwing the blame of his captivity upon the daughters. But the Spirit soon reveals that he had long wished for such an event, and leaves it to be inferred that it was brought about by his direct agency. This subterfuge, to call it by its lightest name, shows that plain truth is not a point of character most strenuously sought after by the Old Spirit.

thing offered me on earth, comes immediately to the side of my lodge." Wassamo saw the women also putting their hands to the side of the lodge, and then handing something around, of which all partook. This he found to be offerings of food made by mortals on earth.

"Daughter," said the Old Spirit Woman, NAUON-GUISK* cannot eat what we eat, so you can procure him what he is accustomed to. "Yes," she replied, and immediately pushed her hand through the side of the lodge, and took a white fish out of the lake, which she prepared for him. She daily followed the same practice, giving every variety of fish he expressed a wish for. Sometimes it was trout, pike, sturgeon, or any other fish the lake furnished. She did the same with regard to meats, or the flesh of any animal or fowl he asked for. For the animals walked over the roof of the lodge, the birds sat upon its poles, and the waters came so near to its side, that the Spirits had only to extend their hands to the outside to procure whatever they wanted.

One day the Old Spirit said (although it was perpetual day with them), "Son-in-law, you must not be surprised at what you will see, for since you have been with us, you have never seen us go to sleep. It was on account of its being summer, which is constant daylight with us. But now what *you* call winter is approaching. It is six months night with us, you will soon see us lie down, and we shall not get up, but for a moment, throughout the whole winter. Take my advice. Leave not the lodge, but try and amuse yourself. You will find all you wish there," raising his arm slowly and pointing. Wassamo said he would obey, and act as he recommended.

On another occasion a thunder storm came on, when every spirit instantly disappeared. When the storm was over, they all again re-entered the lodge. This scene was repeated during every tempest. "You are surprised," said the Old Spirit, "to see us disappear whenever it thunders. The reason is this. A greater Spirit, who lives above, makes those thunders sound and sends his fire. We are afraid, and hide ourselves."

---

*This is a term applied by women to a son-in-law, &c.

The season of sleep approached, and they, one after another, laid themselves down to their long sleep. In the mean time Wassamo amused himself in the best way he could. His relations got up but once during the whole winter, and they then said it was midnight, and laid down again. "Son-in-law," said the Old Spirit, "you can now, in a few days, start with your wife to visit your relations. You can be absent one year, but after that time you must return. When you get to the village you must first go in alone. Leave your wife a short distance from the lodge, and when you are welcome then send for her.* When there, do not be surprised at her disappearance whenever you hear it thunder. You will also prosper in all things, for she is very industrious. All the time that you pass in sleep she will be at work. The distance is short to your village. A road leads directly to it, and when you get there do not forget my wants, as I stated to you before."

Wassamo promised obedience to their directions, and then set out in company with his wife. They travelled in a good road, his wife leading the way, till they got to a rising ground. At the highest point of this, she said, we will soon get to your country. After reaching the summit, they passed, for a short distance, under the lake, and emerged from the water at certain sand banks on the bay of WEKUADONG.†

Wassamo left his wife concealed in a thicket, while he went toward the village alone. On turning the first point of land, who should he meet but his cousin. "Oh Netawis, Netawis," said his cousin, "you have just come in time to save me. They accuse me of having killed you." Words cannot express their joy. The cousin ran off in haste for the village and entered the lodge where Wassamo's mother was. "Hear me," he said, "I have seen him whom you accuse me of having killed. He will be here in a few moments." The village was in instant commotion. All were anxious to see him whom they had thought dead. While the excitement

---

*This is the present ceremonious custom of visiting among the northern Indians, for strangers of their own, or other tribes. Friends proceed directly to the lodges, but it is the privilege of relations only to enter them without invitation at the door.
†Little Traverse Bay of Lake Michigan.

was at its height Wassamo entered the lodge of his parents. All
was joy at the happy meeting. He related all that had happened
to him from the moment of his leaving their temporary night
lodge with the flame on his head. He told them where he had
been, and that he was married. As soon as the excitement of his
reception had abated, he told his mother that he had left his
wife a short distance from the village. She went immediately in
search of her, and soon found her. All the women of the village
conducted her to the lodge of her relations. They were astonished
at her beauty, at the whiteness of her skin, and more so, at her
being able to converse with them in their own language. All was
joy in the village; nothing but feasting could be seen while they
had the means of doing so. The Indians came from different
quarters, to offer them welcome, and to present their tobacco to
the Spirit's daughter.

Thus passed the summer and the fall, and Wassamo's parents
and relations, and the Indians around were prospered in all
things. But his cousin would never leave him, he was constantly
near him, and asking him questions. They took notice that at
every thunder storm his wife disappeared, and that at night, as
well as during the day, she was never idle. Winter was drawing on,
and she told her husband to prepare a lodge for her to pass the
season in, and to inform the Indians beforehand of her father's
request. He did so, and all now began to move off to their winter quarters. Wassamo also prepared for the season. He gave one
half of his lodge to his wife. Before lying down, she said, no one
but yourself must pass on the side of the lodge I am on. Winter
passed slowly away, and when the sap of the maple began to run,
she awoke and commenced her duties as before. She also helped
to make sugar. It was never known before or since that so much
sugar was made during the season. As soon as the Indians had
finished their sugar-making, they left the woods and encamped
at their village. They offered tobacco profusely at the lodge of
Wassamo, asking for the usual length of life, for success as hunters,
and for a plentiful supply of food. Wassamo replied, that he would
mention each of their requests to his father-in-law. So much
tobacco had been offered, that they were obliged to procure two
sacks, made of dressed mooseskin, to hold it. On the outside of

these skins the different totems* of the Indians, who had given the tobacco, were painted and marked, and also those of all persons who had made any request.

When the time arrived for their departure, they told their relatives not to follow them, or see how they disappeared. They then took the two sacks of mooseskin filled with tobacco, and bade adieu to all but Netawis. He insisted on going with them a distance, and when they got to the sand banks he expressed the strongest wish to proceed with them on their journey. Wassamo told him it was impossible, that it was only spirits who could exert the necessary power. They then took an affectionate leave of each other. The young man saw them go into the water and disappear. He returned home and told his friends that he had witnessed their disappearance.

Wassamo and his wife soon reached their home at the grand Sand Hills. The Old Spirit was delighted to see them, and hailed their return with open arms. They presented him with the tobacco, and told him all the requests of the people above. He replied that he would attend to all, but he must first invite his friends to smoke with him. He then sent his MEZHINAUWA,† to invite his friends the Spirits, and named the time for their reception. Before the time arrived he spoke to his son-in-law. "My son," said he, "some of those Manitoes I have invited are very wicked, and I warn you particularly of the one who wished to marry my

---

*Family marks, or arms. This institution has been noticed among the Algonquin tribes from an early day. It is a link in the genealogical chain by which the bands are held together—and a curious trait, whether it be regarded of ancient or modern usage. It has no reference to personal names, but indicates the family or tribal name. All the individuals of a particular family, as the deer, crane, beaver, &c, when called upon for their signature, affix their respective family mark, without regard to specific names. And it is precisely analogous to the existing feudal institutions of coats of arms. *Totame,* or *totem* is the term, and it is a word appealed to by them with pride, and as furnishing evidence of blood relationship. Whatever the institution may be derived from, it is certain that a Benjaminite or an Ephraimite could not appeal to his tribal appellation with more emphasis and dogmatism than do our northern Indians to their *totems.*

†This is an official personage, standing in the light of an aid, or office help, to the chiefs. He carves at feasts, and lights the pipe at councils or ceremonial occasions. He is the verbal messenger of state messages, but not a messenger in the common acceptance of the term. He is an important functionary in all formal business or negotiations with the chiefs.

daughter. Some of them you will, however, find to be friendly. Take my advice, and when they come in, sit close to your wife— so close you must touch her. If you do not you will be lost, for those who are expected to come in are so powerful, that they will draw you from your seat. You have only to observe my words closely, and all will be well." Wassamo said he would obey.

About midday they commenced coming in. There were spirits from all parts of the country. One entered who smiled on him. He was the guardian Spirit of the Ottowas, and he lived near the present GITCHY WEKUADONG.* Soon after, he heard the sounds of the roaring and foaming of waters. Presently they rushed in, and passed through the lodge like a raging tempest. Tremendous pieces of rocks, whole trees, logs, and stumps rolled past, and were borne away by the strong current, with the noise and foaming of some mighty cataract in the spring. It was the guardian spirit of Water-Falls. Again, they heard the roaring of waves, as if beating against a rocky shore. The sounds came rapidly on. In a few moments in rolled the waves of Lake Superior. They were mountain high, and covered with silver-sparkling foam. Wassamo felt their pressure and with difficulty clung to his seat, for they were of frightful appearance, and each one seemed as if it would overwhelm them. This was the last spirit who entered. It was the guardian of Islands in the surrounding lake.

Soon after, the Old Spirit arose and addressed the assembly. "Brothers," he said, "I have invited you to partake with me of the offerings made by the mortals on earth, which have been brought by our relative (pointing to Wassamo). Brothers, you see their wishes and desires (pointing to the figured mooseskins). Brothers, the offering is worthy of our consideration. Brothers, I see nothing on my part to prevent our granting their requests; they do not appear to be unreasonable. Brothers, the offering is gratifying. Our wants for this article are urgent. Shall we grant their requests? One thing more I would say—Brothers, it is this. There is my son-in-law; he is a mortal. I wish to detain him with me, and

---

*Grand Traverse Bay of Lake Michigan.

it is with us jointly to make him one of us." "Hoke! hoke!" ran through the whole company of Spirits.*

The tobacco was then divided equally among them all. They decided to grant the requests of the people on earth, and also respecting the spirit's son-in-law. When the Spirit of Islands passed Wassamo, he looked angrily at him. The guardian spirit of the Ottowa bands said, "it is very strange that he can never appear anywhere without showing his bad disposition."

When the company was dispersed, the Old Spirit told Wassamo that he should once more visit his parents and relatives, and then it should be only for a short time. "It is merely to go and tell them that their wishes are granted, and then to bid them farewell for ever." Sometime after Wassamo and his wife made this visit. Having delivered his message, he said, "I must now bid you all farewell for ever." His parents and friends raised their voices in loud lamentation. They accompanied him to the Sand Banks, where they all seated themselves to see them make their final departure. The day was mild; the sky clear; not a cloud appeared, nor a breath of wind to disturb the bright surface of the water. The most perfect silence reigned throughout the company. They gazed intently on Wassamo and his wife as they waded out into the water, waving their hands. They saw them go into deeper and deeper water. They saw the waves close over their heads. All at once they raised a loud and piercing wail. They looked again, a red flame, as if the sun had glanced on a billow, marked the spot for an instant, but the Feather of Flames and his wife had disappeared for ever.

The preceding tale opens a chapter in Indian demonology, which was narrated by the late chief Chusco, an Ottawa. This individual had performed the office of a seer and necromancer for his tribe for a long

---

*The interjection *Hoh!* is used by these tribes to imply approbation and assent. The change in the word here indicated is to be regarded as one of the points of invention in their tales of demonology.

series of years, and had acquired notoriety and power among them from the successful display of these arts. The story was related after his conversion to Christianity, but he continued to affirm to the last, that his power as a JOSSAKEED, or juggler, was derived from a *direct energy* communicated by the Great Evil Spirit.

OSSEO

or

THE SON OF THE EVENING STAR

An Algonquin Tale

THERE ONCE lived an Indian in the north, who had ten daughters, all of whom grew up to womanhood. They were noted for their beauty, but especially Oweenee, the youngest, who was very independent in her way of thinking. She was a great admirer of romantic places, and paid very little attention to the numerous young men who came to her father's lodge for the purpose of seeing her. Her elder sisters were all solicited in marriage from their parents, and one after another, went off to dwell in the lodges of their husbands, or mothers-in-law, but she would listen to no proposals of the kind. At last she married an old man called OSSEO, who was scarcely able to walk, and was too poor to have things like others. They jeered and laughed at her, on all sides, but she seemed to be quite happy, and said to them, "It is my choice, and you will see in the end, who has acted the wisest." Soon after, the sisters and their husbands and their parents were all invited to a feast, and as they walked along the path, they could not help pitying their young and handsome sister, who had such an unsuitable mate. Osseo often stopped and gazed upwards, but they could perceive nothing in the direction he looked, unless it was the faint glimmering of the evening star. They heard him muttering to himself as they went along, and one of the elder sisters caught the words, "Sho-wain-ne-me-shin nosa."* "Poor old man," said she, "he is talking to his

---

*"Pity me, my father."

father, what a pity it is, that he would not fall and break his neck, that our sister might have a handsome young husband." Presently they passed a large hollow log, lying with one end toward the path. The moment Osseo, who was of the turtle totem, came to it, he stopped short, uttered a loud and peculiar yell, and then dashing into one end of the log, he came out at the other, a most beautiful young man, and springing back to the road, he led off the party with steps as light as the reindeer.* But on turning round to look for his wife, behold, she had been changed into an old, decrepit woman, who was bent almost double, and walked with a cane. The husband, however, treated her very kindly, as she had done him during the time of his enchantment, and constantly addressed her by the term of Ne-ne-moosh-a, or my sweetheart.

When they came to the hunter's lodge with whom they were to feast, they found the feast ready prepared, and as soon as their entertainer had finished his harangue (in which he told them his feasting was in honour of the Evening, or Woman's Star), they began to partake of the portion dealt out, according to age and character, to each one. The food was very delicious, and they were all happy but Osseo, who looked at his wife and then gazed upward, as if he was looking into the substance of the sky. Sounds were soon heard, as if from far-off voices in the air, and they became plainer and plainer, till he could clearly distinguish some of the words.

"My son—my son," said the voice, "I have seen your afflictions and pity your wants. I come to call you away from a scene that is stained with blood and tears. The earth is full of sorrows. Giants and sorcerers, the enemies of mankind, walk abroad in it, and are scattered throughout its length. Every night they are lifting their voices to the Power of Evil, and every day they make themselves busy in casting evil in the hunter's path. You have long been their victim, but shall be their victim no more. The spell you were under is broken. Your evil genius is overcome. I have cast him down by my superior strength, and it is this strength I now exert for your happiness. Ascend, my son—ascend into the skies, and

---

*The *C. Sylvestris* inhabits North America, north of latitude 46°.

partake of the feast I have prepared for you in the stars, and bring with you those you love.

"The food set before you is enchanted and blessed. Fear not to partake of it. It is endowed with magic power to give immortality to mortals, and to change men to spirits. Your bowls and kettles shall be no longer wood and earth. The one shall become silver, and the other wampum. They shall shine like fire, and glisten like the most beautiful scarlet. Every female shall also change her state and looks, and no longer be doomed to laborious tasks. She shall put on the beauty of the starlight, and become a shining bird of the air, clothed with shining feathers. She shall dance and not work—she shall sing and not cry."

"My beams," continued the voice, "shine faintly on your lodge, but they have a power to transform it into the lightness of the skies, and decorate it with the colours of the clouds. Come, Osseo, my son, and dwell no longer on earth. Think strongly on my words, and look steadfastly at my beams. My power is now at its height. Doubt not—delay not. It is the voice of the Spirit of the stars that calls you away to happiness and celestial rest."

The words were intelligible to Osseo, but his companions thought them some far-off sounds of music, or birds singing in the woods. Very soon the lodge began to shake and tremble, and they felt it rising into the air. It was too late to run out, for they were already as high as the tops of the trees. Osseo looked around him as the lodge passed through the topmost boughs, and behold! their wooden dishes were changed into shells of a scarlet colour, the poles of the lodge to glittering wires of silver, and the bark that covered them into the gorgeous wings of insects. A moment more, and his brothers and sisters, and their parents and friends, were transformed into birds of various plumage. Some were jays, some partridges and pigeons, and others gay singing birds, who hopped about displaying their glittering feathers, and singing their songs. But OWEENEE still kept her earthly garb, and exhibited all the indications of extreme age. He again cast his eyes in the direction of the clouds, and uttered that peculiar yell, which had given him the victory at the hollow log. In a moment the youth and beauty of his wife returned; her dingy garments assumed the shining appearance of green silk, and her cane was changed into a silver feather. The lodge again shook and trembled, for they were now passing through the uppermost clouds, and they immediately after found themselves in the Evening Star, the residence of Osseo's father.

"My son," said the old man, "hang that cage of birds, which you have brought along in your hand, at the door, and I will inform you why you and your wife have been sent for." Osseo obeyed the directions, and then took his seat in the lodge. "Pity was shown to you," resumed the king of the star, "on account of the contempt of your wife's sister, who laughed at her ill fortune, and ridiculed you while you were under the power of that wicked spirit, whom you overcame at the log. That spirit lives in the next lodge, being a small star you see on the left of mine, and he has always felt envious of my family, because we had greater power than he had, and especially on account of our having had the care committed to us of the female world. He failed in several attempts to destroy your brothers-in-law and sisters-in-law, but succeeded at last in transforming yourself and your wife into decrepit old persons. You must be careful and not let the light of his beams fall on you, while you are here, for therein is the power of his enchantment; a ray of light is the bow and arrows he uses."

Osseo lived happy and contented in the parental lodge, and in due time his wife presented him with a son, who grew up rapidly, and was the image of his father. He was very quick and ready in learning every thing that was done in his grandfather's domin- ions, but he wished also to learn the art of hunting, for he had heard that this was a favourite pursuit below. To gratify him his father made him a bow and arrows, and he then let the birds out of the cage that he might practise in shooting. He soon became expert, and the very first day brought down a bird, but when he went to pick it up, to his amazement, it was a beautiful young woman with the arrow sticking in her breast. It was one of his younger *aunts*. The moment her blood fell upon the surface of that pure and spotless planet, the charm was dissolved. The boy immediately found himself sinking, but was partly upheld, by something like wings, till he passed through the lower clouds, and he then suddenly dropped upon a high, romantic island in a large lake. He was pleased on looking up, to see all his aunts and uncles following him in the form of birds, and he soon discovered the silver lodge, with his father and mother, descending with its waving barks looking like so many insects' gilded wings. It rested on the highest cliffs of the island, and here they fixed their residence. They all resumed their natural *shapes,* but were diminished to the *size* of fairies, and as a mark of homage to the King of the Evening Star, they never failed, on every pleasant evening, during the summer season, to join hands, and dance upon the top of the rocks. These rocks were quickly observed by the Indians to be covered, in moonlight evenings, with a larger sort of PUK WUDJ ININEES, or Little Men, and were called Mish-in-e-mok-in-ok-ong, or Turtle Spirits, and the island is named from them to this day.* Their shining lodge can be seen in the summer evenings when the moon shines strongly on the pinnacles of the rocks, and the fishermen, who go near those high cliffs at night, have even heard the voices of the happy little dancers.

Michilimackinac, the term alluded to, is the original French orthography of MISH EN I MOK IN ONG, the *local* form (sing. and plu.), of Turtle Spirits.

KWASIND

or

THE FEARFULLY STRONG MAN

PAUWATING* WAS a village where the young men amused themselves very much in ancient times, in sports and ball-playing.

One day as they were engaged in their sports, one of the strongest and most active, at the moment he was about to succeed in a trial of lifting, slipped and fell upon his back. "Ha! ha! ha!" cried the lookers on, "you will never rival Kwasind." He was deeply mortified, and when the sport was over, these words came to his mind. He could not recollect any man of this name. He thought he would ask the old man, the story-teller of the village, the next time he came to the lodge. The opportunity soon occurred.

"My grandfather," said he, "who was Kwasind? I am very anxious to know what he could do."

Kwasind, the old man replied, was a listless idle boy. He would not play when the other boys played, and his parents could never get him to do any kind of labour. He was always making excuses. His parents took notice, however, that he fasted for days together, but they could not learn what spirit he supplicated, or had chosen as the guardian spirit to attend him through life. He was so inattentive to his parents' requests, that he, at last, became a subject of reproach.

"Ah," said his mother to him one day, "is there any young man of your age, in all the village, who does so little for his parents? You neither hunt nor fish. You take no interest in any thing, whether

---

*i. e., Place of shallow cataract, named *Sault de Ste. Marie* on the arrival of the French. This is the *local* form of the word, the substantive proper terminates in EEG.

labour or amusement, which engages the attention of your equals in years. I have often set my nets* in the coldest days of winter, without any assistance from you. And I have taken them up again, while you remained inactive at the lodge fire. Are you not ashamed of such idleness? Go, I bid you, and wring out that net, which I have just taken from the water."

Kwasind saw that there was a determination to make him obey. He did not therefore make any excuses, but went out and took up the net. He carefully folded it, doubled and redoubled it, forming it into a roll, and then with an easy twist of his hands wrung it short off, with as much ease as if every twine had been a thin brittle fibre. Here, they at once saw, the secret of his reluctance. He possessed supernatural strength.

After this, the young men were playing one day on the plain, where there was lying one of those large, heavy, black pieces of rock, which Manabozho is said to have cast at his father. Kwasind took it up with much ease, and threw it into the river. After this, he accompanied his father on a hunting excursion into a remote forest. They came to a place where the wind had thrown a great many trees into a narrow pass. "We must go the other way," said the old man, "it is impossible to get the burdens through this place." He sat down to rest himself, took out his smoking apparatus, and gave a short time to reflection. When he had finished, Kwasind had lifted away the largest pine trees, and pulled them out of the path.

Sailing one day in his canoe, Kwasind saw a large furred animal, which he immediately recognised to be the king of beavers. He plunged into the water in pursuit of it. His companions were in the greatest astonishment and alarm, supposing he would perish. He often dove down and remained a long time under water, pursuing the animal from island to island; and at last returned with the kingly prize. After this, his fame spread far and wide, and no hunter would presume to compete with him.

He performed so many feats of strength and skill, that he excited the envy of the Puck-wudj In-in-ee-sug, or fairies, who conspired against his life. "For," said they, "if this man is suffered to go on, in his career of strength and exploits, we shall presently

---

*Nets are set in winter, in high northern latitudes, through orifices cut in the ice.

have no work to perform. Our agency in the affairs of men must cease. He will undermine our power, and drive us, at last, into the water, where we must all perish, or be devoured by the wicked Neebanawbaig.*

The strength of Kwasind was all concentrated in the crown of his head. This was, at the same time, the only vulnerable part of his body; and there was but one species of weapon which could be successfully employed in making any impression upon it. The fairies carefully hunted through the woods to find this weapon. It was the burr or seed vessel of the white pine. They gathered a quantity of this article, and waylaid Kwasind at a point on the river, where the red rocks jut into the water, forming rude castles— a point which he was accustomed to pass in his canoe. They waited a long time, making merry upon these rocks, for it was a highly romantic spot. At last the wished-for object appeared, Kwasind came floating calmly down the stream, on the after-noon of a summer's day, languid with the heat of the weather, and almost asleep. When his canoe came directly beneath the cliff, the tallest and stoutest fairy began the attack. Others fol-lowed his example. It was a long time before they could hit the vulnerable part, but success at length crowned their efforts, and Kwasind sunk, never to rise more.

Ever since this victory, the Puck Wudj Ininee have made that point of rock a favourite resort. The hunters often hear them laugh, and see their little plumes shake as they pass this scene on light summer evenings.

"My son," continued the old man, "take care that you do not imitate the faults of Kwasind. If he had not so often exerted his strength merely for the sake of *boasting,* he would not, perhaps, have made the fairies feel jealous of him. It is better to use the strength you have, in a quiet useful way, than to sigh after the possession of a giant's power. For if you run, or wrestle, or jump, or fire at a mark, only as well as your equals in years, nobody will envy you. But if you would needs be a Kwasind, you must expect a Kwasind's fate."

---

*A kind of water spirits.

MUDJEE MONEDO
AND
MINNO MONEDO

or

THE SPIRIT OF EVIL
AND THE SPIRIT OF GOOD

A Saginaw Tale

I N A beautiful portion of the country, which was part forest
and part prairie, there lived a bloodthirsty Manito in the
guise of an Indian, who made use of all his arts to decoy men
into his power for the purpose of killing them. Although the
country yielded an abundance of game, and every other production to satisfy his wants, yet it was the study of his life to destroy
human beings, and subsist upon their blood. The country had
once been thickly populated, but he had thinned it off by his
wickedness, and his lodge was surrounded by the bleached bones
of his victims.

The secret of his success lay in his great speed. He had the
power to assume the shape of any quadruped, and it was his custom to challenge persons to run with him. He had a beaten path
on which he ran, leading around a large lake, and he always ran
around this circle, so that the starting and winning point were the
same. At this point stood a post, having a sharp and shining
knife tied to it, and whoever lost the race lost his life. The winner
immediately took up the knife and cut off his competitor's head.
No man was ever known to beat this evil Manito in the race,
although he ran every day; for whenever he was pressed hard, he
changed himself into a fox, wolf, or deer, or other swift-footed
animal, and thus left his competitor behind.

The whole country was in dread of him, and yet, such was the

220

folly and rashness of the young men, that they were continually running with him; for if they refused, he called them cowards, which was a taunt they could not bear. They would rather die than be called cowards. In other respects, the Manito had pleasing manners, and visited the lodges around the country, like others; but his secret object in these visits was to see whether the young boys were getting to be old enough to run with him, and he was careful to keep a watch upon their growth, and never failed to challenge them to run on his race ground. There was no family which had not lost some of its most active members in this way, and the Manito was execrated by all the Indian mothers in the country.

There lived near him a widow, whose husband and ten sons he had killed in this way, and she was now left with an only daughter and a son of ten or twelve years old, named MONEDOWA. She was very poor and feeble, and suffered so much for the want of food, that she would have been glad to die, had it not been for her daughter and her little son, who was not yet able to hunt. The Manito had already visited her lodge to see whether the boy was not sufficiently grown to challenge him. And the mother saw there was a great probability that he would be decoyed and killed as his father and brothers had been. Still, she hoped a better fate would attend him, and strove, in the best way she could, to instruct him in the maxims of a hunter's and a warrior's life. To the daughter she also taught all that could make her useful as a wife, and instructed her in the arts of working with porcupine quills on leather, and various other things, which the Indian females regard as accomplishments. She was also neat and tasteful in arranging her dress according to their customs, and possessing a tall and graceful person, she displayed her national costume to great advantage. She was kind and obedient to her mother, and never neglected to perform her appropriate domestic duties. Her mother's lodge stood on an elevation on the banks of a lake, which gave them a fine prospect of the country for many miles around, the interior of which was diversified with groves and prairies. It was in this quarter that they daily procured their fuel. One day the daughter had gone out to these open groves to pick up dry limbs for their fire, and while admiring the scenery, she strolled farther than usual, and was suddenly startled by the appearance of a young man near her. She would have fled, but was arrested by his pleasing smile, and by hearing herself addressed in her own language. The questions he asked were trivial, relating to her place of residence and family, and were answered with timidity. It could not be concealed, however, that they were mutually pleased with each other, and before parting, he asked her to get her mother's consent to their marriage. She returned home later than usual, but was too timid to say anything to her mother on the subject. The meetings, however, with her admirer on the borders of the prairie, were frequent, and he every time requested her to speak to her mother on the subject of their marriage, which, however, she could not muster the resolution to do. At last the widow suspected something of the kind, from the tardiness of her daughter in coming in, and from the scanty quantity of fuel she sometimes brought. In answer to inquiries, she revealed the circumstance of her meeting the young man, and of his request. After reflecting upon her lonely and destitute situation, the mother gave her consent. The daughter went with a light step to communicate the answer, which her lover heard with delight, and after saying that he would come to the lodge at sunset, they separated. He was punctual to his engagement, and came at the precise time, dressed out as a warrior with every customary decoration, and approached the lodge with a mild and pleasing, yet manly air and commanding step. On entering it, he spoke affectionately to his mother-in-law, whom he called (contrary to the usage), NEEJEE, or *friend.* * She directed him to sit down beside her daughter, and from this moment they were regarded as man and wife.

Early the following morning, he asked for the bow and arrows of those who had been slain by the Manito, and went out a hunting. As soon as he had got out of sight of the lodge, he transformed himself into a PEENA, or partridge, and took his flight in the air. Where or how he procured his food, is unknown; but he returned at evening with the carcasses of two deer. This continued to be his daily practice, and it was not long before the scaffolds near the lodge were loaded with meat. It was observed, however, that

---

*The term *Neejee* is restricted in its use by males to males and cannot, with propriety, be applied by males to females, or by females to males.

he ate but little himself, and that of a peculiar kind of meat, which added to some other particulars, convinced the family of his mysterious character. In a few days his mother-in-law told him that the Manito would come to pay them a visit, to see how the young man prospered. He told her that he should be away that day purposely, but would return the moment the visiter left them. On the day named he flew upon a tall tree, overlooking the lodge, and took his stand there to observe the movement of the Manito. This wicked spirit soon appeared, and as he passed the scaffolds of meat, cast suspicious glances toward them. He had no sooner entered the lodge, stopping first to look, before he went in, than he said— "Why, woman, who is it that is furnishing you meat so plentifully?" "No one," she answered, "but my son—he is just beginning to kill deer." "No, no," said he, "some one is living with you." "Kaween,"* said the old woman, dissembling again, "You are only jesting on my destitute situation. Who do you think would come and trouble themselves about *me?*" "Very well," replied the Manito, "I will go; but on such a day, I will again visit you, and see who it is that furnishes the meat, and whether it is your son or not." He had no sooner left the lodge and got out of sight, than the son-in-law made his appearance with two more deer. On being told of the particulars of the visit, "Very well," said he, "I will be at home next time and see him." They remonstrated against this, telling him of his cruelties, and the barbarous murders he had committed. "No matter," said he, "if he invites me to the race ground, I will not be backward. The result will teach him how to show pity on the vanquished, and not to trample on the widow, and those who are without fathers." When the day of the expected visit arrived, he told his wife to prepare certain pieces of meat, which he pointed out and handed to her, together with two or three buds of the birch-tree which he requested her to put in the pot; and he directed that nothing should be wanting to show the usual hospitality to their guest, although he knew that his only object was to kill him. He then dressed himself as a warrior, putting tints of red on his visage and dress, to show that he was prepared for either war or peace.

---

*"No indeed!"

As soon as the Manito arrived, he eyed this, to him, strange warrior, but dissembled his feelings, and spoke laughingly to the old woman, saying, "Did I not tell you that some one was staying with you, for I knew your son was too young to hunt!" She turned it off by saying that she did not think it necessary to tell him, as he was a Manito and knew before asking. He then conversed with the son-in-law on different topics, and finished by inviting him to the race ground, saying it was a manly amusement—that it would give him an opportunity of seeing other men, and he should himself be pleased to run with him. The young man said he knew nothing of running. "Why," he replied, "don't you see how old I look, while you are young and active. We must at least run to amuse others." "Be it so, then," replied the young man, "I will go in the morning." Pleased with his success, the Manito now wished to return, but he was pressed to remain and partake of the customary hospitalities, although he endeavoured to excuse himself. The meal was immediately spread. But one dish was used. The young man partook of it first, to show his guest that he need not fear to partake, and saying at the same time to him, "It is a feast, and as we seldom meet, we must eat all that is placed on the dish, as a mark of gratitude to the Great Spirit for permitting me to kill the animals, and for the pleasure of seeing you, and partaking of it with you." They ate and conversed until they had eaten nearly all, when the Manito took up the dish and drank the broth. On setting it down, he immediately turned his head and commenced coughing violently, having, as the young man expected, swallowed a grain of the birch tops, which had lodged in his windpipe. He coughed incessantly, and found his situation so unpleasant, that he had to leave, saying, as he quit the lodge, that he should expect the young man at the race ground in the morning.

MONEDOWA prepared himself early in the morning by oiling his limbs, and decorating himself so as to appear to advantage, and having procured leave for his brother to attend him, they repaired to the Manito's race ground. The Manito's lodge stood on an eminence, and a row of other lodges stood near it, and as soon as the young man and his companion came near it, the inmates cried out, "We are visited." At this cry he came out, and descended with them to the starting post on a plain. From this, the course could be seen, as it wound around the lake, and as soon as the people assembled, he began to speak of the race, then belted himself up, and pointed to the knife which hung on the post, and said it was to be used by the winner. "But before we start," said the old man, "I wish it to be understood that when men run with me, I make a bet, and expect them to abide by it. Life against life." He then gave a yell, casting a triumphant glance on the piles of human bones that were scattered about the stake. "I am ready," replied the stranger, as he was called (for no one knew the widow's son-in-law), and they all admired the symmetry and beauty of his limbs, and the fine and bold air which he assumed before his grim antagonist. The shout was given, and they went off with surprising speed, and were soon out of sight. The old man began to show his power by changing himself into a fox, and passing the stranger with great ease, went leisurely along. Monedowa now exerted his magic powers by assuming the shape of a partridge, and lighting a distance ahead of his antagonist, resumed his former shape. When the Manito spied his opponent ahead, "Whoa! whoa!" he exclaimed involuntarily, "this is strange," and immediately changed himself into a wolf, and repassed him. As he went by, he heard a whistling noise in the Manito's throat. He again took flight as a partridge, ascending some distance into the air, and then suddenly coming down with great velocity, as partridges do, lit in the path far ahead. As he passed the wolf, he addressed him thus: "My friend, is this the extent of your speed?" The Manito began to have strong forebodings, for, on looking ahead, he saw the stranger in his natural shape, running along very leisurely. He then assumed alternately the shapes of various animals noted for speed. He again passed the stranger in the shape of a reindeer.* They had now got round the circle of the lake, and were approaching the point of starting, when the stranger

---

*The Cervus Sylvestris, or American species of Reindeer, is confined in its range, north of Lake Huron. No traces of it have been observed south of the parallel of the straits of Michilimackinac, although it is found in the peninsular area between those straits and the south shores of Lake Superior. This animal is called Addick by the Algic race, and is the Caraboo of the Canadian.

again took his flight as a partridge, and lit some distance in advance. To overtake him, the Manito at last assumed the shape of a buffalo, and again got ahead; but it appears this was the last form he could assume, and it was that, in which he had most commonly conquered. The stranger again took his flight as a partridge, and in the act of passing his competitor saw his tongue hanging out from fatigue. "My friend," said he, "is this all your speed?" The Manito answered not. The stranger had now got within a flight of the winning post, when the fiend had nearly caught up to him. "Bakah! bakah! neejee," he vociferated. "Stop, my friend, I wish to talk to you," for he felt that he should be defeated and lose his life, and it was his purpose to beg for it. The stranger laughed, as he replied, "I will speak to you at the starting post. When men run with me, I make a bet, and expect them to abide by it. Life against life." And immediately taking flight, alighted so near to the goal, that he could easily reach it in his natural form. The Manito saw the movement, and was paralyzed. The people at the stake shouted. The stranger ran with his natural speed, his limbs displaying to great advantage, and the war eagle's feathers waving on his head. The shouts were redoubled, hope added to his speed, and amid the din, he leaped to the post, and grasping the shining blade, stood ready to despatch his adversary the moment of his arrival. The Manito came, with fear and cowardice depicted in his face. "My friend," said he, "spare my life," and then added in a low voice, as if he did not wish others to hear it, "give me to live," and began to move off, as if the request was granted. "As you have done to others," replied the noble youth, "so shall it be done to you"; and his bleeding head rolled down the sloping hill. The spectators then drew their knives, and cut his body into numberless pieces. The conqueror then asked to be led to the Manito's lodge, the interior of which had never been seen. Few had ever dared even to ascend the eminence on which it stood. On entering, they saw that it consisted of several apartments. The first was arranged and furnished as Indian lodges usually are. But horror struck upon his mind as they entered the second,—it was entirely surrounded by a wall of human skulls and bones, with pieces of human flesh scattered about. Upon a scaffold the dead bodies of two human beings were hanging, cut open, for the purpose of drying the flesh. The third apartment had its sides beautifully decorated, but horrid to behold, two monsters in the form of black snakes, lay coiled up, one on each side of the lodge. It appears that one of them was the wife, and the other the child of the Manito. They were MISHEGENABIKOES, or Devils. This was also the natural shape of the Manito, but he had assumed the human form only to deceive. The orifice by which they had originally come out of the earth was closed, and escape for them was impossible. The magic knife still glittered in the stranger's hand, and without a moment's delay, he severed both their heads. He then commanded the people to bring together combustibles, which they set fire to, and consumed their remains. When the fire reached their carcasses, a dark smoke ascended from the lodge, and the hideous forms of fiery serpents were seen curling amid the flames.

The mysterious stranger, who had thus proved their deliverer, then commanded them to bring together all the human bones scattered around, and after making due preparations, he chose three magic arrows, and shooting the first into the air, cried, "Arise!" He then shot the second, repeating the cry, and immediately shot the third, uttering aloud, "Arise!" And the bones arose, and stood up covered with flesh, in their natural forms. And they instantly raised a loud and joyous shout of thanks to their deliverer.

The Genius of Benevolence (for such we must now regard him) motioned to all the people to keep silence, and addressed them as follows: "My friends, the Great Spirit who lives above the skies, seeing the cruelties of the Manito I have destroyed, was moved with pity for you, and determined to rid the earth of such a monster. I am the creation of His thinking mind, and therein first appeared, and he gave me such power, that when the word was spoken, it was done. When I wished to have the swiftness of a bird, I flew, and whatever power I wanted was given me. You are witnesses of it, and have seen the Mudjee Monedo killed and burned, and the bones of his victims get up and shout. This is as nothing with Him. It was done to restore your friends. And this will be the way when the earth has an end, for all people will arise again, and friends unite in going to the happy hunting grounds, when they will see who directs all things. My stay with you will be short, for I must return whence I came. During this brief time, I will, however, instruct you, and teach you to live happy."

The whole multitude then followed him to the widow's lodge, where he taught them what to do. They built their lodges around him, forming a very large town. They dug up the earth and planted—they built large houses, and learned many new arts, and were happy. Not as it is now—for all the Indians have forgotten it. Having done this, he ascended into the clouds, leaving his wife the future mother of a son, to whom he referred the people assembled to witness his departure, for subsequent counsel.

———————

Note.—How much of the present fiction is due to ideas communicated to the Indian mind, since the discovery of America, it would be impossible to determine.

It has been found by the examination of the skull of a Saginaw [made by Mr. J. Toulmin Smith], that the organ of destructiveness is very largely developed, exceeding by an inch, in the posterior breadth of the head, that of exhibited specimens of the Caucasian race. This skull, however, exhibited benevolence strongly marked, and the entire groups of the anterior organs, exceeded as 6 to 5½ those of the posterior groups, indicating, so far as the theory is followed, that favourable effects might be anticipated to result from education.

THE PIGEON HAWK
AND TORTOISE

A Fable from the Odjibwa

THE PIGEON hawk bantered the tortoise for a race, but the tortoise declined it, unless he would consent to run several days' journey. The hawk very quickly consented, and they immediately set out. The tortoise knew that if he obtained the victory it must be by great diligence, so he went down into the earth and, taking a straight line, stopped for nothing. The hawk, on the contrary, knowing that he could easily beat his competitor, kept carelessly flying this way and that way in the air, stopping now to visit one, and then another, till so much time had been lost that when he came in sight of the winning point, the tortoise had just come up out of the earth, and gained the prize.

THE CHARMED ARROW

From the Ottowa

This tale is separated from a mass of traditionary matter relating to the origin of wars of the northern Indians, with which, however, it appears to have no historical connexion beyond the existence of a few actual proper names of men and places.

SAGIMAU HAD performed great feats against the enemies of his tribe. He had entirely routed and driven off one of the original tribes from the lakes, and came back to his residence on Lake Huron a conqueror. He was also regarded as a Manito. But, he could not feel easy while he heard of the fame and exploits of Kaubina, a great Chippewa chief and Manito in the north. Kaubina lived on a large island in Lake Superior, and was not only versed in magic himself, but had an aged female coadjutor who was a witch, and went under the name of his grandmother. She lived under Lake Superior, and took care to inform him of every thing that threatened him.

Sagimau determined to measure strength with him. He accordingly thought much about him. One night he dreamed that there was a certain head of a lance, which, if it could be procured, would give him sway over other tribes. This treasure was in the possession of a certain beautiful and majestic eagle, to whom all other birds owed obedience, and who, in consequence of having this weapon, was acknowledged king of birds. The lance was, however, seldom seen, even by those most intimate with the owner. The seer of the village dreamed the same dream. It was much talked about, and made much noise. Sagimau determined to seek for it, as it would make him the greatest hero in the world.

He thought he would first go and see Kaubina, and endeavour to deceive him, or try his skill in necromancy. But he resolved to proceed by stratagem. After several days' travel he crossed the neck of land separating the two great waters, and reached the banks of Lake Superior, opposite a large island, which is now called Grand Island. Here Kaubina lived. Some days before this visit, the witch came into Kaubina's lodge and requested some tobacco. But he happened to be in an ill humour, and refused her, telling her he had none. "Very well," said she, "you will see the time when you may wish you had given me some."

Meantime Sagimau was plotting against him. He resolved to carry off his youngest wife. Having no canoe to cross to the island, he asked his companions whether any of them had ever dreamed of walking in the water. One of the men answered yes. He was therefore selected to accompany him. They went into the water until it came breast high. "You must not have the least doubt," said he to the young man, "but resolve that you can walk under water. If you doubt, you will fail." They both thought strong of it,* and disappeared. When about half way through the strait, they met two monsters, who looked as long as pine trees, and had glistening eyes. But they appeased them by giving them tobacco, and went on. On getting near the island, Sagimau said to his friend, "You must turn yourself into a white stone on the shore, near the path where the women come to dip water. I will assume the shape of a black log of driftwood, and be floating, and thumping on the shore near by."

Kaubina had attended a feast that day, and after he got home to his lodge, complained of thirst. He requested his old wife to get him some water. "My! my!" said she, "It is dark, and why not let that one go, whom you think so much of." He then spoke to the youngest, who immediately got a flambeau, and prepared to go, having first asked the elder wife to accompany her. She declined. Dark as it was, and alone, she pursued the path to the edge of the water. She noticed the white stone, and the wood near it, and

---

*This phraseology is peculiar to the Indian language, and is in accordance with the Indian plan of thought. To "think strong" of a thing implies resolution to the enterprising, and confidence to the doubting.

thought she had never seen them before; but if I return, thought she to herself, with such a story, without the water, they will laugh at me. She made a quick motion to dip the water, but was instantly seized by Sagimau and his companion. They drew her under the water, carried her to the main land, and proceeded one day's journey homeward, when they encamped. Meantime Kaubina waited for his expected drink of water. He at last got up and searched for her on the shore, and in the lodges, but could get no intelligence. He was distressed, and could not rest. Next morning he renewed his search, but in vain. He invoked the name of his grandmother, with due ceremony, making the customary present of tobacco. At length she appeared, and after reminding him of his neglect of her, in her last application for the sacred weed, she revealed to him the whole plot, and also told him the means he must use to recover his lost wife. If you follow my advice, said she, you will get her back in a friendly way, and without bloodshed. Kaubina obeyed the injunctions of the witch. He carried with him a number of young men, and overtook Sagimau at his first night's encampment. When the latter saw him, he assumed a smiling aspect, and came forward and offered his hand. It was accepted. They then sat down and smoked. After this Kaubina said, why did you take my wife. It was only, Sagimau replied, to see how great a Manito you were. Here she is—take her. Now that I know your qualities, we will live in peace. Each concealed the deep hostility he entertained for the other. They parted in peace.

After the interview, Sagimau sent his warriors home to Lake Michigan. He determined to remain in the country and seek the charmed arrow. For this purpose he retired to a remote wood, and transformed himself into a dead moose, which appeared as if the carcass had lain a long period, for worms were in its eyes and nostrils. Very soon eagles, hawks, crows, and other birds of prey, flocked to the carcass. But the skin was so hard and tough that they could not penetrate it with their bills. At length they said, let us go and call WAUB WE NONGA to come and cut a hole for us with his lance. Ze Ghe Nhiew offered to go, but having been told that the dead moose was Sagimau, flew back affrighted. The birds renewed their attempt to pierce the hide, but without success. They then repeated their request to the white vulture-eagle. The latter returned the same wary reply, fearful it was the stratagem of the Manito Sagimau; but when appealed to the third time, with the assurance that worms were in the eyes and nostrils of the carcass, he consented. All the birds were seated around the carcass, eager for the feast. When they heard the sweeping noise of the wings of Waub-we-nonga, the king of the birds, they made a cry of joy. He viewed the carcass from a distance. Two birds older than the rest, screamed out to him to come and cut the skin. He advanced cautiously, and gave a blow, but to no effect, the lance bounded back from the tough hide. The birds set up a loud scream, desiring that he would renew the effort. He did so, and drove the lance in, about a foot. Sagamau immediately caught hold of it and wrenched it from the bird. He instantly resumed his human form and commenced his return to his country. The great bird followed him, entreating him to give it back, and promising, on compliance, that he would grant him any thing that he might desire. Sagimau sternly refused. He knew that it contained magic virtues by which he could accomplish all his purposes, one of the first of which was, to overthrow Kaubina. This resolution he firmly maintained, although the bird followed him all the way back, flying from tree to tree, and renewing its solicitations.

Sagimau had no sooner reached his village with this trophy, than he commenced gathering all the tobacco he could, as presents to the different spirits of the land, whom he deemed it necessary to appease, in consequence of the deception he had used in wrongfully getting possession of the arrow. This sacred offering he carefully put up in cedar bags, and then commenced a journey to such places as he knew they inhabited, to leave his offering, and to obtain the permission of the Manitoes to retain his trophy. He travelled the whole circuit of Lake Michigan, and then went across to Lake Huron, visiting every high place and waterfall, celebrated as the residence of spirits. But he was unfavorably received. None of the spirits would accept his offerings. Every spirit he asked replied, "Waub-we-nonga has passed before you with his complaints, accusing you of a theft, and requesting that the arrow be returned to its lawful owner. We cannot, therefore, hear you. He who has stolen shall again be stolen from." The very same words were used by each. The last spirit he applied to lived in a cleft, on a high point of rock, surrounded by woods, on the summit of the island called Mishinimakinong. He added this sentence. "Hlox has cursed you." Thus foiled at every point, he returned home with all his tobacco. He called all his *jossakeeds,* and medicine-men, and jugglers together, and laid the gift before them, requesting their advice in this emergency. He asked each one to tell him whether his skill could designate the spirit which was meant by that outlandish word uttered on the island. One of the oldest men said, "It has been revealed to me, by my guardian spirit, in a dream. It is the name of a witch living in the bottom of Lake Superior; she is a relative of Waub-we-nonga." Not another word was uttered in the council. Silently they smoked out their pipes, and silently they returned to their lodges.

We must now return to Kaubina. When he had recovered his wife, he went back directly to his lodge on the island, and with due ceremony invoked the counsel and aid of his grandmother. For this purpose he erected a *pointed* lodge,* and covered it close around with bark. He took nothing in with him but his drum, medicine sack, and rattles. After singing for some time, he heard a noise under ground, and the woman appeared. "My grandson," said she, "I am made acquainted with your wishes. Your enemy seeks your blood. Sagimau has obtained the great war bird's arrow, and is preparing the sacred gift of our country† to appease the spirits, and obtain their permission to use it. If he obtains his wishes, he will prevail. But I will use all my power to circumvent him. I have a firm friend among the guardian spirits of our nation, who lives on an island toward the south. Waub-we-nonga himself is my relation. You may rely upon my power. In nine days I shall reappear." At the end of that time she fulfilled her promise, and told him to watch, and that at such a time his enemy would come against him with a large war party in canoes.

In the meantime Sagimau had visited the spirits, and failed in

---

*A high-pointed pyramidal lodge is appropriated to the Indian priesthood or magicians.
†Tobacco.

his design. He would have remained at home, after the result of his council with the old men and sages, had he not continued to hear of the exploits of Kaubina, who was making excursions toward the southwest, and driving back all the tribes who lived on the great lake. He was not only goaded on by envy of his fame, but he thought him the cause of the spirits not accepting his tobacco, and thus rendering useless in his hands the sacred arrow. He mustered a large war party and set off in canoes for the north, for the purpose of attacking the Odjibwas. His old men tried to dissuade him from this expedition, but were not heeded. When the party reached the Great Sand Dunes, Sagimau dreamed that he saw Kaubina on an island, and took him prisoner. He was, therefore, assured of success, and went boldly on. They crossed over to the island to watch the movements of Kaubina, who, at this time, had his village on the main land. This was revealed to the latter by his grandmother, who declared the bloody intentions of the enemy. Kaubina appeared in a moment to forget this advice, for he said to his wife, "Come, let us go over to the island for basswood bark." "Why," said she, "have you not just told me that Sagimau was watching there?" "Well," said he, "I am not afraid. I would have gone if I had not heard this account, and I will go now." While crossing the bay in his canoe, he directed his wife to land him alone, and push out her canoe from the shore, and rest there, so that if any accident occurred, she might immediately cross and arouse the warriors. He directed her, the moment she reached his lodge, to take out his medicine sack, and his fighting skin (which was made out of a large bear skin), and to spread out the latter ready for him, when he arrived, so that he could slip it on in an instant, as he relied on its magic virtues to ensure him an easy victory. Shortly after landing him, while resting on her paddles, she heard the sa-sa-kwan, or war whoop. She immediately paddled for the village, and gave the alarm.

It turned out that when Kaubina landed from the canoe, he stepped ashore near the ambush of Sagimau's party, who arose to a man and instantly made him a prisoner. They immediately tied him to a tree, and pushed over to the main land to secure the village before the alarm spread. They landed very expeditiously, and getting behind the village, approached from that part. The fight had but just commenced when Kaubina appeared. He had been released by Hlox, and invoking his spirit, flew to the rescue of his people. He found his fighting skin ready, and slipping it on hastily, he now felt himself invulnerable. He then cried out to his adversary and challenged him to single combat. Sagimau did not decline. "Here am I," said he. "I defy you." They closed instantly. Blow was answered with blow, without any apparent advantage to either, till about midday, when Sagimau began to give out. He appealed to Kaubina, saying, "My elder brother, it is enough! (nesia me-a-me-nik)". No answer was returned, but the reinvigorated blows of his rival and adversary. Kaubina fought with the rage of a demon, and soon after the scalp of Sagimau was flying in the air. Nearly the whole Ottowa party fell with him. It is said the arrow which Sagimau either forgot to use, or was mysteriously withheld from using, was lost in this combat, and returned to the spirit of the King of the Birds who owned it.

Addik Kum Maig*

or

THE ORIGIN OF THE WHITE FISH

A LONG TIME ago, there lived a famous hunter in a remote part of the north. He had a handsome wife and two sons, who were left in the lodge every day, while he went out in quest of the animals, upon whose flesh they subsisted. Game was very abundant in those days, and his exertions in the chase were well rewarded. The skins of animals furnished them with clothing, and their flesh with food. They lived a long distance from any other lodge, and very seldom saw any one. The two sons were still too young to follow their father to the chase, and usually diverted themselves within a short distance of the lodge. They noticed that a young man visited the lodge during their father's absence, and these visits were frequently repeated. At length the elder of the two said to his mother, "My mother, who is this tall young man that comes here so often during our father's absence?"

"Does he wish to see him? Shall I tell him when he comes back this evening?" "Bad boy," said the mother, pettishly, "mind your bow and arrows, and do not be afraid to enter the forest in search of birds and squirrels, with your little brother. It is not manly to be ever about the lodge. Nor will you become a warrior if you tell all the little things you see and hear to your father. Say not a word to him on the subject." The boys obeyed, but as they grew older, and still saw the visits of this mysterious stranger, they resolved

---

*This term appears to be a derivative from ADDIK—the reindeer—and the plural form of the generic GUMEE—water—implying deer of the waters. To facilitate the reading of this, and other compound derivatives, a capital letter is placed at the head of syllables.

to speak again to their mother, and told her that they meant to
inform their father of all they had observed, for they frequently
saw this young man passing through the woods, and he did not
walk in the path, nor did he carry any thing to eat. If he had any
message to deliver, they had observed that messages were always
addressed to the men, and not to the women. At this, the mother
flew into a rage. "I will kill you," said she, "if you speak of it."
They were again intimidated to hold their peace. But observing
the continuance of an improper intercourse, kept up by stealth,
as it were, they resolved at last to disclose the whole matter to
their father. They did so. The result was such as might have been
anticipated. The father, being satisfied of the infidelity of his
wife, watched a suitable occasion, when she was separated from
the children, that they might not have their feelings excited, and
with a single blow of his war-club despatched her. He then buried
her under the ashes of his fire, took down the lodge, and removed,
with his two sons, to a distant position.

But the spirit of the woman haunted the children, who were
now grown up to the estate of young men. She appeared to them
as they returned from hunting in the evening. They were also terrified in their dreams, which they attributed to her. She harassed
their imaginations wherever they went. Life became a scene of
perpetual terrors. They resolved, together with their father, to
leave the country, and commenced a journey toward the south.
After travelling many days along the shores of Lake Superior,
they passed around a high promontory of rock where a large
river issued out of the lake, and soon after came to a place called
PAUWA-TEEG.*

They had no sooner come in sight of these falls, than they
beheld the skull of the woman rolling along the beach. They were
in the utmost fear, and knew not how to elude her. At this
moment one of them looked out, and saw a stately crane sitting
on a rock in the middle of the rapids. They called out to the bird.
"See, grandfather, we are persecuted by a spirit. Come and take
us across the falls, so that we may escape her."

---

*Sault Ste. Marie.

This crane was a bird of extraordinary size and great age. When first descried by the two sons, he sat in a state of stupour, in the midst of the most violent eddies. When he heard himself addressed he stretched forth his neck with great deliberation, and lifting himself by his wings, flew across to their assistance. "Be careful," said the crane, "that you do not touch the back part of my head. It is sore, and should you press against it, I shall not be able to avoid throwing you both into the rapids." They were, however, attentive on this point, and were safely landed on the south shore of the river.

The crane then resumed his former position in the rapids. But the skull now cried out, "Come, my grandfather, and carry me over, for I have lost my children, and am sorely distressed." The aged bird flew to her assistance. He carefully repeated the injunction that she must by no means touch the back part of his head, which had been hurt, and was not yet healed. She promised to obey, but soon felt a curiosity to know where the head of her carrier had been hurt, and how so aged a bird could have received so bad a wound. She thought it strange, and before they were half way over the rapids, could not resist the inclination she felt to touch the affected part. Instantly the crane threw her into the rapids. "There," said he, "you have been of no use during your life, you shall now be changed into something for the benefit of your people, and it shall be called Addik Kum Maig." As the skull floated from rock to rock, the brains were strewed in the water, in a form resembling roes, which soon assumed the shape of a new species of fish, possessing a whiteness of colour, and peculiar flavour, which have caused it, ever since, to be in great repute with the Indians.

The family of this man, in gratitude for their deliverance, adopted the crane as their totem, or mark; and this continues to be the distinguishing tribal sign of the band to this day.

OWASSO AND WAYOOND

or

THE MANITO FOILED

A Saginaw Tale

O WASSO AND Wayoond were sons of the Thunder that rules in the northern hemisphere.* Their father had left them at an early age, after having suffered greatly from the power of some horrid Weendigoes, or man-eaters, against whom he prevailed at last. Wayoond was the youngest of the two, and was but a mere boy when his father left them, and ascended into the skies; but he was intrusted to the care of his elder brother. And he left them his parting advice. They lived in a large country, where there were lakes and open fields, and often amused themselves in playing ball. Game was very plenty at that time, and they had no difficulty in killing as many animals and birds as they wanted. For their father had been a great medicine man, and had given them powerful spirits to aid them in all they undertook.

Some time after the father's ascent, the young men went to amuse themselves by playing ball near the shores of a beautiful lake. They played and laughed with great spirit, and the ball was seldom allowed to touch the ground. In this lake happened to be a wicked old Manito, who looked at them playing, and was very much pleased with their beauty and activity. He thought to himself, what shall I do to get them to accompany me—he willed that one

---

*Thunder is invariably *personified* by the Algic Indians. There is no other mode of describing it in their vocabulary.

of them should hit the ball sideways, and that it should fall into
his canoe. It so happened. When the boys saw the old man they
were surprised, as they had not noticed him before. "Bring
the ball to us," they both cried out, "come to the shore." "No,"
answered the old man. He, however, came near enough for either
of them to wade out to him. "Come, come," he said, "come and
get your ball." They insisted on his coming ashore, but he would
not consent. "Very well," said the eldest, "I will go and get it,"
and he jumped into the water and approached the old man.
"Hand it to me," he said, touching the canoe. "Ha," answered the
old man, "reach over and get it yourself." The young man did so,
and as he was in the act of reaching, the old Manito pushed him
into the canoe, and uttering the words, *maujaun chemaun!* off
they flew, cutting the water so fast, that the spray fell over them.
In a short time they reached the old man's lodge.

He then took the young man by the arm and led him to his
lodge. "My daughter," he said, to his eldest, as they entered the
lodge, "I have brought you a husband." The young woman
smiled, for she soon saw what a fine looking young man he was.
The old man told him to take his seat near her, and the ceremony
was soon ended that made them man and wife.

The young man felt for his poor brother, but it was out of his
power, at that time, to render him any assistance. He remained
very happy with his wife, and they were blessed with a son. She
told him that her father was a magician, and had a magic canoe,
and was wicked. He, one day, asked his son-in-law to go out a
fishing with him. They started, for the magician had only to
speak, and off went the canoe. They reached a rocky island and
fished round it. The young man had fastened his spear in a very
large sturgeon, who was making violent efforts to extricate himself from the barbs. The old man thought this a very favourable
opportunity to drown his son-in-law, and by aiding the canoe as
it rocked outwards, plunged the young man head foremost into
the lake. He then spoke to his canoe, and in a very few moments
was out of sight. The young man knew that this would happen,
but being gifted with limited magic powers, he knew also how to
relieve himself. He spoke to the fish and told him to swim toward
the lodge, while he carried him along, which he did with great

velocity. Once he told the sturgeon to rise near the surface of the water, so that he might catch a glimpse of the magician. He did so, and the young man saw him busy, in another direction, fishing. He proceeded and reached the beach, near the magician's lodge, in advance of him. He then spoke to the fish, not to be angry for his having speared him, as he was created to be meat for man. He then drew the fish on shore, and went up and told his wife to dress it and pull out the gristly part and cook it immediately. She did so, and when it was cooked the magician arrived. "Your grandfather is arrived," said the woman to her son, "go and see what he brings, and eat this as you go," handing him some of the gristle. The boy went, and the magician immediately asked him, "What are you eating? and who brought it?" He replied, "My father brought it." The magician had his doubts and felt perplexed; he, however, put on a grave face, and entering the lodge, acted as if nothing unusual had transpired.

Some days elapsed when he again requested his son-in-law to accompany him. The young man said, "Yes!" His wife had then told him the true character of her father, and the number of times he could exercise his magic powers. They went out, and arrived at a solitary island composed entirely of rocks. The magician said, "Go on shore and pick up all the gulls' eggs you can find." The rocks were covered with them, and the air resounded with the cry of the gulls, who saw the robbery committed on them. The magician took the opportunity to speak to the gulls. "I have long wished," said he, "to offer you something. I now give you this young man for food." He then uttered the charm to his canoe, and it shot out of sight, abandoning the young man to his fate. The gulls flew in immense numbers around him, and were ready to devour him. He addressed them and said—"Gulls, you know you were not formed to eat human flesh, and man was not made to be the prey of birds; obey my words. Fly close together, a sufficient number of you, and carry me on your backs to the magician's lodge." They obeyed him, and he soon found himself swiftly gliding toward home.

It appears that the magician in telling his canoe to go, often limited it, in point of time, or distance, till he ordered it forward again. In this instance he fell asleep, and the canoe stood still, for the young man in his flight over the lake saw him lying on his back in the canoe, taking a nap, as the day was calm and delightful. The gulls, as they passed over him, treated him with great disrespect. He jumped up and exclaimed, "It is always so with these double pierced birds!" Owasso reached the lodge in safety, and killed two or three of the gulls for the sake of their feathers to ornament his son's head. When the magician arrived, his grandson met him with his head covered with feathers. "Where did you get these?" he asked. "My father brought them," he answered. He felt perplexed and uneasy, but said nothing. He entered the lodge in silence, and sat down to meditate upon some new plan for destroying his son-in-law. He reflected that he had tried two of his charms without effect, and had but two more left. He again asked the young man to go with him to get young eagles, he said he wished to tame them, and keep them as pets. They started on the trip, and after traversing an immense waste of water, at length reached a desolate island in the centre of the lake. They landed and soon found an eagle's nest. The young man obeyed his father-in-law's wishes, by climbing up to get the young ones. He had nearly reached the nest, when he heard the magician's voice addressing the tree, saying, "Grow up," and the tree instantly reached an extraordinary height. "Now, eagles!" said he, "I promised you food, and I give you this young man to feed upon." Then he said to the canoe, "Go!" and away he went, leaving the young man at the mercy of the eagles. The birds were enraged at seeing their young in danger—they flew round him with their beaks open, and their claws distended, ready to tear him in pieces. His power, however, extended to them also, and he got them to fly back with him to the lodge. His wife was rejoiced to think that he had escaped the third charm, and told him it was now his turn to ask the magician to go out, fearing that the old man would not repeat the invitation himself. She gave him all necessary directions, which he promised to follow.

When the magician arrived, his surprise and consternation was at its height, finding that his third effort had failed, and that he had but a single charm more in his power.

One evening as Owasso and his wife were sitting on the banks of the lake, and the soft breeze swept over it, they heard a song, as if sung by some one at a great distance. The sound continued some time and then died away in perfect stillness. "Oh! 'tis the voice of my brother," cried the young man. "If I could only see him!" and he hung down his head in deep anguish. His wife felt for him, and to console him, she proposed that they should attempt to make their escape on the morrow. The plan was laid. The younger sister was to offer to comb her father's hair during the warm and sultry part of the day, and pick the hairs clean, and in so doing, it was supposed he would fall asleep. The plan succeeded, and as soon as he slept, the young man and family embarked in the magic canoe, then saying *majaun chemaun!* off the canoe started. They had nearly reached the land, and could distinctly hear the voice of the young man, singing, as before, when the magician awoke. He suspected something, and looking for his canoe immediately found it gone. He spoke his magic words, extended his sinewy arm in the air, and drew it in. The charm was irresistible—the young man and his wife saw, with anguish, when almost within reach of the shore, that the canoe suddenly turned back. They soon reached the lodge. The magician stood on the beach, and drew up his canoe. He did not utter a word. The young couple entered the lodge in silence.* Autumn was now near its close, and winter soon set in. Soon after the first fall of snow, the young man asked the magician to go out hunting deer, as they could now easily be tracked. They set out together, and after several days' journey, arrived at a fit place for their object. They busied themselves in hunting all day, but without success. At evening they built themselves a lodge of pine branches to sleep in. The night was bitterly cold, but the young man took off his leggings and moccasins and hung them up to dry. The magician did the same, carefully hanging his own in a separate place, and they laid down to sleep. During the night the magician got up and went out, remaining some time. As the young man suspected him, and knew, indeed, what kind of a trick the old

---

*This taciturnity is characteristic of the American Indians, who seldom speak or manifest any emotion when events of this nature take place in actual life, especially if hard feelings have been excited in either party.

man meant to play him, he took this opportunity to get up and change the moccasins and leggings, putting his own in the place of the magician's, depending on the darkness of the lodge to impose on him. Afterward they both laid down and slept. Near daylight the magician got up to rekindle the fire, and slyly reached down his own leggings and moccasins with a stick, thinking they were the young man's, and dropped them into the fire, at the same instant throwing himself down, pretending he still wanted to sleep.

The leather leggings and moccasins soon drew up and were burnt. Instantly jumping up, and rubbing his eyes, the magician cried out, "Son-in-law, your moccasins are burning." Owasso got up deliberately and unconcerned. "No, my friend," said he, "here are *mine*," taking them down and putting them on. "It is *your* moccasins that are burning." The magician dropped his head in vexation to think that he had been foiled in all his attempts. Nothing was now left, and he knew that no mercy would be shown him. The young man left him to meditate on all his crimes of blood, and to meet that fate from the want of covering for his feet and legs, which he had prepared for him. He reached home in safety in a few days, notwithstanding the cold, and resolved to quit the place for ever, and go in search of his brother. Although the weather was cold, the lake had not yet frozen over, and the young hunter and his family resolved to embark immediately, the younger sister went with them in the hope of getting a husband. Word was given to the magic canoe, and they went swiftly on their way to the opposite shore. Owasso soon heard his younger brother's well-known voice, as the sounds were wafted on the breeze, singing the following words:

Ni si ai
Ni si ai
A ko nau gud dau o un
A ko nau gud dau o un
Ash i gun ai a he ee
Ni mau en gun e wee
Ash i gun ai a he ee
Ni mau en gun e wee.

"My brother—my brother! Since you left me going in the canoe, a-hee-ee, I am half changed into a wolf, E-wee—I am half changed into a wolf, E-wee." This he kept repeating as they neared the shore. The sounds were very distinct. On the sand they saw the tracks of a wolf, as if departing. They also saw the prints of human hands; and they soon saw Wayoond himself, half man and half wolf, running along shore. Owasso ran after him, crying, "Ni she ma! Ni she ma!" but the partly transformed object jumped on the bank and looked back for some time, repeating the former words, and disappeared in the woods.

The women built a lodge at the spot, and got everything comfortable for a long stay. The man was, however, very uneasy, and exerted his power to regain his brother—for he kept near the lodge at night, singing in a most pitiful strain. They always left food for him some distance from the lodge, which he ate in the night.

The unmarried woman, who was something of a mud-jee-kee-kuá-wis, proposed to dig a pit and cover it with light sticks and leaves, for the purpose of placing the meat on, that when he came to eat it he might fall in. Her plan succeeded, and when they came next morning to examine it, they were rejoiced to find the half wolf in the pit. The man had been fasting previously, and he brought his medicines and charms, and threw some over his brother, who, after some time, resumed his human shape. He was taken to the lodge, but it was some time before the change was perfect, and still longer before he was restored to health. His disposition, however, was soured, for he always sat and looked very gloomy, and felt no pleasure in the society of his friends. He recommended hunting, in which he was very successful, for he always hung the tail of a wolf to his girdle at his back, or at his leg-bands or garters, which gave him great speed and vigour in overtaking animals of the deer kind.

MAUJEEKIKUAWIS was forward in her advances toward him. He, however, paid no attention to it, and shunned her. She continued to be very assiduous in attending to his wants, such as cooking, and mending his moccasins. She felt hurt and displeased at his indifference, and resolved to play him a trick. Opportunity soon offered. The lodge was spacious, and she dug a hole in the ground, where the young man usually sat, covering it very carefully. When

the brothers returned from the chase, the young man threw himself down carelessly at the usual place, and fell into the cavity, his
head and feet remaining out, so that he was unable to extricate
himself. "Ha! ha!" cried Maujeekikuawis, as she helped him out,
"you are mine, I have caught you at last, and I did it on purpose."
A smile came over the young man's face, and he said, "So be it, I
will be yours": and from that moment they lived happily as man
and wife.

They all lived contented and happy after this, for a length of
time. The elder brother's son grew up to manhood, and was noted
for his beauty, bravery, and manliness. He was very expert in the
chase, and supplied them abundantly with food.

One evening the brothers mentioned their desire of visiting a
very high mountain in the vicinity, in order, as they said, to gratify their curiosity, and see the country which lay beyond it. The
women tried to dissuade them, and expressed their fears lest some
accident might befall them; but their opposition was unavailing.
The men prepared to depart, and gave their parting advice to
their wives and children, telling them, that should anything serious
happen, Owasso's elder son was now fully capable of supporting
them, and that the time was not far distant when they should
all meet each other in those happy hunting grounds toward the
setting sun.

The night after this parting address they left the lodge. It was
very dark, still not a breath of air could be felt—when lo! flashes
of lightning appeared, and the noise of rumbling thunder was
suddenly heard advancing from the north (where their father had
gone) and the quietude of the night gave place to one of the most
terrible tempests. The dark air was lit up with flashes of vivid and
forked lightning, and the roar of that ear-stopping thunder was
incessant. At the same time the south wind rushed on with a
tremendous noise, laying the most stately trees level with the earth.

The young men never returned, but tradition says that they
were taken up by their father from the mountain's top, and aided
him in wreaking just vengeance on all Weendigoes and magicians. For it appears that after he was fixed in his ethereal abode,
he beheld with horror the bad actions of these wicked men. And
he resolved to destroy them, and rid the earth of such monsters,

as well as to take vengeance for what he had himself suffered from them. To this end he exerted the power the Great Spirit had given him, by sending thunder and lightning to destroy them all. From this period the Indian world has been free from them. Still the imaginations of our old and young men often dwell upon their former power, and they are led to believe that the hills, and caves, and forests, occupied by these once visible, are still possessed by invisible demons.

Note.—This story, it will be perceived, very much resembles, in some of its incidents, one previously inserted from the Odjibwa. It also embraces one of the principal incidents in the allegory of the "Forsaken Boy," from the same source.

SHAWONDASEE

From the Mythology of the Odjibwas

M UDJEKEWIS AND nine brothers conquered the Mammoth Bear, and obtained the Sacred Belt of Wampum, the great object of previous warlike enterprise, and the great means of happiness to men. The chief honour of this achievement was awarded to Mudjekewis, the youngest of the ten, who received the government of the West Winds. He is therefore called KABEYUN, the father of the winds. To his son, WABUN, he gave the East; to SHAWONDASEE, the South, and to KABIBONOKKA, the North. Manabozho, being an illegitimate son, was left unprovided. When he grew up, and obtained the secret of his birth, he went to war against his father, KABEYUN, and having brought the latter to terms, he received the government of the Northwest Winds, ruling jointly with his brother KABIBONOKKA the tempests from that quarter of the heavens.

Shawondasee is represented as an affluent, plethoric old man, who has grown unwieldy from repletion, and seldom moves. He keeps his eyes steadfastly fixed on the north. When he sighs, in autumn, we have those balmy southern airs, which communicate warmth and delight over the northern hemisphere, and make the *Indian Summer.*

One day, while gazing toward the north, he beheld a beautiful young woman of slender and majestic form, standing on the plains. She appeared in the same place for several days, but what most attracted his admiration, was her bright and flowing locks of yellow hair. Ever dilatory, however, he contented himself with gazing. At length he saw, or fancied he saw, her head enveloped in a pure white mass like snow. This excited his jealousy toward his brother Kabibonokka, and he threw out a succession of short and rapid sighs—when lo! the air was filled with light filaments of a silvery hue, but the object of his affections had for ever vanished. In reality, the southern airs had blown off the fine-winged seed-vessels of the prairie dandelion.

"My son," said the narrator, "it is not wise to differ in our tastes from other people; nor ought we to put off, through slothfulness, what is best done at once. Had Shawondasee conformed to the tastes of his countrymen, he would not have been an admirer of *yellow* hair; and if he had evinced a proper activity in his youth, his mind would not have run flower-gathering in his age."

THE LINNET AND EAGLE

A Fable from the Odjibwa

THE BIRDS met together one day, to try which could fly the highest. Some flew up very swift, but soon got tired, and were passed by others of stronger wing. But the eagle went up beyond them all, and was ready to claim the victory, when the gray linnet, a very small bird, flew from the eagle's back, where it had perched unperceived, and being fresh and unexhausted, succeeded in going the highest. When the birds came down, and met in council to award the prize, it was given to the eagle, because that bird had not only gone up nearer to the sun than any of the larger birds, but it had carried the linnet on its back.

Hence the feathers of the eagle are esteemed the most honourable marks for a warrior, as it is not only considered the bravest bird, but also endowed with strength to soar the highest.

THE MOOSE AND WOODPECKER

or

MANABOZHO IN DISTRESS

From the Pillagers*

FTER MANABOZHO had killed the Prince of Serpents, he was living in a state of great want, completely deserted by his powers, as a deity, and not able to procure the ordinary means of subsistence. He was at this time living with his wife and children, in a remote part of the country, where he could get no game. He was miserably poor. It was winter, and he had not the common Indian comforts.

He said to his wife, one day, I will go out a walking, and see if I cannot find some lodges. After walking some time he saw a lodge at a distance. The children were playing at the door. When they saw him approaching they ran into the lodge, and told their parents that Manabozho was coming. It was the residence of the large red-headed Woodpecker. He came to the lodge door and asked him to enter. He did so. After some time, the Woodpecker, who was a magician, said to his wife, Have you nothing to give Manabozho, he must be hungry. She answered, No. In the centre of the lodge stood a large white tamarack tree. The Woodpecker flew on to it, and commenced going up, turning his head on each side of the tree, and every now and then driving in his bill. At last he drew something out of the tree, and threw it down, when, behold! a fine, fat raccoon on the ground. He drew out six or seven

---

*A warlike tribe of the Algic stock located at the sources of the Mississippi.

more. He then descended, and told his wife to prepare them. Manabozho, he said, this is the only thing we eat. What else can we give you? It is very good, replied Manabozho. They smoked their pipes and conversed with each other. After eating, the great spirit-chief got ready to go home. The Woodpecker said to his wife, Give him the remaining raccoons to take home for his children. In the act of leaving the lodge he dropped intentionally one of his mittens, which was soon after observed. Run, said the Woodpecker to his eldest son, and give it to him. But don't give it into his hand; throw it at him, for there is no knowing him, he acts so curiously. The boy did as he was bid. Nemesho (my grandfather), said he, as he came up to him, you have left one of your mittens—here it is. Yes, said he, affecting to be ignorant of the circumstance, it is so. But don't throw it, you will soil it in the snow. The lad, however, threw it, and was about to return. List, said Manabozho, is that all you eat,—do you eat nothing else with the raccoon. No, replied the young Woodpecker. Tell your father, he answered, to come and visit me, and let him bring a sack. I will give him what he shall eat with his raccoon meat. When the young one reported this to his father, the old man turned up his nose at the invitation. What does the old fellow think he has got! exclaimed he.

Some time after the Woodpecker went to pay a visit to Manabozho. He was received with the usual attention. It had been the boast of Manabozho, in former days, that he could do what any other being in the creation could, whether man or animal. He affected to have the sagacity of all animals, to understand their language, and to be capable of exactly imitating it. And in his visits to men, it was his custom to return, exactly, the treatment he had received. He was very ceremonious in following the very voice and manner of his entertainers. The Woodpecker had no sooner entered his lodge, therefore, than he commenced playing the mimic. He had previously directed his wife to change his lodge, so as to enclose a large dry tamarack tree. What can I give you, said he to the Woodpecker; but as we eat, so shall you eat. He then put a long piece of bone in his nose, in imitation of the bill of this bird, and jumping on the tamarack tree, attempted to climb it, doing as he had seen the Woodpecker do. He turned his head first on one side, then on the other. He made awkward efforts to ascend, but continually slipped down. He struck the tree with the bone in his nose, until at last he drove it so far up his nostrils that the blood began to flow, and he fell down senseless at the foot of the tree. The Woodpecker started after his drum and rattle to restore him, and having got them, succeeded in bringing him to. As soon as he came to his senses, he began to lay the blame of his failure to his wife, saying to his guest, Nemesho, it is this woman relation of yours,—*she* is the cause of my not succeeding. She has rendered me a worthless fellow. Before I took her I could also get raccoons. The Woodpecker said nothing, but flying on the tree, drew out several fine raccoons. Here, said he, this is the way *we* do, and left him with apparent contempt.

Severe weather continued, and Manabozho still suffered for the want of food. One day he walked out, and came to a lodge, which was occupied by the Moose (Möz). The young Mozonsug* saw him and told their father Manabozho was at the door. He told them to invite him in. Being seated they entered into conversation. At last the Moose, who was a Meeta, said, What shall we give Manabozho to eat? We have nothing. His wife was seated with her back toward him, making garters. He walked up to her, and untying the covering of the armlet from her back, cut off a large piece of flesh from the square of her shoulder.† He then put some medicine on it, which immediately healed the wound. The skin did not even appear to have been broken, and his wife was so little affected by it, that she did not so much as leave off her work, till he told her to prepare the flesh for eating. Manabozho, said he, this is [what] we eat, and it is all we can give you.

After they had finished eating Manabozho set out for home, but intentionally, as before, dropped one of his *minjekawun,* or

---

*Diminutive form, plural number, of the noun *Möz.*

†The dress of the females in the Odjibwa nation consists of sleeves, open on the inner side of the arm from the elbow up, and terminating in large square folds, falling from the shoulders, which are tied at the back of the neck with ribbon or binding. The sleeves are separately made, and not attached to the breast garment, which consists of square folds of cloth, ornamented and sustained by shoulder straps. To untie the sleeves or armlets, as is here described, is therefore to expose the shoulders, but not the back—a simple devise, quickly accomplished, by which the magician could readily exercise his art almost imperceptibly to the object.

mittens. One of the young Moose took it to him, telling him that his father had sent him with it. He had been cautioned not to hand it to him, but to throw it at him. Having done so, contrary to the remonstrance of Manabozho, he was going back when the latter cried out BAKAH! BAKAH!* Is *that*† the only kind of meat you eat? Tell me. Yes, answered the young man, that is all, we have nothing else. Tell your father, he replied, to come and visit me, and I will give him what you shall eat with your meat. The old Moose listened to this message with indignity. I wonder what he thinks he has got, poor fellow!

He was bound, however, to obey the invitation, and went accordingly, taking along a cedar sack, for he had been told to bring one. Manabozho received him in the same manner he had himself been received,—repeating the same remarks, and attempted to supply the lack of food in the same manner. To this end he had requested his wife to busy herself in making garters. He arose and untied the covering of her back as he had seen the Moose do. He then cut her back shockingly, paying no attention to her cries or resistance, until he saw her fall down, from the loss of blood. Manabozho, said the Moose, you are killing your wife. He immediately ran for his drum and rattle, and restored her to life by his skill. He had no sooner done this than Manabozho began to lay the blame of his ill success on his wife. Why, Nemesho, said he, this woman, this relation of yours—she is making me a most worthless fellow. Formerly, I procured my meat in this way. But now I can accomplish nothing.

The Moose then cut large pieces of flesh off his own thighs, without the least injury to himself, and gave them to Manabozho, saying with a contemptuous air, this is the way *we* do. He then left the lodge.

---

*"Stop! stop!"

†It is difficult to throw into the English pronoun the whole of the meaning of the Indian. Pronouns in this language being, like other parts of speech, transitive, they are at once indicative both of the actor, personal, and relative, and the nature of the object, or subject of the action, or relation. *This* and *that* are not used in the elementary form these pronouns invariably possess in the English. Inflections are put to them indicating the class of natural objects to which they refer: a noun masculine or feminine, requiring an animate pronoun; a noun inanimate, a pronoun inanimate.

After these visits Manabozho was sitting pensively in his lodge one day, with his head down. He heard the wind whistling around it, and thought, by attentively listening, he could hear the voice of some one speaking to him. It seemed to say to him; Great chief, why are you sorrowful. Am not I your friend—your guardian Spirit? He immediately took up his rattle, and without leaving his sitting posture, began to sing the chant which at the close of every stanza has the chorus of "WHAW LAY LE AW." When he had devoted a long time to this chant, he laid his rattle aside, and determined to fast. For this purpose he went to a cave, and built a very small fire near which he laid down, first telling his wife, that neither she nor the children must come near him, till he had finished his fast. At the end of seven days he came back to the lodge, pale and emaciated. His wife in the meantime had dug through the snow, and got a small quantity of the root called truffles. These she boiled and set before him. When he had finished his repast, he took his large bow and bent it. Then placing a strong arrow to the string, he drew it back, and sent the arrow, with the strength of a giant, through the side of his bark lodge. There, said he to his wife, go to the outside, and you will find a large bear, shot through the heart. She did so, and found one as he had predicted.

He then sent the children out to get red willow sticks. Of these he cut off as many pieces, of equal length, as would serve to invite his friends to a feast. A red stick was sent to each one, not forgetting the Moose and the Woodpecker.

When they arrived they were astonished to see such a profusion of meat cooked for them, at such a time of scarcity. Manabozho understood their glances and felt a conscious pride in making such a display. Akewazi, said he, to one of the oldest of the party, the weather is very cold, and the snow lasts a long time. We can kill nothing now but small squirrels. And I have sent for you to help me eat some of them. The Woodpecker was the first to put a mouthful of the bear's meat to his mouth, but he had no sooner begun to taste it, than it changed into a dry powder, and set him coughing. It appeared as bitter as ashes. The Moose felt the same effect, and began to cough. Each one, in turn, was added to the number of coughers. But they had too much sense of decorum, and respect for their entertainer, to say any thing. The meat looked very fine. They thought they would try more of it. But the more they ate, the faster they coughed and the louder became the uproar, until Manabozho, exerting his former power, which he now felt to be renewed, transformed them all into the ADJIDAMO, or squirrel, an animal which is still found to have the habit of barking, or coughing, whenever it sees any one approach its nest.

WEENG

From the Mythology of the Chippewas

LEEP IS personified by the Algic race under the name of Weeng.* But the power of the Indian Morpheus is executed in a peculiar manner, and by a novel agency. Weeng seldom acts directly in inducing sleep, but he exercises dominion over hosts of gnome-like beings, who are everywhere present, and are constantly on the alert. These beings are invisible to common eyes. Each one is armed with a tiny puggamaugon, or club, and when he observes a person sitting or reclining under circumstances favourable to sleep, he nimbly climbs upon his forehead and inflicts a blow. The first blow only creates drowsiness, the second makes the person lethargic, so that he occasionally closes his eyelids, the third produces sound sleep. It is the constant duty of these little emissaries to put every one to sleep whom they encounter—men, women, and children. And they are found secreted around the bed, or on small protuberances of the bark of the Indian lodges. They hide themselves in the GUSHKEE-PITAUGUN, or smoking pouch of the hunter, and when he sits down to light his pipe in the woods, are ready to fly out and exert their sleep-compelling power. If they succeed, the game is suffered to pass, and the hunter obliged to return to his lodge without a reward.

In general, however, they are represented to possess friendly dispositions, seeking constantly to restore vigour and elasticity to the exhausted body. But being without judgment, their power is

---

*This word has the g sounded hard, as if it were followed by a half sound of k—a common sound for g final in the Odjibwa.

258

sometimes exerted at the hazard of reputation, or even life. Sleep may be induced in a person carelessly floating in his canoe, above a fall; or in a war party, on the borders of an enemy's country; or in a female, without the protection of the lodge circle. Although their peculiar season of action is in the night, they are also alert during the day.

While the forms of these gnomes are believed to be those of *ininees,* little or fairy men, the figure of Weeng himself is unknown, and it is not certain that he has ever been seen. Most of what is known on this subject, is derived from Iagoo, who related, that going out one day with his dogs to hunt, he passed through a wide range of thicket, where he lost his dogs. He became much alarmed, for they were faithful animals, and he was greatly attached to them. He called out, and made very exertion to recover them in vain. At length he came to a spot where he found them asleep, having incautiously ran near the residence of Weeng. After great exertions he aroused them, but not without having felt the power of somnolency himself. As he cast up his eyes from the place where the dogs were lying, he saw the Spirit of Sleep sitting upon a branch of a tree. He was in the shape of a giant insect, or *mon-etoas,* with many wings from his back, which made a low deep murmuring sound, like distant falling water. But Iagoo himself, being a very great liar and braggart, but little credit was given to his narration.

Weeng is not only the dispenser of sleep, but it seems, he is also the author of dulness, which renders the word susceptible of an ironical use. If an orator fails, he is said to be struck by Weeng. If a warrior *lingers,* he has ventured too near the sleepy god. If children begin to nod or yawn, the Indian mother looks up smilingly, and says, "they have been struck by Weeng," and puts them to bed.

Iagoo

From the Mythology of the Chippewas

I AGOO IS THE NAME of a personage noted in Indian lore for having given extravagant narrations of whatever he had seen, heard, or accomplished. It seems that he always saw extraordinary things, made extraordinary journeys, and performed extraordinary feats. He could not look out of his lodge and see things as other men did. If he described a bird, it had a most singular variety of brilliant plumage. The animals he met with were all of the monstrous kind; they had eyes like orbs of fire, and claws like hooks of steel, and could step over the top of an Indian lodge. He told of a serpent he had seen, which had hair on its neck like a mane, and feet resembling a quadruped; and if one were to take his own account of his exploits and observations, it would be difficult to decide whether his strength, his activity, or his wisdom should be most admired.

Iagoo did not appear to have been endowed with the ordinary faculties of other men. His eyes appeared to be magnifiers, and the tympanum of his ears so constructed that what appeared to common observers to be but the sound of a zephyr, to him had a far closer resemblance to the noise of thunder. His imagination appeared to be of so exuberant a character, that he scarcely required more than a drop of water to construct an ocean, or a grain of sand to form an earth. And he had so happy an exemption from both the restraints of judgment and moral accountability, that he never found the slightest difficulty in accommodating his facts to the most enlarged credulity. Nor was his ample thirst for the marvellous ever quenched by attempts to reconcile statements the most strange, unaccountable, and preposterous.

Such was Iagoo, the Indian story-teller, whose name is associated with all that is extravagant and marvellous, and has long been established in the hunter's vocabulary as a perfect synonym for liar, and is bandied about as a familiar proverb. If a hunter or warrior, in telling his exploits, undertakes to embellish them; to overrate his merits, or in any other way to excite the incredulity of his hearers, he is liable to be rebuked with the remark, "So here we have Iagoo come again." And he seems to hold the relative rank in oral narration which our written literature awards to Baron Munchausen, Jack Falstaff, and Captain Lemuel Gulliver.

Notwithstanding all this, there are but a few scraps of his actual stories to be found. He first attracted notice by giving an account of a water lilly, a single leaf of which, he averred, was sufficient to make a petticoat and upper garments for his wife and daughter. One evening he was sitting in his lodge, on the banks of a river, and hearing the quacking of ducks on the stream, he fired through the lodge door at a venture. He killed a swan that happened to be flying by, and twenty brace of ducks in the stream. But this did not check the force of his shot; they passed on, and struck the heads of two loons, at the moment they were coming up from beneath the water, and even went beyond and killed a most extraordinary large fish called Moshkeenozha.* On another occasion he had killed a deer, and after skinning it, was carrying the carcass on his shoulders, when he spied some stately elks on the plain before him. He immediately gave them chase, and had run, over hill and dale, a distance of half a day's travel, before he recollected that he had the deer's carcass on his shoulders.

One day, as he was passing over a tract of *mush-keeg,* or bog-land, he saw musquitoes of such enormous size, that he staked his reputation on the fact that a single wing of one of the insects was sufficient for a sail to his canoe, and the proboscis as big as his wife's shovel. But he was favoured with a still more extraordinary

---

*The muscalunge.

sight, in a gigantic ant, which passed him, as he was watching a beaver's lodge, dragging the entire carcass of a hare.

At another time, for he was ever seeing or doing something wonderful, he got out of smoking weed, and in going into the woods in search of some, he discovered a bunch of the red willow, or maple bush, of such a luxuriant growth, that he was industriously occupied half a day in walking round it.

THE GRAVE LIGHT

or

ADVENTURES OF A WARRIOR'S SOUL

From the Odjibwa

THERE WAS once a battle between the Indians, in which many were killed on both sides. Among the number was the leader of the Odjibwas, a very brave man, who had fought in many battles; but while he was shouting for victory, he received an arrow in his flesh, and fell as if dead. At last his companions *thought he was dead,* and treated him as if he were. They placed his body in a sitting posture, on the field of battle, his back being supported by a tree, and his face toward the enemies' country. They put on him his head-dress of feathers, and leaned his bow against his shoulders, for it was before the white men had brought guns for the Indians. They then left him and returned to their homes.

The warrior, however, heard and saw all they did. Although his body was deprived of muscular motion, his soul was living within it. He heard them lament his death, and felt their touch as they set him up. "They will not be so cruel as to leave me here," he thought to himself. "I am certainly not dead. I have the use of my senses." But his anguish was extreme, when he saw them, one after another depart, till he was left alone among the dead. He could not move a limb, nor a muscle, and felt as if he were buried in his own body. Horrid agonies came over him. He exerted himself, but found that he had no power over his muscles. At last he appeared to leap out of himself. He first stood up, and then followed his friends. He soon overtook them, but when he arrived at their camp no one noticed him. He spoke to them, but no one answered. He seemed to be *invisible* to them, and his voice appeared to have no *sound.* Unconscious, however, of his body's being left behind, he thought their conduct most strange. He determined to follow them, and exactly imitated all they did, walking when they walked, running when they ran, sleeping when they slept. But the most unbroken silence was maintained as to his presence.

When evening came he addressed the party. "Is it possible," said he, "that you do not see me, nor hear me, nor understand me? Will you permit me to starve when you have plenty? Is there no one who recollects me?" And with similar sentiments he continued to talk to them, and to upbraid them at every stage of their homeward journey, but his words seemed to pass like the sounds of the wind.

At length they reached the village, and the women and children, and old men, came out, according to custom, to welcome the returning war party. They set up the shout of praise. "Kumaudjing! kumaudjing! kumaudjing! They have met, fought, and conquered," was heard at every side. Group after group repeated the cry.

> Kumaudjing! kumaudjing! kumaudjing!
> They have met, fought, and conquered
>   The strong and the brave,
> See the eagle plumes nod,
>   And the red trophies wave.
>   Kumaudjing! kumaudjing!
>   The war-banner waves,
>   They have fought like our fathers,
>   And scorn to be slaves,
>   The sons of the noble,
>   They scorn to be slaves.
> And he—where is he, who has led them to fight,
>   Whose arrow was death,
>   And whose war-club was might.
>   Kumaudjing! kumaudjing!
>   The hero is near,
> He is tying his enemies' scalp to his robe,
> And wiping the enemies' blood from his spear.

He is near—he is near,
And, hark, his Sa-sa-kwan*
Now bursts on the ear.

The truth, however, was soon revealed; although it caused a momentary check, it did not mar the *general* joy. The sight of scalps made every tongue vocal. A thousand inquiries were made, and he heard his own fate described, how he had fought bravely, been killed, and left among the dead.

"It is not true," replied the indignant chief, "that I was killed and left upon the field of battle. I am here. I live. I move. See me." Nobody answered. He then walked to his own lodge. He saw his wife tearing her hair, and lamenting his fate. He asked her to bind up his wounds. She made no reply. He placed his mouth close to her ear, and called for food. She did not notice it. He drew back his arm and struck her a blow. She felt nothing.

Thus foiled he determined to go back. He followed the track of the warriors. It was four days' journey. During three days he met with nothing extraordinary. On the fourth, toward evening, as he drew near the skirts of the battle field, he saw a fire in the path. He stepped on one side, but the fire had also moved its position. He crossed to the other side, but the fire was still before him. Whichever way he took, the fire appeared to bar his approach. At this moment he espied the enemy of his fortunes in the moccasin, or flat-headed snake. "My son," said the reptile, "you have heretofore been considered a brave man—but beware of this fire. It is a strong spirit. You must appease it by the sacred gift." The warrior put his hand to his side, but he had left his sack behind him. "Demon," he exclaimed, addressing the flame, "why do you bar my approach. Know that I am a spirit. I have never been defeated by my enemies, and I will not be defeated by you."

So saying, he made a sudden effort and leaped through the flames. In this effort *he awoke from his trance*. He had lain eight days on the battle field. He found himself sitting on the ground, with his back supported by a tree, and his bow leaning against his

---

*War cry.

shoulder, as his friends had left him. He looked up and beheld a
large Gha Niew, or war eagle, sitting in the tree, which he immediately recognised as his guardian spirit, or personal Manito.
This bird had watched his body, and prevented the other birds of
prey from devouring it.

He arose and stood for a few minutes, but found himself weak
and emaciated. By the use of simples and such forest arts as our
people are versed in, he succeeded in reaching his home. When
he came near, he uttered the Sa sa kwan, or war cry, which threw
the village into an uproar. But while they were debating the
meaning of so unexpected a sound, the wounded chief was ushered
into their midst. He related his adventures as before given. He
concluded his narrative by telling them that it is pleasing to the
spirits of the dead to have a fire lit up on their graves at night,
after their burial. He gave as a reason, that it is four days' travel
to the place appointed for the residence of the soul, and it
requires a light every night at the place of its encampment. If the
friends of the deceased neglect this rite, the spirit is compelled to
build a fire for itself.

Light up the fire upon my grave
　　　When I am dead.
'Twill softly shed its beaming rays,
To guide the soul its darkling ways,
And ever, as the day's full light
Goes down, and leaves the world in night,
These kindly gleams, with warmth possest,
Shall show my spirit where to rest
　　　When I am dead.

Four days the funeral rite renew,
　　　When I am dead.
While onward bent, with typic woes,
I seek the red man's last repose;
Let no rude hand the flame destroy,
Nor mar the scene with festive joy;
While night by night, a ghostly guest,
I journey to my final rest,
　　　When I am dead.

No moral light directs my way
        When I am dead.
A hunter's fate—a warrior's fame,
A shade, a phantom, or a name,
All life-long through my hands have sought,
Unblest, unlettered, and untaught:
Deny me not the boon I crave—
A symbol-light upon my grave,
        When I am dead.

PAUGUK

From the Mythology of the Chippewas

I N A peculiar class of languages like the native American, in
which symbols are so extensively used, it might be anticipated that Death should be thus denoted.

I asked SHAGUSH KODA WAIKWA, from whom this allegory is
derived, whether the Northern Indians discriminated between a
corpse, a ghost, a spirit, an angel, and death, considered as a personification. The answer was affirmative, and I received the name
for each.

Pauguk, according to this authority, is the personification of
death. He is represented as existing without flesh or blood. He
is a hunter, and besides his bow and arrows, is armed with a
puggamagon, or war-club. But he hunts only men, women, and
children. He is an object of dread and horror. To see him is a sure
indication of death. Some accounts represent his bones as covered by a thin transparent skin, and his eye sockets as filled with
balls of fire.

Pauguk never speaks. Unlike the JEEBI or ghost, his limbs
never assume the rotundity of life, neither is he to be confounded
in form with the numerous class of minor Manitoes, or spirits.
He does not possess the power of metamorphosis. Unvaried in
repulsiveness, he is ever an object of fear; and often, according to
Indian story, has the warrior, flushed with the ardour of battle,
rushing forward to seize the prize of victory, clasped the cold and
bony hand of PAUGUK.

"I shall never forget the fate of OWYNOKWA," continued the
narrator. "She was a widow of my native village, who had been
left with six sons. One after the other, as they became of suitable
age, they had joined the war parties who went out against their

enemies and fallen in battle. At last but one was left; he was her only stay and comfort, supplying her with good and protection in her old age. But he too, as he became old enough, spurning the dull life of a hunter, followed the war drum of his tribe, and went out against our enemies in the West. The absence of such a war party, is a time of anxiety and suspense with the women of a village. To relieve this, and at the same moment to prepare them for more particular intelligence, the returning party gives the war-cry of triumph, and the death-wail indicating the number slain, as soon as they come within hearing. On the present occasion, Owynokwa rushed from her lodge, the moment she caught the first sound. She stood with her lips parted, in an attitude of intense and agonized suspense; and as soon as the death-wail broke upon her ear, despair appeared to rivet her to the spot. She heeded nothing; not a muscle moved; she neither inquired nor heard, who were the slain, but sank slowly to the earth in the place where she stood. She was carried into her lodge, and the next morning showed signs of reanimation, but they were slight and brief—the rigidity of death soon seized upon her frame, and she followed her son to the land of spirits. Her son was indeed among the slain, but mortal tongue had not communicated the fact. It was generally supposed she had met the glare of Pauguk at the moment the death-wail, or *Chee kwau dum,* had broke on her ear."

THE VINE AND OAK

An Allegory in the Manner of the Algics

A VINE was growing beside a thrifty oak, and had just reached that height at which it requires support. "Oak," said the ivy vine, "bend your trunk so that you may be a support to me." "My support," replied the oak, "is naturally yours, and you may rely on my strength to bear you up, but I am too large and too solid to bend. Put your arms around me, my pretty vine, and I will manfully support and cherish you, if you have an ambition to climb, even as high as the clouds. While I thus hold you up, you will ornament my rough trunk with your pretty green leaves and shining scarlet berries. They will be as frontlets to my head, and I shall stand in the forest like a glorious warrior, with all his plumes. We were made by the Master of Life to grow together, that by our union the weak should be made strong, and the strong render aid to the weak."

"But I wish to grow *independently,*" said the vine, "why cannot you twine around me, and let me grow up straight, and not be a mere dependant upon *you.*" "Nature," answered the oak, "did not *so* design it. It is impossible that you should grow to any height *alone,* and if you try it, the winds and rain, if not your own weight, will bring you to the ground. Neither is it proper for you to run your arms hither and yon, among the trees. The trees will begin to say— "It is not my vine—it is a stranger—get thee gone, I will not cherish thee." By this time thou wilt be so entangled among the different branches, that thou canst not get back to the oak; and nobody will *then* admire thee, or pity thee."

"Ah me," said the vine, "let me escape from such a destiny," and with this, she twined herself around the oak, and they both grew and flourished happily together.

A CATALOG OF SELECTED
DOVER BOOKS
IN ALL FIELDS OF INTEREST

A CATALOG OF SELECTED DOVER
BOOKS IN ALL FIELDS OF INTEREST

CONCERNING THE SPIRITUAL IN ART, Wassily Kandinsky. Pioneering work by father of abstract art. Thoughts on color theory, nature of art. Analysis of earlier masters. 12 illustrations. 80pp. of text. 5⅜ x 8½. 23411-8 Pa. $4.95

ANIMALS: 1,419 Copyright-Free Illustrations of Mammals, Birds, Fish, Insects, etc., Jim Harter (ed.). Clear wood engravings present, in extremely lifelike poses, over 1,000 species of animals. One of the most extensive pictorial sourcebooks of its kind. Captions. Index. 284pp. 9 x 12. 23766-4 Pa. $14.95

CELTIC ART: The Methods of Construction, George Bain. Simple geometric techniques for making Celtic interlacements, spirals, Kells-type initials, animals, humans, etc. Over 500 illustrations. 160pp. 9 x 12. (USO) 22923-8 Pa. $9.95

AN ATLAS OF ANATOMY FOR ARTISTS, Fritz Schider. Most thorough reference work on art anatomy in the world. Hundreds of illustrations, including selections from works by Vesalius, Leonardo, Goya, Ingres, Michelangelo, others. 593 illustrations. 192pp. 7⅛ x 10¼. 20241-0 Pa. $9.95

CELTIC HAND STROKE-BY-STROKE (Irish Half-Uncial from "The Book of Kells"): An Arthur Baker Calligraphy Manual, Arthur Baker. Complete guide to creating each letter of the alphabet in distinctive Celtic manner. Covers hand position, strokes, pens, inks, paper, more. Illustrated. 48pp. 8¼ x 11. 24336-2 Pa. $3.95

EASY ORIGAMI, John Montroll. Charming collection of 32 projects (hat, cup, pelican, piano, swan, many more) specially designed for the novice origami hobbyist. Clearly illustrated easy-to-follow instructions insure that even beginning papercrafters will achieve successful results. 48pp. 8¼ x 11. 27298-2 Pa. $3.50

THE COMPLETE BOOK OF BIRDHOUSE CONSTRUCTION FOR WOODWORKERS, Scott D. Campbell. Detailed instructions, illustrations, tables. Also data on bird habitat and instinct patterns. Bibliography. 3 tables. 63 illustrations in 15 figures. 48pp. 5¼ x 8½. 24407-5 Pa. $2.50

BLOOMINGDALE'S ILLUSTRATED 1886 CATALOG: Fashions, Dry Goods and Housewares, Bloomingdale Brothers. Famed merchants' extremely rare catalog depicting about 1,700 products: clothing, housewares, firearms, dry goods, jewelry, more. Invaluable for dating, identifying vintage items. Also, copyright-free graphics for artists, designers. Co-published with Henry Ford Museum & Greenfield Village. 160pp. 8¼ x 11. 25780-0 Pa. $10.95

HISTORIC COSTUME IN PICTURES, Braun & Schneider. Over 1,450 costumed figures in clearly detailed engravings—from dawn of civilization to end of 19th century. Captions. Many folk costumes. 256pp. 8⅜ x 11¾. 23150-X Pa. $12.95

STICKLEY CRAFTSMAN FURNITURE CATALOGS, Gustav Stickley and L. & J. G. Stickley. Beautiful, functional furniture in two authentic catalogs from 1910. 594 illustrations, including 277 photos, show settles, rockers, armchairs, reclining chairs, bookcases, desks, tables. 183pp. 6½ x 9¼. 23838-5 Pa. $11.95

AMERICAN LOCOMOTIVES IN HISTORIC PHOTOGRAPHS: 1858 to 1949, Ron Ziel (ed.). A rare collection of 126 meticulously detailed official photographs, called "builder portraits," of American locomotives that majestically chronicle the rise of steam locomotive power in America. Introduction. Detailed captions. xi + 129pp. 9 x 12. 27393-8 Pa. $12.95

AMERICA'S LIGHTHOUSES: An Illustrated History, Francis Ross Holland, Jr. Delightfully written, profusely illustrated fact-filled survey of over 200 American lighthouses since 1716. History, anecdotes, technological advances, more. 240pp. 8 x 10¾. 25576-X Pa. $12.95

TOWARDS A NEW ARCHITECTURE, Le Corbusier. Pioneering manifesto by founder of "International School." Technical and aesthetic theories, views of industry, economics, relation of form to function, "mass-production split" and much more. Profusely illustrated. 320pp. 6⅛ x 9¼. (USO) 25023-7 Pa. $9.95

HOW THE OTHER HALF LIVES, Jacob Riis. Famous journalistic record, exposing poverty and degradation of New York slums around 1900, by major social reformer. 100 striking and influential photographs. 233pp. 10 x 7⅞. 22012-5 Pa. $11.95

FRUIT KEY AND TWIG KEY TO TREES AND SHRUBS, William M. Harlow. One of the handiest and most widely used identification aids. Fruit key covers 120 deciduous and evergreen species; twig key 160 deciduous species. Easily used. Over 300 photographs. 126pp. 5⅜ x 8½. 20511-8 Pa. $3.95

COMMON BIRD SONGS, Dr. Donald J. Borror. Songs of 60 most common U.S. birds: robins, sparrows, cardinals, bluejays, finches, more—arranged in order of increasing complexity. Up to 9 variations of songs of each species. Cassette and manual 99911-4 $8.95

ORCHIDS AS HOUSE PLANTS, Rebecca Tyson Northen. Grow cattleyas and many other kinds of orchids—in a window, in a case, or under artificial light. 63 illustrations. 148pp. 5⅜ x 8½. 23261-1 Pa. $4.95

MONSTER MAZES, Dave Phillips. Masterful mazes at four levels of difficulty. Avoid deadly perils and evil creatures to find magical treasures. Solutions for all 32 exciting illustrated puzzles. 48pp. 8¼ x 11. 26005-4 Pa. $2.95

MOZART'S DON GIOVANNI (DOVER OPERA LIBRETTO SERIES), Wolfgang Amadeus Mozart. Introduced and translated by Ellen H. Bleiler. Standard Italian libretto, with complete English translation. Convenient and thoroughly portable—an ideal companion for reading along with a recording or the performance itself. Introduction. List of characters. Plot summary. 121pp. 5¼ x 8½. 24944-1 Pa. $3.95

TECHNICAL MANUAL AND DICTIONARY OF CLASSICAL BALLET, Gail Grant. Defines, explains, comments on steps, movements, poses and concepts. 15-page pictorial section. Basic book for student, viewer. 127pp. 5⅜ x 8½. 21843-0 Pa. $4.95

CATALOG OF DOVER BOOKS

BRASS INSTRUMENTS: Their History and Development, Anthony Baines. Authoritative, updated survey of the evolution of trumpets, trombones, bugles, cornets, French horns, tubas and other brass wind instruments. Over 140 illustrations and 48 music examples. Corrected and updated by author. New preface. Bibliography. 320pp. 5⅜ x 8½. 27574-4 Pa. $9.95

HOLLYWOOD GLAMOR PORTRAITS, John Kobal (ed.). 145 photos from 1926-49. Harlow, Gable, Bogart, Bacall; 94 stars in all. Full background on photographers, technical aspects. 160pp. 8⅜ x 11¼. 23352-9 Pa. $12.95

MAX AND MORITZ, Wilhelm Busch. Great humor classic in both German and English. Also 10 other works: "Cat and Mouse," "Plisch and Plumm," etc. 216pp. 5⅜ x 8½. 20181-3 Pa. $6.95

THE RAVEN AND OTHER FAVORITE POEMS, Edgar Allan Poe. Over 40 of the author's most memorable poems: "The Bells," "Ulalume," "Israfel," "To Helen," "The Conqueror Worm," "Eldorado," "Annabel Lee," many more. Alphabetic lists of titles and first lines. 64pp. 5 3/16 x 8¼. 26685-0 Pa. $1.00

PERSONAL MEMOIRS OF U. S. GRANT, Ulysses Simpson Grant. Intelligent, deeply moving firsthand account of Civil War campaigns, considered by many the finest military memoirs ever written. Includes letters, historic photographs, maps and more. 528pp. 6⅛ x 9¼. 28587-1 Pa. $12.95

AMULETS AND SUPERSTITIONS, E. A. Wallis Budge. Comprehensive discourse on origin, powers of amulets in many ancient cultures: Arab, Persian Babylonian, Assyrian, Egyptian, Gnostic, Hebrew, Phoenician, Syriac, etc. Covers cross, swastika, crucifix, seals, rings, stones, etc. 584pp. 5⅜ x 8½. 23573-4 Pa. $12.95

RUSSIAN STORIES/PYCCKNE PACCKA3bl: A Dual-Language Book, edited by Gleb Struve. Twelve tales by such masters as Chekhov, Tolstoy, Dostoevsky, Pushkin, others. Excellent word-for-word English translations on facing pages, plus teaching and study aids, Russian/English vocabulary, biographical/critical introductions, more. 416pp. 5⅜ x 8½. 26244-8 Pa. $9.95

PHILADELPHIA THEN AND NOW: 60 Sites Photographed in the Past and Present, Kenneth Finkel and Susan Oyama. Rare photographs of City Hall, Logan Square, Independence Hall, Betsy Ross House, other landmarks juxtaposed with contemporary views. Captures changing face of historic city. Introduction. Captions. 128pp. 8¼ x 11. 25790-8 Pa. $9.95

AIA ARCHITECTURAL GUIDE TO NASSAU AND SUFFOLK COUNTIES, LONG ISLAND, The American Institute of Architects, Long Island Chapter, and the Society for the Preservation of Long Island Antiquities. Comprehensive, well-researched and generously illustrated volume brings to life over three centuries of Long Island's great architectural heritage. More than 240 photographs with authoritative, extensively detailed captions. 176pp. 8¼ x 11. 26946-9 Pa. $14.95

NORTH AMERICAN INDIAN LIFE: Customs and Traditions of 23 Tribes, Elsie Clews Parsons (ed.). 27 fictionalized essays by noted anthropologists examine religion, customs, government, additional facets of life among the Winnebago, Crow, Zuni, Eskimo, other tribes. 480pp. 6⅛ x 9¼. 27377-6 Pa. $10.95

FRANK LLOYD WRIGHT'S HOLLYHOCK HOUSE, Donald Hoffmann. Lavishly illustrated, carefully documented study of one of Wright's most controversial residential designs. Over 120 photographs, floor plans, elevations, etc. Detailed perceptive text by noted Wright scholar. Index. 128pp. 9¼ x 10¾. 27133-1 Pa. $11.95

THE MALE AND FEMALE FIGURE IN MOTION: 60 Classic Photographic Sequences, Eadweard Muybridge. 60 true-action photographs of men and women walking, running, climbing, bending, turning, etc., reproduced from rare 19th-century masterpiece. vi + 121pp. 9 x 12.   24745-7 Pa. $10.95

1001 QUESTIONS ANSWERED ABOUT THE SEASHORE, N. J. Berrill and Jacquelyn Berrill. Queries answered about dolphins, sea snails, sponges, starfish, fishes, shore birds, many others. Covers appearance, breeding, growth, feeding, much more. 305pp. 5¼ x 8¼.   23366-9 Pa. $8.95

GUIDE TO OWL WATCHING IN NORTH AMERICA, Donald S. Heintzelman. Superb guide offers complete data and descriptions of 19 species: barn owl, screech owl, snowy owl, many more. Expert coverage of owl-watching equipment, conservation, migrations and invasions, etc. Guide to observing sites. 84 illustrations. xiii + 193pp. 5⅜ x 8½.   27344-X Pa. $8.95

MEDICINAL AND OTHER USES OF NORTH AMERICAN PLANTS: A Historical Survey with Special Reference to the Eastern Indian Tribes, Charlotte Erichsen-Brown. Chronological historical citations document 500 years of usage of plants, trees, shrubs native to eastern Canada, northeastern U.S. Also complete identifying information. 343 illustrations. 544pp. 6½ x 9¼.   25951-X Pa. $12.95

STORYBOOK MAZES, Dave Phillips. 23 stories and mazes on two-page spreads: Wizard of Oz, Treasure Island, Robin Hood, etc. Solutions. 64pp. 8¼ x 11.
                                                                              23628-5 Pa. $2.95

NEGRO FOLK MUSIC, U.S.A., Harold Courlander. Noted folklorist's scholarly yet readable analysis of rich and varied musical tradition. Includes authentic versions of over 40 folk songs. Valuable bibliography and discography. xi + 324pp. 5⅜ x 8½.
                                                                              27350-4 Pa. $9.95

MOVIE-STAR PORTRAITS OF THE FORTIES, John Kobal (ed.). 163 glamor, studio photos of 106 stars of the 1940s: Rita Hayworth, Ava Gardner, Marlon Brando, Clark Gable, many more. 176pp. 8⅜ x 11¼.   23546-7 Pa. $12.95

BENCHLEY LOST AND FOUND, Robert Benchley. Finest humor from early 30s, about pet peeves, child psychologists, post office and others. Mostly unavailable elsewhere. 73 illustrations by Peter Arno and others. 183pp. 5⅜ x 8½. 22410-4 Pa. $6.95

YEKL and THE IMPORTED BRIDEGROOM AND OTHER STORIES OF YIDDISH NEW YORK, Abraham Cahan. Film Hester Street based on Yekl (1896). Novel, other stories among first about Jewish immigrants on N.Y.'s East Side. 240pp. 5⅜ x 8½.   22427-9 Pa. $6.95

SELECTED POEMS, Walt Whitman. Generous sampling from *Leaves of Grass.* Twenty-four poems include "I Hear America Singing," "Song of the Open Road," "I Sing the Body Electric," "When Lilacs Last in the Dooryard Bloom'd," "O Captain! My Captain!"–all reprinted from an authoritative edition. Lists of titles and first lines. 128pp. 5¹⁄₁₆ x 8¼.   26878-0 Pa. $1.00

THE BEST TALES OF HOFFMANN, E. T. A. Hoffmann. 10 of Hoffmann's most important stories: "Nutcracker and the King of Mice," "The Golden Flowerpot," etc. 458pp. 5⅜ x 8½. 21793-0 Pa. $9.95

FROM FETISH TO GOD IN ANCIENT EGYPT, E. A. Wallis Budge. Rich detailed survey of Egyptian conception of "God" and gods, magic, cult of animals, Osiris, more. Also, superb English translations of hymns and legends. 240 illustrations. 545pp. 5⅜ x 8½. 25803-3 Pa. $13.95

FRENCH STORIES/CONTES FRANÇAIS: A Dual-Language Book, Wallace Fowlie. Ten stories by French masters, Voltaire to Camus: "Micromegas" by Voltaire; "The Atheist's Mass" by Balzac; "Minuet" by de Maupassant; "The Guest" by Camus, six more. Excellent English translations on facing pages. Also French-English vocabulary list, exercises, more. 352pp. 5⅜ x 8½. 26443-2 Pa. $9.95

CHICAGO AT THE TURN OF THE CENTURY IN PHOTOGRAPHS: 122 Historic Views from the Collections of the Chicago Historical Society, Larry A. Viskochil. Rare large-format prints offer detailed views of City Hall, State Street, the Loop, Hull House, Union Station, many other landmarks, circa 1904-1913. Introduction. Captions. Maps. 144pp. 9⅜ x 12¼. 24656-6 Pa. $12.95

OLD BROOKLYN IN EARLY PHOTOGRAPHS, 1865-1929, William Lee Younger. Luna Park, Gravesend race track, construction of Grand Army Plaza, moving of Hotel Brighton, etc. 157 previously unpublished photographs. 165pp. 8⅞ x 11¾. 23587-4 Pa. $13.95

THE MYTHS OF THE NORTH AMERICAN INDIANS, Lewis Spence. Rich anthology of the myths and legends of the Algonquins, Iroquois, Pawnees and Sioux, prefaced by an extensive historical and ethnological commentary. 36 illustrations. 480pp. 5⅜ x 8½. 25967-6 Pa. $10.95

AN ENCYCLOPEDIA OF BATTLES: Accounts of Over 1,560 Battles from 1479 B.C. to the Present, David Eggenberger. Essential details of every major battle in recorded history from the first battle of Megiddo in 1479 B.C. to Grenada in 1984. List of Battle Maps. New Appendix covering the years 1967-1984. Index. 99 illustrations. 544pp. 6½ x 9¼. 24913-1 Pa. $16.95

SAILING ALONE AROUND THE WORLD, Captain Joshua Slocum. First man to sail around the world, alone, in small boat. One of great feats of seamanship told in delightful manner. 67 illustrations. 294pp. 5⅜ x 8½. 20326-3 Pa. $6.95

ANARCHISM AND OTHER ESSAYS, Emma Goldman. Powerful, penetrating, prophetic essays on direct action, role of minorities, prison reform, puritan hypocrisy, violence, etc. 271pp. 5⅜ x 8½. 22484-8 Pa. $7.95

MYTHS OF THE HINDUS AND BUDDHISTS, Ananda K. Coomaraswamy and Sister Nivedita. Great stories of the epics; deeds of Krishna, Shiva, taken from puranas, Vedas, folk tales; etc. 32 illustrations. 400pp. 5⅜ x 8½. 21759-0 Pa. $12.95

BEYOND PSYCHOLOGY, Otto Rank. Fear of death, desire of immortality, nature of sexuality, social organization, creativity, according to Rankian system. 291pp. 5⅜ x 8½. 20485-5 Pa. $8.95

A THEOLOGICO-POLITICAL TREATISE, Benedict Spinoza. Also contains unfinished Political Treatise. Great classic on religious liberty, theory of government on common consent. R. Elwes translation. Total of 421pp. 5⅜ x 8½. 20249-6 Pa. $9.95

CATALOG OF DOVER BOOKS

MY BONDAGE AND MY FREEDOM, Frederick Douglass. Born a slave, Douglass became outspoken force in antislavery movement. The best of Douglass' autobiographies. Graphic description of slave life. 464pp. 5⅜ x 8½. 22457-0 Pa. $8.95

FOLLOWING THE EQUATOR: A Journey Around the World, Mark Twain. Fascinating humorous account of 1897 voyage to Hawaii, Australia, India, New Zealand, etc. Ironic, bemused reports on peoples, customs, climate, flora and fauna, politics, much more. 197 illustrations. 720pp. 5⅜ x 8½. 26113-1 Pa. $15.95

THE PEOPLE CALLED SHAKERS, Edward D. Andrews. Definitive study of Shakers: origins, beliefs, practices, dances, social organization, furniture and crafts, etc. 33 illustrations. 351pp. 5⅜ x 8½. 21081-2 Pa. $8.95

THE MYTHS OF GREECE AND ROME, H. A. Guerber. A classic of mythology, generously illustrated, long prized for its simple, graphic, accurate retelling of the principal myths of Greece and Rome, and for its commentary on their origins and significance. With 64 illustrations by Michelangelo, Raphael, Titian, Rubens, Canova, Bernini and others. 480pp. 5⅜ x 8½. 27584-1 Pa. $9.95

PSYCHOLOGY OF MUSIC, Carl E. Seashore. Classic work discusses music as a medium from psychological viewpoint. Clear treatment of physical acoustics, auditory apparatus, sound perception, development of musical skills, nature of musical feeling, host of other topics. 88 figures. 408pp. 5⅜ x 8½. 21851-1 Pa. $10.95

THE PHILOSOPHY OF HISTORY, Georg W. Hegel. Great classic of Western thought develops concept that history is not chance but rational process, the evolution of freedom. 457pp. 5⅜ x 8½. 20112-0 Pa. $9.95

THE BOOK OF TEA, Kakuzo Okakura. Minor classic of the Orient: entertaining, charming explanation, interpretation of traditional Japanese culture in terms of tea ceremony. 94pp. 5⅜ x 8½. 20070-1 Pa. $3.95

LIFE IN ANCIENT EGYPT, Adolf Erman. Fullest, most thorough, detailed older account with much not in more recent books, domestic life, religion, magic, medicine, commerce, much more. Many illustrations reproduce tomb paintings, carvings, hieroglyphs, etc. 597pp. 5⅜ x 8½. 22632-8 Pa. $12.95

SUNDIALS, Their Theory and Construction, Albert Waugh. Far and away the best, most thorough coverage of ideas, mathematics concerned, types, construction, adjusting anywhere. Simple, nontechnical treatment allows even children to build several of these dials. Over 100 illustrations. 230pp. 5⅜ x 8½. 22947-5 Pa. $8.95

DYNAMICS OF FLUIDS IN POROUS MEDIA, Jacob Bear. For advanced students of ground water hydrology, soil mechanics and physics, drainage and irrigation engineering, and more. 335 illustrations. Exercises, with answers. 784pp. 6⅛ x 9¼. 65675-6 Pa. $19.95

SONGS OF EXPERIENCE: Facsimile Reproduction with 26 Plates in Full Color, William Blake. 26 full-color plates from a rare 1826 edition. Includes "TheTyger," "London," "Holy Thursday," and other poems. Printed text of poems. 48pp. 5¼ x 7. 24636-1 Pa. $4.95

OLD-TIME VIGNETTES IN FULL COLOR, Carol Belanger Grafton (ed.). Over 390 charming, often sentimental illustrations, selected from archives of Victorian graphics–pretty women posing, children playing, food, flowers, kittens and puppies, smiling cherubs, birds and butterflies, much more. All copyright-free. 48pp. 9¼ x 12¼. 27269-9 Pa. $7.95

CATALOG OF DOVER BOOKS

THE INFLUENCE OF SEA POWER UPON HISTORY, 1660–1783, A. T. Mahan. Influential classic of naval history and tactics still used as text in war colleges. First paperback edition. 4 maps. 24 battle plans. 640pp. 5⅜ x 8½. 25509-3 Pa. $14.95

THE STORY OF THE TITANIC AS TOLD BY ITS SURVIVORS, Jack Winocour (ed.). What it was really like. Panic, despair, shocking inefficiency, and a little heroism. More thrilling than any fictional account. 26 illustrations. 320pp. 5⅜ x 8½. 20610-6 Pa. $8.95

FAIRY AND FOLK TALES OF THE IRISH PEASANTRY, William Butler Yeats (ed.). Treasury of 64 tales from the twilight world of Celtic myth and legend: "The Soul Cages," "The Kildare Pooka," "King O'Toole and his Goose," many more. Introduction and Notes by W. B. Yeats. 352pp. 5⅜ x 8½. 26941-8 Pa. $8.95

BUDDHIST MAHAYANA TEXTS, E. B. Cowell and Others (eds.). Superb, accurate translations of basic documents in Mahayana Buddhism, highly important in history of religions. The Buddha-karita of Asvaghosha, Larger Sukhavativyuha, more. 448pp. 5⅜ x 8½. 25552-2 Pa. $12.95

ONE TWO THREE . . . INFINITY: Facts and Speculations of Science, George Gamow. Great physicist's fascinating, readable overview of contemporary science: number theory, relativity, fourth dimension, entropy, genes, atomic structure, much more. 128 illustrations. Index. 352pp. 5⅜ x 8½. 25664-2 Pa. $8.95

ENGINEERING IN HISTORY, Richard Shelton Kirby, et al. Broad, nontechnical survey of history's major technological advances: birth of Greek science, industrial revolution, electricity and applied science, 20th-century automation, much more. 181 illustrations. ". . . excellent . . ."–*Isis*. Bibliography. vii + 530pp. 5⅜ x 8¼. 26412-2 Pa. $14.95

DALÍ ON MODERN ART: The Cuckolds of Antiquated Modern Art, Salvador Dalí. Influential painter skewers modern art and its practitioners. Outrageous evaluations of Picasso, Cézanne, Turner, more. 15 renderings of paintings discussed. 44 calligraphic decorations by Dalí. 96pp. 5⅜ x 8½. (USO) 29220-7 Pa. $4.95

ANTIQUE PLAYING CARDS: A Pictorial History, Henry René D'Allemagne. Over 900 elaborate, decorative images from rare playing cards (14th–20th centuries): Bacchus, death, dancing dogs, hunting scenes, royal coats of arms, players cheating, much more. 96pp. 9¼ x 12¼. 29265-7 Pa. $12.95

MAKING FURNITURE MASTERPIECES: 30 Projects with Measured Drawings, Franklin H. Gottshall. Step-by-step instructions, illustrations for constructing handsome, useful pieces, among them a Sheraton desk, Chippendale chair, Spanish desk, Queen Anne table and a William and Mary dressing mirror. 224pp. 8⅛ x 11¼. 29338-6 Pa. $13.95

THE FOSSIL BOOK: A Record of Prehistoric Life, Patricia V. Rich et al. Profusely illustrated definitive guide covers everything from single-celled organisms and dinosaurs to birds and mammals and the interplay between climate and man. Over 1,500 illustrations. 760pp. 7½ x 10⅛. 29371-8 Pa. $29.95

Prices subject to change without notice.

Available at your book dealer or write for free catalog to Dept. GI, Dover Publications, Inc., 31 East 2nd St., Mineola, N.Y. 11501. Dover publishes more than 500 books each year on science, elementary and advanced mathematics, biology, music, art, literary history, social sciences and other areas.